D1060298

HOW TO COOK A TAPIR

At Table

HOW TO COOK A TAPIR

A Memoir of Belize

JOAN FRY

UNIVERSITY OF NEBRASKA PRESS
LINCOLN AND LONDON

Library of Congress
Cataloging-in-Publication Data
Fry, Joan.
How to cook a tapir: a memoir of Belize /
Joan Fry.
p. cm.
ISBN 978-0-8032-1903-8 (cloth: alk. paper)
1. Kekchi Indians—Social life and customs.
2. Kekchi Indians—Rites and ceremonies.
3. Maya cookery.   I. Title.
F1465.2.K5F78   2009
305.897′423097282092—dc22
[B]
2008039683

Set in Minion by Bob Reitz.
Designed by Ashley Muehlbauer.

For Helen and Will Mebius, my mother and father, who watched their only child go off to live in the rainforest, and for Don Owen-Lewis, who picked up where they left off.

If the world has any ends, British Honduras [modern Belize] would certainly be one of them.

ALDOUS HUXLEY, *Beyond the Mexique Bay*

CONTENTS

ILLUSTRATIONS

PREFACE

All the events in this book happened. My former husband *was* the first American anthropologist to study the Kekchi Maya of southern Belize. The cooks who prepared the dishes described in this book or gave me the recipes are real people, and I have used their real names. The rest of the characters are real, too. But to avoid any unpleasantness—including but not limited to legal action—I have changed a few names.

I freely admit that I also, with frivolous abandon, altered the timeline. For example, the Monkey Dance was held in April, but in the book I say it was held in November. (In actuality, the Katarina was held in November.) In other words, I changed the calendar. The ancient Maya, with their passion for charting the exact movements of the sun and moon, would have been scandalized, but I'll risk it.

Since I lived in British Honduras, it has disappeared. The country now calls itself Belize, and the village of Rio Blanco is officially Santa Elena. With three exceptions I use names that were current at the time I lived there. One: the black Caribs, descended from escaped black African slaves and "red" (or "yellow") Carib Indians, have identified with their African ancestors, distancing themselves from their man-eating

Caribbean ones. (The Caribs, indigenous to the Caribbean islands, were reputedly cannibals.) They now call themselves Garifuna, and I have honored their preference. Two: when I lived there, the capital of British Honduras was Belize. The capital of the present-day country of Belize is Belmopan; its largest city is Belize City. To avoid confusion I call the old capital Belize City. Three: since the word "Indian" is inaccurate, I have tried to call the Maya "the Maya" whenever possible, although everyone, including the Maya themselves, called them Indians.

I use the recipes that Kekchi women cooked when I lived there. I've seen modern recipes for *escabeche,* for example, that call for frying the chicken before adding it to the soup. Some of today's Kekchi cooks make flour *tortillas* by adding baking powder, which makes them puff up like omelets and gives them a breadlike texture. Neither recipe is traditional, and I chose not to include them. They are available on the Internet, along with plenty of bad advice. (You do not need to "kneed" your flour *tortilla* dough. Most cooks use their hands.) I did include an updated version of Maya beans simply because most families prefer them this way. (So do I.) I added pasta to my chickpea soup recipe because if I'd *had* pasta—or known how to make it—I would have added it. The same is true of the recipes for green corn dumplings, *callaloo*, and pumpkin soup.

The food items I specify are available in most American supermarkets. *Samat* (Eryngium foetidum) is the only exception. I have never seen it for sale, fresh or dried, anywhere, under any name. The seeds, however, are available on the Internet under the name *culantro*. (Do not confuse it with *cilantro*.)

Every day Belize becomes more and more popular as a must-see tourist spot, but unless tourists actively seek out Maya villages, they will encounter the Maya only in market towns or around archaeological sites, hawking trinkets. Incredibly, Rio Blanco and other villages in Toledo and Stann Creek districts still get their drinking water from the river, and the women still do laundry there. Many towns, including Rio Blanco, *still* lack electricity. When I lived there, the last of the Kekchi cultural beliefs and rituals—those handed down from their ancient Maya ancestors—were already vanishing, but for the most part I was oblivious. One reason I wrote this book is to give back some of those forgotten rituals, and to share the Kekchis' traditional recipes before they, too, disappear.

ACKNOWLEDGMENTS

I am deeply indebted to Pamela Malpas for prodding me to think about what metaphoric associations "food" and "cooking" have for me. My thanks to the members of the Belize Forums who helped me with recipes, and to the Staff Development Committee of Antelope Valley College, which funded part of my research. I'm very grateful to my writer friends—Gina Cresse, Marilyn Hanes, Linda Holley, Carol Kaylor, Dave Lewis, Gail Lofdahl, Margaret Priddy, and Peggy Touchstone, and my poet friend Charles Hood—as well as to my cooking friend, Barbara Davis, who helped me re-create some of the recipes. Special thanks to Heather Lundine, Ann Baker, and Robin DuBlanc, my editors, for their insightful guidance.

My abiding gratitude to Francisca Bardalez, interpreter, recipe finder, and friend, for making me part of her extended family. And to John, who taste-tested each dish I cooked regardless of how many times he had tasted it before.

Finally, *to ho cre* to the Kekchi cooks who contributed recipes for this book and/or taught me how to prepare them. My heartfelt thanks to them all.

NEIGHBORS

Like their ancestors, the present-day Maya inhabit eastern Mexico—including the Yucatan peninsula—Belize, Guatemala, and parts of Honduras and El Salvador. Between 5 and 6 million people speak one or more of the two dozen–plus known Mayan languages, although there is plenty of scholarly bickering about whether certain local dialects are really "languages." (Some estimates put the number of Mayan languages as high as seventy.) Most Mayan speakers in Belize are Kekchi. Others speak Yucatec Maya, while a few—concentrated in and around the village of San Antonio—speak Mopan Maya. There are ethnic differences as well. Since the Kekchi originated in the mountains of Guatemala, where the weather is considerably more bracing than it is in the tropical rainforest of Belize, Kekchi women wore long, heavy skirts and were inordinately fond of *caldo*, or soup.

In Rio Blanco, half my neighbors were Kekchi and the other half were Mopan. Even though intermarriage was common, the languages are so different that the Kekchi can't speak or understand Mopan and vice versa. When I describe people as "ethnically Kekchi" or "ethnically Mopan," I'm referring to the language they spoke as well as to their other cultural preferences, including the food the women cooked and the way they prepared it. One of my best students, Maxiana Choc, had a Mopan father and a Kekchi mother. She grew up speaking Kekchi and considered herself Kekchi, even though her last name was Mopan. Maxiana is "ethnically Kekchi."

Both groups used the Spanish word *ladino* to designate someone half Maya and half "Spanish" (a Guatemalan, Honduran, etc.) who spoke Spanish and/or English and preferred to work as someone's employee rather than live in a bush house in the jungle and depend on the family corn crop to survive. In other words, people of mixed blood could *choose* their ethnicity. Some chose to be Mopan, others chose to be Kekchi, and some opted out of being Maya altogether and chose to be *ladinos*. Occasionally the term was applied to a full-blooded Maya, like Maxiana's older brother Evaristo, who had made that choice.

I have followed current academic convention and use the word *Maya* for the people themselves, both singular and plural, and as an adjective. The only time I use the word *Mayan* is in reference to their language.

Modern Kekchi has not yet been standardized in written form. *Kekchi* can also be spelled *K'ekchi* or *Q'eqchi*. The apostrophe designates a glottal stop, which is a cross between a cough and a hiccup.

Our neighbors, listed alphabetically by first name:

Aprimo Tux (Kekchi). My student, the oldest of José and Ana Tux's many grandchildren.

Arcenio Garcia (Kekchi), another of my best students. His father is Sebastian Garcia (Kekchi and Guatemalan Spanish, ethnically Kekchi); his mother is Kekchi. Arcenio's younger brother Secondino and his two sisters, Adelaida and Epijenia, are my students.

Cirila Chub (Kekchi and Honduran Spanish, ethnically Kekchi), Don Owen-Lewis's housekeeper. Huni Hun is Cirila's son (ethnically Kekchi), and Gloria Che (Kekchi) is Don's goddaughter.

Cresencio Choc (ethnically Mopan). He and his younger brother, "little" Julian, are both my students. His parents are Silvaria and Enriques Choc. Dolores's husband, Joaquin Choc, is one of his older brothers.

Dolores (Mopan) and Joaquin Choc (ethnically Mopan). No relation to Evaristo Choc's family. Their children Paulina, Eluterio (nicknamed Lute), and Valeria are my students.

Don Owen-Lewis (British), Amerindian development officer.

Evaristo Choc (trilingual; a *ladino* by choice, not ethnicity), man about town. The oldest son of Candelaria (Kekchi) and Marto Choc (Mopan).

Jesús and Gregoria Boh (Kekchi), our closest, our *very* closest, neighbors. Their son Silvario is my student. Living in the same house is Jesús's brother Florentino Boh (Kekchi) and his wife Goyita (Mopan). Their oldest son is my student Francisco.

Father John Paul Cull (ethnically American), a Jesuit from St. Louis. My boss.

José Tux (Kekchi) and his wife Ana (Kekchi), lived in Rio Blanco before it was a town. Their children include Aleja (married to Evaristo Choc), Francisco (married to Rosaria Choc, one of Evaristo's sisters), and my students Paulina, Nicasio, and Crisantos.

Juanita and Jaime Bul (Mopan). One of the families that moved into Rio Blanco when Aaron and I were in Guatemala over Christmas.

Julian Jimenez, "big" Julian (Kekchi and Honduran Spanish), is Silvaria Choc's bachelor brother. Part-time *ladino*, ethnically a misfit.

Lucia (trilingual but ethnically Mopan) and Crispino Bah (Kekchi). Their only child is Natalia, my student. Lucia's older brother is Evaristo Choc.

Luis Choc (ethnically Mopan). Lucia and Maxiana are his sisters. One of my students.

Manuel and Petrona Xi (Kekchi), Don's good friends and our neighbors in Crique Sarco.

Martín (Kekchi) and Fernanda (Mopan) Ical. Martín is one of José Ical's two brothers. The other is Mateo.

Marto Choc (Mopan) and his wife, Candelaria (Kekchi). Their children include Evaristo, Lucia (Bah), Rosaria (Tux), and my students Maxiana and Luis.

Mateo Ical (Kekchi), the *mayordomo*, or head honcho, of Rio Blanco. Married to Micalia (Kekchi). Their son is my student Saturnino.

Maxiana Choc (ethnically Kekchi), my student. Evaristo is her brother and Lucia Bah is her sister.

Natalia Bah (ethnically Kekchi), my student. The only child of Lucia and Crispino Bah. Maxiana is her aunt.

Paulina Choc (ethnically Mopan). The oldest of Dolores and Joaquin's four children. She, her brother Eluterio (nicknamed Lute), and her sister Valeria are my students.

Silvaria (Kekchi and Honduran Spanish; ethnically Kekchi) and Enriques Choc (Mopan). Their grown sons, all ethnically Mopan, include Joaquin (married to Dolores), Florencio, and Asunción.

British Honduras, July 1962

ONE

Hurricane

Whistle shrieking, the *Heron H*—a small tramp cargo ship that resembled a tugboat—labored out of the Belize City harbor. Her hold was crammed with hogs. To clear my head of their mud and sewage stink, I sat on the railing, my back against a beam and my legs straight out in front of me, so I wouldn't flash my underpants. I watched in fascination as Belize City retreated building by building, then disappeared entirely, replaced by palm trees and an occasional tin-roofed shack.

Our cabin, where Aaron, my new husband, had stashed our suitcases, was directly across from me. It was the size of a closet and had two bunk beds nailed to the wall, each covered with a stained, inch-thick mattress. No sheets. No pillows. I had already made up my mind to stay awake the entire trip rather than sleep on one of those filthy mattresses.

Farther down the deck, just outside the head, an enormous brindle bull was tied to the railing by his horns. Anyone using the head had to yank the door open and dash inside before the bull kicked the door shut in his face. I was twenty years old, born and raised in the New Jersey suburbs, and had never seen an animal with testicles the size of cantaloupes before. I couldn't stop staring at them.

As the scenery slid by—no more shacks, just sea and sky and a bank of greenery dense as fog—a black man wearing creased trousers and a see-through white shirt shuffled past me. He'd been back and forth a few times already, flipping through a deck of cards, asking people if they wanted a game.

But this time he stopped, cocked his head, and regarded me as the oddity I was: the only white woman on board. He was skinny and very black—a Garifuna, I decided. The Creoles in Belize City tended to be toast-colored and better fed. I refused to make eye contact, hoping he'd leave me alone. My escape from Verona, New Jersey, into the rainforest was a fantasy come true, and I wanted to savor it in private.

The Garifuna held out his hand. "You would shake hands with a black man in his own country?" His voice wasn't belligerent; he was just asking. He didn't even sound especially hopeful.

Idealistic to the core—although not the radical leftist Aaron was—I leaned forward, my hand extended. "Of course!"

We shook. More accurately, the Garifuna pumped my hand once, then dropped it. "What you doing here? You Peace Corps?"

"No."

"Papal Volunteer?"

"No."

"What you could be, then?"

Good question. How could I explain that I was the wife of an anthropologist who planned to spend the next year studying the Kekchi Maya? How could I explain an anthropologist? Or that I was running away from home to grow up? "I'm a teacher," I said in a burst of inspiration. Only a small technicality. I *would* be a teacher, once Aaron and the local priest decided on an appropriate village. As of now, I was simply Mrs. Aaron Ward.

The Garifuna nodded his approval. "Where you going teach?"

"Toledo District."

"Ahh—you going to Punta Gorda then!"

Punta Gorda was a small coastal town where Aaron and I and the

Heron would part company. "No. I mean yes, that's where we're going. But that's not where I'm teaching."

"Barranco?"

"No."

Subtly his features rearranged themselves. "You going teach Indians, then."

"The Maya. Yes."

"But they backward, Missus. They eat pure corn and beans, just so. Why you want it live in a trash house in the bush and eat corn and beans?" He gestured wordlessly toward the bow, where a dozen barefoot Maya sat stoically on wooden benches, their faces as blank as a platter of pork chops. The Garifuna's expression said he'd seen my future and it made him squeamish. "Good day to you, Missus." And off he went, in search of a better class of person to play cards with.

Late that afternoon the wind came up, although the day was still bright and calm with no clouds. I abandoned my front-row seat on the railing when the *Heron* started to pitch and decided I'd sit—nothing more, just *sit*—on the lower bunk. Through the open door I watched sapphire blue waves, their crests smoking with foam, slap the *Heron* from side to side with a crack like a tree splitting. Then I watched one of the passengers heave his lunch just outside our cabin.

Aaron materialized next to me on the bunk. "Do you believe this weather? The purser said we're getting slammed by the tail end of a hurricane." Then he took a good look at me. "Uh-oh. You don't look so good, Squirrel. How're you feeling?"

"Not good." I slumped against him, watching the horizon climb the door frame and then swoop out of sight as though it had never existed. My stomach followed the lurch of the horizon line. The air inside the cabin was stifling.

"Buster Hunter wants to know if we'll take tea with him."

I groaned. Buster Hunter was the captain, a hulking, white-haired bull of a man, dressed in grimy, oil-soaked pants and a vest like one of his own deckhands. "You go. I'll stay here."

"Poor Squirrel. That's one thing we never thought of packing—seasick pills." Gently Aaron wrapped his arm around my shoulders and rocked me. He smelled salty, with undertones of pig. His role model was Robert Jordan, the protagonist of Ernest Hemingway's *For Whom the Bell Tolls*. I couldn't recall any of Hemingway's heroes traveling on pig boats.

I kissed the pale, tight skin under Aaron's jaw and gingerly lay down on the mattress, trying not to touch it, my cheek against my folded hands. "I'll be fine. Go have tea with Captain Hunter. Tell him I'm flattered but indisposed."

By the time the *Heron* dropped anchor at Stann Creek that night, I'd thrown up so many times my ribcage ached. Cockroaches scurried up and down my bare legs. I hardly had enough strength to pick my head up and look out the door. Aaron lay in the upper bunk, snoring.

The *Heron* wallowed at a long, ramshackle wharf, pitching so hard I was surprised that the people trying to board her didn't lose their footing and drown. Women teetered on pilings, handing boxes and crates and children to people already on board. The wharf itself was nothing more than a string of oil drums lashed together, lit by a beacon hung from the mast of a derelict sailing schooner. People yelled back and forth in Creole, Spanish, Mayan, Garifuna, English. The beacon on the schooner turned blue, then white, then orange.

A Maya man with a sloping forehead, a sensuous, down-turned mouth, and a machete strapped around his waist like a sword was trying to wedge a treadle sewing machine against the rail. Garifuna women swayed down the passageway, baskets of fresh fruit on their heads, bracelets cascading down their arms like rivers of silver. Buster Hunter stood on the *Heron*'s upper deck, his face changing color with the light, his hair radiating from his head in little wisps, like flames. He looked like Satan directing a scene in hell.

Moaning, I curled into a ball and prayed for a quick death.

When I had announced my wedding plans to my parents, they were appalled. They disapproved of Aaron's politics. They disapproved of the fact that he, an older man—he was a graduate student—was taking me, a sophomore at the University of Michigan, on a "working honeymoon" for a year in the jungle. Like most people, they had no idea where British Honduras was. Africa? An island off the coast of China? Only my German-born grandfather, who had run away to sea at fourteen, knew it was a tiny Central American country the size of Massachusetts, south of Mexico and east and north of Guatemala. Its entire eastern border faced the Caribbean as though the country were sprawled on its side, facing the azure half-moon of the earth's second-largest barrier reef. Along its spine grew some of Central America's most pristine rainforest. That's where Aaron and I were going—where the Maya lived.

"We used to ship mahogany out of Stann Creek," my grandfather had said, chewing thoughtfully on his pipe. When I was a kid, his tales about life on the high seas enthralled me. It was my fervent wish to grow up and be a sailor like Grandpa Brombach. But along with adolescence came the dawning realization that girls didn't sign on as sailors in order to see the world. I'd have to manage it some other way.

So I got married.

The morning of the third day the sea subsided. The *Heron* had slowed to a crawl, and I felt well enough to venture out on deck and find out why. A man in a handmade wooden dory wielded his oars to keep his little boat from colliding with the *Heron* while the man next to him held up a string of fish. A thin, elderly Creole wearing a grimy apron hung over the *Heron*'s rail, talking to them. The fish and some money changed hands, and the men rowed back to shore. I couldn't see a town. I couldn't see a house. I couldn't even see a trickle of smoke streaming skyward.

Aaron showed up a few minutes later. "How do you feel? Are you in the mood for breakfast at the captain's table?"

"Yes, I am," I said, surprising myself. "I'm starving."

Bear-Bear grinned. "I'm glad to hear that."

Confidently he bounded ahead of me up the ladder to the upper deck. He always moved as though he expected inanimate objects to get out of his way. An expert skier, he had a sturdy build, brown hair, leaf-green eyes, and a complexion that turned red and peeled before it tanned. The ladder was slick with sea spray and hard to hold on to. Self-consciously I glanced down to see if any of the Maya were peering up my skirt. Skirts were a sore point between me and Aaron. I would have been much happier wearing jeans, but he wouldn't allow it. "Only Kekchi men wear trousers, Squirrel. The women wear skirts. Why draw attention to yourself and confuse them when there's no need to?"

His argument was logical but not persuasive. I couldn't explain—because I wasn't consciously aware of it—how vulnerable a woman accustomed to wearing jeans could feel in a skirt. But the fight I had really minded losing was over cigarettes. Aaron had argued that since the Maya women didn't smoke cigarettes, neither could I. He didn't tell me they smoked *puros* instead—small, smelly, hand-rolled cigars.

The Maya were eating dabs of what looked like raw dough with their fingers. Not one of them even glanced in my direction, and the women—whose own skirts were so long they grazed the deck—didn't seem to care how a white woman climbing a ladder was dressed.

Breakfast with the captain was Creole bread, scrambled eggs, and fried fish. I scooped some eggs on my plate, a few slices of bread, and two fish. Before tackling the fish, I cut their heads off and maneuvered them discreetly behind the eggs so I wouldn't have to look into their poached, milky eyes.

Buster Hunter was wearing the same clothes he'd had on in Stann Creek. From the smell of the cabin, he'd probably been wearing them a great deal longer than that. But he had a wonderful view from up here, and while he talked I gazed over his shoulder at the jungle that stretched in an unbroken green line from the shore to the horizon.

"My only real competition's the *Caribe*," Hunter rasped. We had passed the *Caribe*, a decrepit tramp freighter that also hauled passengers, during the night. She had run aground on a sandbar. "Owned by a bunch of Creoles from Belize City. Got greedy, they did." He emitted a short, unexpected laugh. "Greedy choke puppy. *Heron*'s my boat, and

Belize City to Puerto Barrios is my run. I carry the mail. They'll learn."
He shoveled a forkful of fish and eggs into his mouth. "I own stock in
Brodie's," he added, as if that clinched the argument—which it did.
Brodie's was the colony's biggest general store.

The fish were crunchy on the outside, moist and sweet on the inside.
Since I saw nothing on the table that resembled a napkin, I wiped my
mouth using the back of my hand the way Hunter had. "Who were
they?"

He swung his massive head toward me, scowling. "What's that?"

I slid closer to Aaron. Up close, Hunter looked even bigger and more
alarming than he had from a distance. "Those men who sold your cook
the fish. Who were they?"

"Half-breeds. Must be a dozen of 'em back in the bush there. Mother's
Kekchi, father's Garifuna."

"But where do they live? There's nothing *there!*"

Hunter laughed again, smacking the table so hard all the dishware
jumped. His fist was the size of a ham. "There isn't, except the Indians.
Took some Brits down earlier this month, bigwigs from Belize Estates,
and all they did was bellyache. Turns out they'd hired a Maya work-
force. They're hard workers, I'll give 'em that, but when it came time
to plant corn, every last one of 'em dropped his tools and disappeared.
Went home to make plantation. If I'd known they were going to hire
Indians, I could have set 'em straight quick-time. The Maya don't eat
with knives and forks, believe in every kind of heathen mumbo jumbo,
and won't let anything come between them and their cornfields. They
say they whisper in the ear of the ancients when they plant. Bunch of
savages, if you ask me."

I felt Aaron stiffen. Under different circumstances he would have joked
that the Maya were *noble* savages, like the ones the French philosopher
Jean-Jacques Rousseau had described. That was the main reason he
wanted to study the Kekchi—to find out who they really were. As for
me, I had never seen people like the Maya before. I'd never seen anybody
like Buster Hunter before. And, for all the time I'd spent exploring the

woods as a kid, I had never seen wilderness like this before, either. Did the rainforest where Aaron planned to take me look this isolated, this unwelcoming? And what if the Kekchi really *were* savages?

But I should have asked him those questions when we first discussed honeymooning among the Maya. Now it was too late. For better or worse, I was already here.

Don Owen-Lewis, the Amerindian development officer, met us in Punta Gorda and drove us to his house in Machaca Creek. The road was muddy, a single lane defined by tire tracks. Toledo District had no paved roads and no electricity, although Don lived in a sprawling, Western-style house with beds and fluffy pillows and indoor plumbing. Machaca Creek was even hotter and more humid than Belize City had been.

"Tommygoff will kill you quick-time," Don informed me after dinner that night, his yellow-flecked hazel eyes alight with mischief. He had a long, skinny build, a ribald sense of humor, and black hair that stuck straight up on his head like a rooster comb.

This man has lived in the bush too long, I thought. Don's job was to integrate the Maya, subsistence farmers who practiced slash-and-burn agriculture, into the colony's market economy. He had lived here eight years—Aaron had met him the previous summer. Since I couldn't tell if he was trying to amuse me or scare me, I didn't react. Also I didn't know what a tommygoff was.

"Man in Crique Sarco stepped over his threshold one day and tommy-goff bit him on the foot," Don continued gleefully. "Sat down with his back against his house and lit a cigarette. Dead before he finished it." Don himself was smoking at a furious rate, as though to emphasize his point.

"Is that so," I said mildly. Okay—a tommygoff was a snake. And Crique Sarco was a Kekchi village where Aaron and I would spend the next three weeks. Last summer Aaron had lived there with Manuel and Petrona Xi, a young Kekchi couple and their children. (Don's first home had been in Crique Sarco; Manuel and Petrona were his next-door neighbors.)

According to Aaron, Crique Sarco would be the perfect place to get me acclimated to living among the Maya. Otherwise I was apt to come down with culture shock—he made it sound like the measles—and cry hysterically, begging to go back to the States.

I felt much better; at least the ground had stopped moving. I decided Don's snake story was deliberate hyperbole. He was teasing, trying to get a reaction out of me. I lit a cigarette of my own, one I'd bummed from him. It was a Colonial, locally made—stubby, unfiltered, and so strong it hurt to inhale. Snakes, even venomous ones, didn't scare me. Spiders scared me. And the prospect of cooking.

"Your plantain turn black, you stone the John Crow." Don wasn't letting up.

Of course then I had to ask what a plantain was.

"Banana. *Big* banana," he replied—inaccurately, as it turned out. Plantains did resemble big bananas, but most people cooked them before eating them.

"What's John Crow?"

"Vultures. We have two of the bloody—sorry—buggers here. Ones with the white heads are the king vultures. Don't often see that lot."

Bloody. Don had veered from Creole back to the vocabulary of a British civil servant. Both languages were incomprehensible to me, yet both purported to be English. I wondered which version the Maya spoke.

The day before Aaron and I left for Crique Sarco, I stood next to Cirila, Don's Kekchi housekeeper, in her sunny, spacious kitchen, looking at raw corn dough. I was supposed to be learning how to make corn *tortillas*. Cirila seemed civilized to me. A slender, pretty woman with a delicate aquiline nose and eyes that reminded me of half-closed windows, she smelled like soap and flowers. I never saw her wear anything but Western-style dresses—housedresses, my mother would have called them. Huni, her eight-year-old son, was outside, playing airplane and dive-bombing the dogs. Gloria, an orphaned Kekchi girl of about five who lived with them—Don was her godfather—leaned against the doorjamb as Cirila explained, in her careful English, how this blob of dough had come to be.

First she had stripped the dried corn from the cob with her hands. Then she had soaked it in lime water. (Lime the mineral, not the fruit.) After rinsing it she ground it, mated it deftly with a precise amount of water, and pulled off small pieces like the ones the passengers on the *Heron* had been eating, using her hands to pat each one into a precise circle.

Her demonstration made the process seem easy, but she'd been making *tortillas* since she was Gloria's age. To me it seemed like way too much work. Gloria, her thumb in her mouth up to the last knuckle, watched us silently, her small, pretty face severe as a nun's.

Cirila tossed a *tortilla* on her *comal*, an iron skillet with no sides or handle. When the top of the *tortilla* separated from the bottom and poofed out, Cirila flipped it as easily as I'd fold a napkin, using the very tips of her fingers.

When it was my turn, I had a premonition that my *tortilla* wouldn't turn into a moist, fragrant circle of dough like Cirila's—I had added too much water. My premonition was correct.

I tried not to feel stupid, but this was my second household fiasco. Earlier Cirila had asked me to help her cut out material for a dress, and I botched it. I didn't lay the pattern out correctly, and as a result she didn't have enough material to finish the dress. I apologized, knowing she'd have to make a trip to Punta Gorda, where, if she was lucky, she'd find a remnant of the same material.

Cirila looked at my *tortilla*. It resembled a runny pancake. Then she looked at me, an expression of pity on her face.

My stomach flip-flopped. Who did she feel sorry for? Me? Or Aaron?

TWO

Bush Bride

I wrote my parents a letter from Crique Sarco in longhand because I'd left my typewriter at Don's house. "We're back from Guatemala City, where Aaron registered for classes at the Universidad de San Carlos in order to keep his student deferment." Unless Aaron was officially enrolled as a student *somewhere*, he was prime draft material for Vietnam. "At the moment we're living in the first house Don built in this country. It has regular walls made out of painted lumber and a wooden floor, but the roof is thatch. The outhouse also has a thatch roof. I have a two-burner kerosene stove but carry water up from the river in a bucket, the way the Kekchi women do. I have black-and-blue marks on both shins."

I decided not to mention the frog eggs I scooped off the cooking water every morning before making breakfast, or the dead spiders and two-inch cockroach carcasses I swept out the door with a broom made of palm fronds.

What we eat depends on who gave us food that day—tortillas from Don's former neighbors Manuel and Petrona Xi, pineapple from somebody else, a few eggs, and an assortment of canned goods Don calls tins. (Even the margarine comes in a tin, like lard.) We drink tea because that's all Don has here. I am very much looking forward to a cup of coffee again. Since Aaron doesn't like tortillas, we put margarine and peanut butter on them. Flour tortillas we eat with margarine and jelly. Petrona gave us some fresh fish last night, and to reciprocate I'm going to bake some Bisquick biscuits. I wonder what she'll do to them before she considers them edible.

Like most Kekchi women, Petrona wears her hair in a single braid down her back—her hair is waist-length—and an ankle-length blue plaid skirt. Aaron says the skirts are handwoven from nine yards of material, and that in Guatemala you can tell what language group a woman belongs to by her skirt pattern.

Also like most Kekchi women, Petrona went topless. I decided not to mention that, either.

As soon as school lets out hoards of kids dash in our front door to watch us. They don't think I can do anything right. Yesterday while I was sweeping, a little girl grabbed the broom out of my hands and cleaned the house while another ran to the river and filled my water bucket. When I tried to thank them in Kekchi, they giggled. (It's a guttural language, full of gasps and glottal stops.) The people are friendly, but their favorite occupation is staring. They watch us cook, bathe in the river, eat—probably even sleep, because to shut the door is considered an unfriendly act. Most don't say anything, they just materialize and stare and take off again unless I do something that strikes them funny. Then they laugh. Two little boys are watching as I write this.

The weather is miserable. It's been raining for three days solid.

But on the fourth day the sun came out, and after breakfast I followed a muddy path to the schoolhouse so I could watch a *real* teacher in action. (At Michigan I was an English major, not an education major.)

Mr. Zuniga, the head teacher, was a big, amiable Garifuna with a deep voice that sounded like claps of thunder. He believed in rote recitation and that left-handed children should write using their right hand.

"One times two is two," his advanced students chanted in unison, one eye on him, the other on me—a blue-eyed blond wearing her hair in a ponytail, a blouse, and a knee-length flowered skirt. "Two times two is four. Three times two is six. Four times two is eight."

The kids were pretty good at this, considering they were in a one-room schoolhouse where six-year-olds were mixed in with fourteen-year-olds. They made it all the way up to twelve times two before starting with "One times three is three."

Suddenly I spotted a pack of Raleighs on Mr. Zuniga's desk. They were the only brand of American cigarettes sold in the colony, and the back of my throat prickled with lust. Aaron and I were still bickering about cigarettes—I kept bumming them from other smokers. I admitted it was a character flaw. I *should* stop smoking. But I couldn't. While Raleighs weren't my brand—I was a Marlboro girl—I craved one of Mr. Zuniga's Raleighs as desperately as only an addicted, two-pack-a-day smoker could crave a single hit of tobacco.

The children were singing "God Save the Queen." Feeling suddenly very wide awake—my hammock, donated by one of the Kekchi men, was too small for me and I slept fitfully at night, when I slept at all—I grabbed my notebook and pencil and tried to distract myself by scoring the melody and jotting down the words. I'd have to teach the song to my own students in addition to the usual three Rs.

But all I could think about was that pack of Raleighs on Mr. Zuniga's desk. I hunched over my notebook, pressing down on my pencil so hard the point snapped, and wrote myself a note: "'The Alphabet Song': a good way to introduce English to the kids."

Didn't Mr. Zuniga take a midmorning break? Wasn't he about due for one?

Aaron knew everybody in Crique Sarco and was always tramping off to somebody's *milpa*, or cornfield (English-speakers called it a plantation), or sitting with a group of people, notebook in hand, asking questions. One afternoon after school let out, an elderly man wearing glasses—Aaron called him Pedro but didn't introduce us—stopped by to say his sister-in-law wanted us to come to her house for *lab*. Aaron accepted.

"You didn't *ask* me if I want to come," I pointed out when Pedro left.

"Don't you?"

"Not particularly. You speak Kekchi and I don't. And what, exactly, is *lab*?"

"Corn gruel. They boil it with wild honey or sugarcane juice."

"Mmm—sounds tasty," I said. "Pass."

"Squirrel, you have to go."

"Why?"

"Because you're my wife. Pedro asked both of us."

"No, he asked *you*. And you said yes without asking me." While I liked the idea of being married to the Answer Man, and knowing that the Answer Man had chosen to marry *me*, that knowledge didn't prevent me from arguing with him. It was nothing personal. I argued with everybody. But the skirt business and the cigarette business were still festering. *They* were personal.

"Well, his sister-in-law expects both of us now. So both of us are going."

"Even though I don't want to."

Aaron looked at me sadly, his green eyes reproachful. "This is how it's going to be, Squirrel. You married an anthropologist."

We went to Pedro's sister-in-law's house to drink *lab*.

When we arrived, a crowd had already assembled, the men outside, the women in the house. After poking his head inside the door, Aaron told me to go on in and make myself comfortable. He would be outside with the men.

"But . . ." Was he going to just *abandon* me?

He was. "I'll be right outside, Squirrel. You'll be fine."

I wasn't so sure about that. I'd been here less than a week and didn't know anybody except Petrona—who apparently hadn't been invited. The air was so thick with smoke and unfamiliar food smells it was hard to breathe. Babies hung from the rafters in miniature cloth hammocks called *lepup-eb* while their mothers cooked.

None of the women wore blouses, and I didn't know where to look. I hadn't seen so many bare breasts since high school gym class. Breasts so long they hung like cucumbers past the old women's waists. Small, high, round breasts on the young women. Swollen shapely ones etched with blue veins on nursing mothers, their dark nipples as big as cabbage roses.

But I couldn't talk to them—nobody spoke English. Unlike the Maya passengers on the *Heron*, they were all intensely curious about me. They kept smiling, even the toothless old women. Big, wide smiles as they hurled questions at me in Kekchi. After each question they crowded closer.

Another half-naked woman—she looked about fourteen—scurried through the doorway, her baby in a *lepup* on her back. As soon as she saw me she uttered a loud "Ayiii!" Before I knew what was happening, she had rushed over and was stroking the blond hair on my arms the way I'd pet a cat, but the wrong direction, so the hairs stood up. She seemed hypnotized, standing so close to me I could smell the baby shit in the *lepup*.

I bolted out the door. Aaron was where he said he'd be, sitting with the men, and I squeezed in next to him, my heart jitterbugging against my ribs.

The men ignored me. They were caught up with teasing a good-looking young man named Ricardo, who grinned and ducked his head every so often, as if in contrition. After a few minutes the women came out carrying dried calabash gourds filled with *lab*. Aaron and I were served first. I took a swallow and gagged. *Lab* tasted like sugar-flavored spit.

That night I tried to tell Aaron why I had run out of the house—how claustrophobic I had felt as the *only* white woman in a very small house, the *only* woman wearing a blouse, the *only* woman who didn't speak Kekchi. "But it won't happen again," I vowed. "I don't want to jeopardize your research."

Aaron lay in his hammock next to me, but it was so dark I couldn't see him. My father, an amateur astronomer who had made himself a telescope and ground his own lens, would have loved it here—he would have loved the *sky*, at least. Except for the brilliance of the far-flung stars, the sky was as black as a cast-iron skillet. No light pollution. No lights, except for an occasional flickering fire.

"You'll get used to them," Aaron said. "I had to. Don said it got to him at first, too. They have no concept of personal space."

I'd noticed that.

"Ricardo just took a second wife. All the other men are jealous as hell and won't stop humbugging him. They probably didn't even notice you."

"Was he the young guy who kept grinning?"

"Don said it's not common, but one of the men said he knew of some other guy with two wives near San Antonio." Aaron seemed pretty smitten with the idea himself.

And that was the extent of our conversation about culture shock.

According to *Betty Crocker's New Picture Cook Book*—which Aaron's father had given to me as a Christmas present and which I had left in Verona—if I ever found myself in a situation where I didn't know what silverware to use, I should watch my hostess. With the Maya this wasn't a problem—they used their hands or *tortillas* to convey whatever they were eating into their mouth. But Mrs. Zuniga, the teacher's wife, had invited us for dinner and handed me a plate of *tamales*. At each place setting was a knife, fork, and spoon, and I watched Mrs. Zuniga surreptitiously until she picked up her fork.

Meat of any kind was scarce in the village, and I was flattered that she considered us worthy of slaughtering a chicken. The *tamale*, the first I'd ever eaten, was delicious. My family's idea of ethnic food was pizza. I complimented Mrs. Zuniga. She smiled and gave me another one.

I unwrapped it from the husk and cut off a chunk with my fork. It made a big mouthful, and when I took my first bite, something hard scratched the inside of my cheek. Furtively I returned what had been in my mouth back to my plate and attempted to cut it in half.

This time I encountered scales.

Mr. Zuniga was talking to Aaron, and when his wife turned away from the table to one of their children, I pulled the *tamale* apart and discovered a chicken foot, complete with toenails. Was I supposed to eat it? Surely not the toenails!

I looked around the table. Everybody was still preoccupied, so I loosened the corn mixture from the chicken foot with my fingers and ate that.

As Aaron and I walked back to Don's house, I told him what I'd found in my *tamale*.

"They're poor—they don't waste anything. You ate it, I hope?"

I stopped walking. "You're kidding."

Aaron looked surprised. "No, I'm not, Squirrel. We have to live the way they do, or they won't accept us. And if they don't accept us, I can't study their culture. Our time here will be wasted."

"Even the bottom parts of the feet with tread on them? Do you know how that feels against your tongue? And how about the toenails? Bear-Bear, there was *dirt* under those toenails! Please don't tell me I'm supposed to eat the toenails!"

"I'd try. At the very least I'd slip them in my pocket while nobody was looking."

"Skirts don't have pockets."

Aaron sighed deeply and took my hand. "Come on, Squirrel. Let's go home. Arguing in public won't help anything."

"How about arguing in private?"

"Did I tell you I saw Gloria's old house today?"

"Who's Gloria?"

"Don's goddaughter. Huni and Gloria—the two kids? Remember? Somebody killed her father about eight weeks ago, and from the looks of the house, the stepmother packed up the kids and left the same day it happened."

I stopped walking again. "'Killed' as in 'murdered'? On purpose?"

"Squirrel, at this rate we'll never get back. Can you walk and talk at the same time? Come on—give it a try."

This was more like it. This was the Bear-Bear I had married, affectionate and boyish, teasing me and inviting me to tease him back—unlike Robert Jordan in *For Whom the Bell Tolls*, who bedded Maria but was too committed to a higher truth to banter with her. Hemingway's book had even inspired the nicknames Aaron and I gave each other. I bumped him with my hip. "I'll keep walking only if you tell me what happened. Who killed him?"

"Another Kekchi. One of his neighbors."

"Why?"

"The guy claims it was self-defense."

"Did it happen here? In Crique Sarco?"

"Yes."

"And?"

Aaron bumped me back. "And what?"

"What happened to him?"

"Who?"

"The guy who killed Gloria's father!"

"Nothing. Nobody brought charges against him. Come on. We're not home yet."

"You mean he's still *here*?"

"Where else would he be?"

I was so shocked I couldn't force my next question out of my mouth. Had this man been sitting outside with us, drinking *lab*?

"Gloria's family came from San Pedro Carchá in Guatemala," Aaron continued, oblivious. "Manuel told me how the Kekchi build houses there. It's an interesting construction—they seal the walls with clay halfway up, probably to conserve heat." We were approaching Don's house. Aaron dropped my hand.

"Hey," I protested.

"You need to be more observant, Squirrel. Haven't you noticed that married couples, even very young ones, aren't demonstrative in public? Women nuzzle their babies, and little kids often walk around holding hands, but not husbands and wives."

I stopped walking again. Few American couples—at least those my parents' age—kissy-faced in public either. But no holding hands? No hugging? "Wait a minute. I want to get this straight." I was surprised at how angry I felt. "In order to fit in we have to eat chicken feet *and* no more cuddly fun-stuff?"

"Squirrel, let's *go*. I want to sketch Che's house before I forget what it looks like."

And we'd be living among the Maya for an entire year? How far was Aaron planning to take this "we have to fit in" business? That's what *I* wanted to talk about. But Aaron wanted to talk about house construction, so "we" were talking about house construction.

I had a lot to learn about being a wife.

"Tuck in, you lot," Don urged us. He'd come up the Temax River to Crique Sarco by motorboat, carrying fresh meat. My three-week crash course in cultural immersion was over.

I had already cadged a Colonial from him. Tomorrow morning he would take us back to his house in Machaca Creek, and Aaron would talk to Father Cull about what villages needed a teacher. Aaron apparently didn't associate my behavior—running out of a strange woman's kitchen—with culture shock because he didn't mention it to Don, who assumed I had passed with flying colors. To Don this was an important rite of passage, and he wanted to help me celebrate.

I was touched, even though his idea of a celebration was "Let's make it as much like a proper British meal as possible—a joint of meat, a vegetable, and a sweet for dessert." He was all prepared—that's why he'd shot a *waree*, a wild boar, that morning.

Since Don was more adept at coaxing heat out of the stove than I was, I let him roast a rack of *waree* ribs. The vegetable was tinned celery, which tasted more like tin than celery. As soon as Petrona spotted him, she brought over some ripe plantains deep-fried in lard, her pretty, moon-round face creased with smiles. Dessert.

When Don pronounced the ribs done, he cut them apart and doled them out. I looked at mine dubiously. It was as long as my thighbone and teetered precariously on my plate. The meat was scorched in parts and blood red by the bone. I loved red meat—in its place. But its place was next to a baked potato with a salad on the side, or between two hamburger buns. What if this *waree* were diseased? It probably had worms—everything had worms here, even the children. And what about trichinosis?

But after watching Don and Aaron "tuck in" with obvious gusto, holding the ribs with both hands as if they were eating corn on the cob, I bit into mine.

To my surprise the *waree* didn't taste gamey, or even like pork. There just wasn't very much of it, and after gnawing the bone down to the nub, I was immediately hungry again. Without a very sharp knife or fangs, eating *waree* was like eating dental floss.

Father John Paul Cull, my new boss, was an American Jesuit of American Indian ancestry, a kind, fanatical man who often forgot to eat. He had a degree in geology and the stamina and intractability of a mule. In spite of his deficiencies—he didn't speak either Kekchi or Mopan Maya—he knew everybody in the district. Without him the Maya villages would have had no teachers at all.

Even though I wasn't Catholic, my two years of college made me one of the best-educated people in the colony, and Father Cull wanted me for a teacher. And somehow he got it done.

One night Aaron and I sat down with him in the rectory at San Antonio. He needed teachers in several villages, he told Aaron. But Aaron found something wrong with all of them—too remote, or the people were Mopan, not Kekchi—until Father Cull mentioned Santa

Elena. (Out of his hearing the Maya called it by its old name, Rio Blanco.) During dry season, he said, it was about a four-hour hike from San Antonio. The village was fairly new, mixed Kekchi and Mopan, and they'd had one teacher, a Garifuna man. The Indians had built a school and a house for him, both less than two years old, but he hadn't stayed. On the minus side, only seventy-plus people lived there, including children. The village was so small it had no *alcalde*, or mayor. It didn't even have a church. When Father Cull came, he celebrated mass in the schoolhouse.

Aaron thought Santa Elena would probably work, but before he committed himself he wanted to go see it. "I'll only be gone a day or two, Squirrel," he told me. "No sense in you tagging along. You'll just slow me down. You can wait in San Antonio until I come back."

"But where will I stay? I don't want to impose on Don again."

"There's a Garifuna nurse here, maybe you could stay with her. Or maybe Father Cull's housekeeper would be willing to take in a guest—she lives in town somewhere. Staying with Father Cull probably wouldn't be a good idea."

It wasn't—he never even offered. But neither did he suggest staying with the nurse, his housekeeper, or any of the teachers. So I stayed in the *cabildo*, a Spanish word usually translated as "town hall." But in Toledo District it meant the jail, which—luckily for me—happened to be vacant at the moment. It had four bunk beds, two on either side, that reminded me of the ones on the *Heron* except the mattresses were clean. One of the teachers told me that the last person to stay here had been a Mopan man who'd gotten drunk and started a fight with his neighbor, and the two "played machete." The winner had been the previous occupant. The loser had stumbled to the nurse's house with his arm sliced halfway off at the shoulder.

During the day I sat in on classes, where I learned catechism, the Hail Mary, and the Act of Contrition so I could teach them to my students. I also learned a song called "The Children's Mass." *Good thing I can carry a tune*, I thought. I hadn't realized it would be a job requirement.

After school let out, I stayed in the *cabildo* and read or wrote letters so I wouldn't have to talk to anybody. When it got dark I went to bed. There was an outhouse not far from the *cabildo* that I used as little as possible—tarantulas love dark, damp corners, and I was terrified even of small spiders, let alone ones the size of potholders. I wasn't too crazy about the outhouse itself, either. Perched on the edge of a ravine, it was so old I was afraid that if I sneezed it would break away from the hillside and crash into the rocks below with me bouncing around inside.

My second night in the *cabildo* the villagers held a festival. Father Cull insisted it was in celebration of the Virgin's birthday. To me it looked more like one of the dances the sixteenth-century Spanish priests had taught their Maya converts, complete with costumes and masks, a drum, a flute, and a marimba—all handmade—and rum. A *lot* of rum.

"I got into a wrangle about original sin with Father Cull this afternoon," I wrote to Barbara Davis, my best friend since childhood. "Mistake. He thinks all Maya girls ought to be married by fifteen so they won't live in 'enforced concubinage.' By that he means common-law marriage. I wonder if he knows about Ricardo's second wife."

Twice a day I cooked something over my single-burner Primus stove—instant oatmeal for breakfast and Knorr's dried soup for dinner—and thought about what I had gotten myself into. An only child with two working parents, I'd grown up to be a very private person who valued silence. The Maya valued neither. The only foreign country I had ever visited was Canada, where people spoke English and the women wore clothes above their waist. I knew how to boil water. What I didn't know was how to put something *in* the water and cook it.

But I did know one thing. In the short time I'd lived here, I realized that nothing I had learned in high school home economics applied to the Maya. Cooking was not a matter of consulting recipes and preparing food in an interesting and appealing fashion. To the Maya, cooking was a survival skill.

XX

CONVICT SOUP

1 package of Knorr's dried soup mix, any variety
water

Before buying the soup, hold the package up to the light and check for pinholes. After opening it, inspect the mix itself for black specks. If you see holes or black specks, the cockroaches beat you to the soup. Discard and try another package.

Add more water than the directions tell you to and boil the hell out of the soup for twenty minutes because nobody drinks the water in places like this without boiling it first.

Eat it anyway.

THREE

At Home in the Jungle

It was scarcely daylight when Aaron showed up in front of the *cabildo* with four men, a horse, and two mules. I was so relieved to see him I wanted to throw my arms around his neck and climb him like a tree. But he read my intentions and shook his head. Not in public.

Chastened, I watched the men load our belongings, realizing for the first time how much *stuff* we had. A lot of books: fat ones—like *The Merck Manual of Medical Information* (not recommended reading when you're bored and a day away from the nearest doctor)—and skinny ones, like *Ethnology of the Mayas of Southern and Central British Honduras* by J. Eric Thompson (an archaeologist who had lived near San Antonio while excavating the ruins of Lubaantun in the 1930s). We had magazines. We had clothes, Aaron's rifle, my typewriter, the Primus stove, and other cookware. And we had food. Not only staples like salt and instant coffee, but a year's worth of freeze-dried meals designed for astronauts that our mothers had packed for us. The horse and mules were laden like prospectors' burros.

It was hot and humid and the beginning of rainy season, and the road to Santa Elena was so muddy it looked like pureed prunes. Everything around us dripped—trees, leaves, underbrush, the sky. Since I didn't wear socks with my sneakers, my feet immediately broke out in blisters. Aaron wore laced paratrooper boots—his feet stayed unblistered and dry. So did the feet of the two Maya men wearing knee-high rubber boots. The other two were barefoot.

The trail wound around *milpas* and descended into valleys broken by small, cold streams. In the distance I could see the Maya Mountains, pale blue and hugging the horizon like smoke. Except for the watery sky, everything was green. Even the random, humpbacked hills that surrounded us, symmetrical as a child's drawing, were green.

After we passed Santa Cruz—Rio Blanco was the next town, if we ever got there—the trail narrowed and turned into sludge. The mud, churned up by mules and puddled with urine, came halfway to my knees and made obscene sucking noises as I slogged through it. I took my sneakers off—each one weighed at least five pounds—knocked the mud off them, tied the laces together, and slung them over my shoulder.

"That's not smart," Aaron told me.

"So what?" I snarled. My feet hurt and I was feeling sorry for myself.

"You don't know what's in that mud," Aaron said, as though he did. "You'll get worms."

"Those guys aren't wearing shoes."

"They're used to it."

"And how did they get used to it? By not wearing shoes."

Aaron frowned at me in warning. "Have it your way. *Be* stubborn. But don't say I didn't warn you."

"Don't worry. I won't." I felt like an eight-year-old squabbling with another eight-year-old.

The Maya acted as though none of them had understood the exchange. But a few miles farther on Evaristo, the good-looking one, stopped abruptly. "Look, Mr. World. You see the ants?"

Mr. World? I thought. Where had *that* come from? We all stopped to watch two lines of ants scurrying side by side like cars in traffic, running briefly parallel to the trail before disappearing into the bush. Each in-going ant held a piece of vegetation over its head like a tiny green umbrella. The men murmured among themselves.

"Are they dangerous?" I asked Aaron, as scenes from jungle adventure movies (all featuring tarantulas and snakes as thick as soup cans) flashed through my head. "Should we just be *standing* here?" As opposed to running the movie backward—back to the *cabildo*, back to Crique Sarco, back to Don's house, back to Belize City, back to Michigan, where I could smoke and wear jeans?

"They're leaf-cutter ants. Completely harmless," Aaron said curtly. He was still smarting from our shoe exchange. In *For Whom the Bell Tolls* Maria always deferred to her man. "The dangerous ones are the army ants. When they're on the move, they can strip the meat off your bones in a matter of minutes if you don't get out of their way."

"Ants like this we call wee-wees," Evaristo said, looking at Aaron. "No good. They go into one man's *milpa* and the next day, when the man come back, his corn is gone. Everything. Gone." Now he was looking straight at me.

I wasn't expecting that—a Maya talking to me while making eye contact. All I could think of to say was, "In one night?"

"Yes, Missus. Just so. One night."

I looked back at him. Evaristo had a distinctive, triangular face with high cheekbones and a ready smile, and was Aaron's height. In fact—I took a quick look around to confirm this—several of the men were Aaron's height. Did that mean I might finally have a hammock big enough to *sleep* in?

Even though I'd gone barefoot every summer of my life, my feet were no match for rainforest mud. By the time we caught sight of the Rio Blanco River, they were so mutilated I was limping. Everybody stopped in the shallow river crossing to drink. "Go ahead, Squirrel," Aaron said. "It's good water."

Too tired to think up a decent retort, I splashed water on my face and drank from my cupped hands. The water *was* good—cold and rich with minerals. I wanted to roll in it. Here at the crossing, the streambed was a flat sheet of limestone, swept clean of sediment, shadowed on both sides by ancient, wide-branched trees. Up close I could distinguish individual shrubs and vines, which I hadn't been able to do from the *Heron*. But it was so dense, so thick with vegetation, that if a jaguar had been crouching a foot away from me I wouldn't have seen it. There was the river—a light, translucent green—and the sky. The rest was jungle, without daylight, without movement, without sound.

I took a final drink. As I raised my hands to my mouth, tiny, inchworm-sized fish slithered though my fingers back into the river. I sank to my knees, coughing and gasping and trying not to imagine what swallowing them would feel like. Aaron grabbed my elbow. "What's wrong?"

"There are . . . I almost . . . nothing."

José Tux, the old man who seemed to be in charge, interrupted the other men, who were teasing one another, and told them to get moving. Heavy-handed teasing was a common Maya pastime that Don, no slacker at it himself, called "humbugging." The men rolled up their pants' legs and waded across the river. I rewound my ponytail to get the hair out of my face and followed them.

As soon as we arrived at the other side, two ragged children spotted us. They shrieked, then clapped their hands over their mouths and ran in the opposite direction. The next sound I heard was a mournful, long-drawn-out *wooo*.

I broke out in goose bumps. "What was *that*?"

"Conch shell," replied the Answer Man. "The ancient Maya used them—Thompson calls them 'conch trumpets' in his book. I think the *mayordomo* just announced our arrival."

The trail wound uphill from the river. Here and there I saw wooden houses with thatched roofs. Some families had citrus trees in their yard, or cacao trees, or coffee bushes. More children ran out to stare at us, accompanied by their parents. The men wore the same long-sleeved, Western-style shirts the Kekchi had in Crique Sarco, with unbelted trousers the color of tea. But the women—I stared at them, then away—wore long skirts in various shades of buttercup yellow, pink, and purple. They resembled layered petticoats, some with ruffles. A few women wore a type of *huipil*, white blouses decorated around the neck and sleeves with elaborate black hand-stitching. But most women were bare-breasted.

"Why aren't they wearing Kekchi skirts?" I whispered to Aaron.

"Mopan skirts are cheaper. That's the Kekchi for you—pragmatic."

When the trail leveled out, Aaron stopped. "There's the school," he said, pointing. "That big building. And here we are. This is it."

"It" was the teacher's house—my first house as a married woman.

Carefully I stepped through a gaping hole in the front wall, past two men who knelt on the ground while they laced saplings together with tie-ties—thin, supple vines. Our new front door?

The house was the size of my parents' living room. The walls were rough-hewn vertical planks held together with tie-ties. It had no windows. (Neither did anybody else's house.) The floor was dirt, and the roof was thatched with overlapping layers of palm fronds. One of the corner posts had sprouted—my very own indoor weed patch.

"It had a sleeping platform originally." Aaron was talking faster than he normally did, probably to make up for the fact that I was too stunned to say anything. "That's what the Garifuna prefer. Of course a lot of people in Crique Sarco slept on platforms, too, but Manuel told me that was to protect them from vampire bats."

Vampire bats? I closed my eyes and took several deep breaths. Were there any here in Rio Blanco? We hadn't brought mosquito netting. And those flesh-eating ants—had Aaron been humbugging me?

"But I asked them to take it out so we'd have room to string our hammocks," Aaron continued. He *sounded* sincere. "It didn't have a back door, either, so they're going to cut out a portion of the wall and make us one. Everybody's really excited to have a teacher here again."

"Where's the outhouse?"

Aaron cleared his throat. "Well, I asked Mateo Ical—he's the headman, the *mayordomo*, the guy going through my pack over there—and he said the ground is too rocky to dig a latrine. The Peace Corps built a communal latrine here last year but nobody uses it. Well—they do, but as a dump. You know. Cans and whatnot."

It seemed as though all seventy villagers were crammed inside our house. We were clearly the most interesting thing that had happened in Rio Blanco in years, but rather than ask direct questions, the Maya stood around and stared at us.

Don had told me that the Maya "this side" of Toledo District, meaning north of Crique Sarco, had all seen white men before—Don himself, Father Cull, the bishop of British Honduras, various British army officers. But most had never seen a white woman.

"I asked one of the men to make you a hammock," Aaron continued. The more he talked, the less he sounded like anybody I knew. He sounded like a used-car salesman. "But it won't be ready for a while yet. I guess we'll both have to sleep in mine for the time being."

His hammock was woven out of colorful Yucatec yarn and was big enough for two people—in theory. In practice I tend to thrash in my sleep and had elbowed him in the eye our first night in Crique Sarco. That was why I had slept by myself in a too-short hammock.

"Well?" Aaron asked finally, his voice thick with apprehension.

"Where's the rest of it?" I was so dismayed I didn't even feel the sand flies boring into my skin until I went to bed that night. By then my ankles were rimmed with blood-specked welts that wouldn't stop itching. "Where's the *stove*?"

I hadn't expected a refrigerator, but a table and chairs would have been nice. And water—how would I get water? How would I wash clothes? In Crique Sarco I had washed them by hand in a metal tub using a washboard, but the tub and washboard belonged to Don, so I'd left them there. "What about our clothes? Do they just stay in boxes? And the flour and our cooking stuff—where do we put it all? And if we don't have an outhouse, what do we *do*?" My voice had risen to a wail.

"What the Maya do." Aaron sounded as though he were pleading with me. "Go bush."

I didn't have to be told what that meant. I would walk outside carrying a roll of toilet paper until I reached a spot far enough away from my neighbors that nobody could see me. Rain and the pigs would take care of the rest.

As I absorbed the fact that I would be living without a stove, a sink, a shower, running water, and a bathroom—let alone electricity—for the next year, a slender Mopan woman staggered through what would be our front door, clutching a smooth, flat rock. None of the men offered to help her. She, too, was topless, her skirt a faded bubblegum pink.

"For you, Teacher. For to cook," she panted, looking at me sideways. She was our next-door neighbor, Dolores Choc.

I started to ask how a flat rock was supposed to help me cook when a younger, slimmer version of Dolores—except she wore a soiled green dress—lurched in with another, even bigger rock. Dolores said something to her in Mopan, and the girl, her daughter Paulina, set the rock down, slipped out silently, and returned a few minutes later carrying yet a third rock and a rusty machete blade.

Kneeling, Dolores dug a shallow trench into the floor using the machete. After balancing one stone upright on its long side like a package of bacon, she dug two additional trenches and fitted the other stones against them. Assembled, they formed a three-sided enclosure about twenty inches high. For the final flourish, Dolores laid the machete blade across the open end of what I, a former Girl Scout with an Outdoor Cooking badge, finally recognized as a rudimentary fireplace.

Another barefoot woman came through the doorway, carrying a plate of hot corn *tortillas*. She was bare-breasted, too, except for a colorful beaded necklace with a safety pin dangling from it. She had a pretty face, dark, intelligent eyes, and wore a glossy magenta skirt. "For you," she murmured, handing me the plate. I found out later—when I found out who Dolores was—that her name was Lucia, and that she was Evaristo's sister. When she spoke to me, she looked me in the face the same way he did.

But before I could thank either woman, a young boy rushed up, so agitated and out of breath his words came out in spurts.

"Damn," Aaron murmured as the villagers tore out of our house like stampeding horses. "I hope that hog pen is on the other side of the village."

"What's wrong?"

"A jaguar just attacked somebody's pig."

Maybe I *had* been a foot away from a jaguar at the river crossing. I closed my eyes again, hoping that when I opened them I'd be someplace else—New Jersey, even. No such luck.

Only one little boy, naked except for a dusty brown shirt, remained in the house, staring at us. When he realized he was all by himself, he rushed out the doorway with both arms outstretched, howling for his mother. I knew exactly how he felt.

It was getting dark out. "We need some light," Aaron said, heading for the hacked-out hole in the back wall that would someday be a door. "Why don't you look through those boxes and see what you can find?"

"Wait! Where are you going?" I ran after him.

"Mateo's, to get firewood."

As soon as I stepped outside, I saw something I hadn't noticed before. Five houses, including ours, were clustered around the school. From here I could look straight through the front door of Dolores's house, Lucia's house, and Mateo's house—and they, presumably, could look straight into ours. There was also a fourth house, directly behind us, so close it looked as though ours were casting a shadow. Around each house was a cleared space, and beyond the clearing was jungle. Downtown Rio Blanco.

I had never felt so alone in my life.

By the time Aaron returned with an armload of wood, I had found the flashlight, turned it on, and set it on a box. Aaron dropped the wood and started to lay a fire. Then he sat back and we stared at one another. We had firewood and a stove, but nothing to cook.

While Aaron held the flashlight, I rummaged through more boxes until I found a can equipped with its own key—no need to stab it open with a machete.

XXX

SARDINE SURPRISE

> 1 can whole sardines, packed in oil
> ground *chile* pepper (optional)
> hot-off-the-*comal tortillas*

Lay a strip of sardines down the center of the *tortilla* and fold the ends of the *tortilla* over until they meet. If you prefer, roll the *tortilla* up tube fashion, the way you would a rug.

Feeds 1½ people.

FOUR

The Village Idiot

Aaron and I had just finished our instant oatmeal the following morning—I was sitting on a box of books while Aaron reclined in his hammock—when a teenage boy arrived with a load of firewood. He looked as though his mother had put a bowl over his head and then snipped around it with blunt scissors. He had entered without asking, and after depositing the wood inside the door, he flipped his hair out of his face long enough to give us a quick, thorough once-over. Then, eyes downcast, he left.

"Why don't they look us in the face?" I asked as I made myself another, stronger cup of instant coffee. It was still a novelty after three weeks of tea, but it didn't even begin to make me feel better about being here.

"It's a way of showing deference," the Answer Man said, his voice kindly. I must not have stuck my elbow in his eye the previous night. "We do the same thing—who we feel free to touch, for example, as opposed to someone of higher status we would never consider touching."

I lowered myself into his hammock and stretched out next to him. What I wanted to do was pound my fists on his chest and demand to be taken home. Instead, I slid one bare foot slowly up his leg. "Who do *you* feel free to touch?"

He looked at me sideways. "Or who we feel free to interrupt."

"I never interrupt you."

He almost grinned. "You interrupt me all the time."

"So if they look you in the eye, like Evaristo and Lucia, they consider you equals?"

"Right."

"I wonder if it's part of their culture or a behavior colonialism imposed on them."

"Of course it's colonialism! Damn Brits—the Kekchi have darker skin, live in 'primitive' houses, have 'primitive' skills. Never mind that their forebears developed the most elaborate civilization in the New World, to say nothing of having created a written language, come up with the concept of zero, and were such brilliant astronomers they developed a calendar almost as precise as our own. Look at the British in India—different people, same dynamic. Identical."

I wondered if Don Owen-Lewis were perpetuating this "dynamic." The only time I had seen him exert his authority had been on my behalf, the day we arrived in Crique Sarco. Several young Kekchi men had immediately sauntered into his house and made themselves at home, lolling in the hammocks and bantering with him while Aaron took me to meet Manuel and Petrona Xi. On our way back, Aaron detoured to the latrine and I walked into the porch alone. Seeing that all the hammocks were occupied, I hesitated in the doorway. The young men broke off their conversation to stare at me.

"*Elen re li ab*," Don said sharply. Get out of the hammock. Looking surprised, the man closest to me rose reluctantly so I could sit down. Don wasn't teaching them to feel inferior. He was teaching them manners—it was part of his job.

Aaron jarred me back to the here and now. "I want to get the men together this morning to clear the bush around the school. I have to get moving, Squirrel."

"Right now? I thought we could maybe—*relax* a little? Together? I haven't seen you for four days!"

Aaron rubbed noses with me—another Squirrel and Bear-Bear ritual—then pushed himself out of the hammock. "Have you taken a good look at the walls? To say nothing about our nonexistent back door? We'll have to wait until it gets dark to 'relax.' We try anything during daylight hours and we'll have the entire village gawking at us."

He was right. The chinks between the boards were wide enough to slide my hand through.

"As for not seeing me for a couple of days, don't forget I'm studying the Kekchi of Toledo District, not only the Kekchi here in Rio Blanco." Aaron strapped on his machete. "I'll be gone a lot."

"I know. You told me that." We had just gotten here. Was he already talking about abandoning me again?

"Okay, then." Aaron leaned down to kiss me. "Good-bye, Squirrel."

He was.

Over the next few days the house lost some of its primitivism as we acquired furniture, bush-style. A rough but recognizable table appeared, courtesy of Aaron and some of the men who had built our doors. One leg was shorter than the other three; I slid a piece of cardboard under it. Somebody gave us two backless wooden seats, or *bancos*, that resembled footrests. Courtesy of Evaristo, long, picnic-style benches lined the walls on either side of the front door. A small, three-tiered wooden shelf materialized against the wall by the fireplace. My pantry. Although it was an effort—I loathed getting out of my hammock in the morning—I unpacked some boxes. Flour, margarine, onions, and lard went on the bottom shelf. Instant coffee—which the Maya called *café listo*, Spanish for "ready" coffee—and dried soup mixes went on the next shelf. But after stacking my blue and white tin dishes on the top shelf—I saved the smoothest section for a cutting board—I didn't have anyplace to put pots.

Speculatively I eyed the corner post, the one sprouting leaves. I asked Aaron to hammer a few nails into it and hung the pots from them. Every time I used one, I inspected it for cockroach droppings. Half a dried calabash floated in a water bucket on the floor at the other end of the shelves. We drank from the calabash, used it as a measuring cup and as a small basin when we brushed our teeth and washed our faces. I felt as though I were camping in the woods with no adult supervision.

Every afternoon I emptied the water that remained in the bucket and trudged barefoot down to the river to bring back fresh water. It was a longer hike than it had been in Crique Sarco, and my shins were taking such a beating that I used both hands to hug the pail against my stomach. The women all laughed at me. Like Petrona, they carried their water buckets on their heads.

When more tie-tie vines materialized, Aaron assembled, from leftover saplings, a framework to hold our clothes, still in cardboard boxes. It reminded me of a poor man's vertical closet organizer.

Finally someone brought over a hammock for me. Unlike Aaron's, it was a quiet, subdued tan, woven out of henequen so intricately that it looked crocheted. Every morning I woke up with diamond-shaped patterns embedded in my face.

But it was too small for me.

I lit the kerosene lamp, adjusted the wick, and was squinting at the directions on a box of Tang when I saw a female figure loitering outside our closed front door. She'd seen me, too. "*Caba nu*," she said softly.

Aaron was awake—he'd just asked me what we were having for breakfast. Instant oatmeal. What did he think we were having? "Aaron? What should I do?"

"Invite her in. She just greeted you in Kekchi. Oh shit—wait!" He rolled out of his hammock, simultaneously pulling on his pants. "Okay."

I opened the door, trying not to let my annoyance show. Why couldn't these people knock? They either sauntered in without an invitation, or they lurked outside until somebody noticed them.

The woman was very young. She held a piece of paper in one hand and a child by the other, a little boy with a large, pale face, his hair slicked back with water. Shyly she smoothed the paper flat on the table. It was a birth certificate, and it said that the little boy's name was Aprimo Tux and that his father was Eustaquio Tux, one of the many sons of José Tux. José was one of the oldest men in the village and by far the most prolific. When school started two days later, Aprimo, who was five, arrived with his uncle Crisantos, also five—the old man's youngest child.

"*Aha*," I told Aprimo's mother. "Yes" was one of the few Kekchi words I knew. Aprimo was old enough to go to school.

The woman's eyes grazed my face and she nodded back in corroboration, reaching for her son's hand again. "*Uss.*" Good.

This ritual had been going on for days. At least a dozen mothers had trooped in with children in tow, asking if the child could attend school. According to Father Cull, schooling was compulsory for all children six to fourteen. Most parents wanted their children in class. But not Dolores Choc, our neighbor. "Paulina need it one husband," she told me earnestly, pronouncing the word "whosban." "Too old for school."

I still had trouble talking to bare-breasted women—I stared instead at the uneven part in Dolores's long, braided hair. But I took teaching seriously. If Paulina was younger than fourteen—and my guess was twelve or thirteen, in spite of her shapely body—she was going to school. "How old is she?"

"Well, I don't know, Teacher."

"Do you have her birth certificate?"

Dolores's expression turned coy. "No," she said, smiling broadly. Her teeth were a mossy greenish-brown.

"I bet we can figure it out. Valeria is six—we decided that yesterday." Valeria was Dolores's youngest daughter. "And Eluterio is eight."

Dolores nodded reluctantly.

"How much older is Paulina than Eluterio?" I prodded.

"Well, I don't know. Maybe five rains?"

"Then she should be in school." The Maya used "rains" to calculate age, so if Paulina had lived through five more rainy seasons than her brother, she was thirteen.

Dolores looked unhappy. She was probably wishing she hadn't gone through all the trouble of building me a fireplace that first day—this wasn't how neighbors were supposed to repay favors. "But we need she in the *milpa*, to back corn!"

Aaron interrupted our discussion. "Dolores, how much would you charge to make us *tortillas* for lunch?"

His question clearly caught her off guard. It caught me off guard, too. Ever since Aaron and I had arrived here, I'd been inhaling the fragrant, corn-chip aroma of freshly made *tortillas* wafting from the women's houses and salivating.

Dolores frowned. "What you say?"

"My wife doesn't have time to make *tortillas*. How much would you charge to make us *tortillas* for lunch every day?"

After several offers and counteroffers, she and Aaron agreed he would pay her fifty cents BH (British Honduras) a week, and in exchange she'd cook a few extra *tortillas* at lunchtime and give them to us.

As if to seal the bargain, she came back around noon with a stack of fresh *tortillas* and a plate of rice and beans. I suspected she hadn't given up on Paulina, but that was between her and Father Cull. As far as I was concerned, Paulina was one of my students.

Aaron had assured me—and attempted to reassure my mother—that we wouldn't die of malnutrition in the jungle. The staple diet of the Maya was corn and beans, and had been for centuries. Each food filled some essential niche missing in the other. Nutrition-wise, it was the perfect diet.

Taste-wise it was another story. Maya beans weren't the tender string beans or buttery wax beans of my childhood. They were dried, and the women cooked them by reconstituting them with water and simmering them into submission until they had a runny pink stew. The main difference between their beans and Creole stew beans was *chile* pepper—an essential ingredient in Maya cooking. (Stew beans traditionally include a can of coconut cream and a pig's tail.)

I had never been a dried bean fan. When I was small my mother once told me to eat the lima beans on my plate, or else. I forced a few down and promptly threw up all over the table. That's why I cooked white rice—which the Maya had started growing as a cash crop only a few years earlier—before I learned to cook beans. I had watched my mother and knew that making rice required even less effort than making instant oatmeal. Aaron liked beans and *tortillas* with his rice. I liked mine with margarine—hold the beans.

Thanks to Aaron our food situation had improved considerably, but I still had to get water every day, and I still had to do laundry. One morning I waylaid Lucia on her way to the river and asked if she would teach me how to wash clothes. I could have asked Dolores, but I liked Lucia better. She was smart, like her brother Evaristo, said exactly what was on her mind, and didn't gawk at me. And her teeth weren't green. Like Dolores, she came from San Antonio. Both women spoke good English in low, sonorous voices. But while Dolores was tall and lithe with a slim back and straight, slender legs, Lucia was short and squat and slightly bowlegged. While Dolores swished languidly from place to place with her skirt swirling around her ankles, Lucia wrapped her skirt around her legs, hiked it to her knees, and tucked the hem into her waistband. By nature she was more reserved than Dolores, and more careful to conceal what she was thinking—in this case, that Teacher must be a halfwit. Why else would a lady (a Creole word—all women were ladies) of my advanced age not know how to wash clothes?

"How you could do like so in your country?" she demanded.

"*Re li máquina*," I told her. Using a machine.

"*In'ca*," she exclaimed, disbelief coloring her words in spite of her best efforts. No way.

"It's true. The machine does everything."

A machine that washed clothes? That was *too* unthinkable. Lucia flashed me the look people give liars—contempt tempered by pity—and said she'd be doing laundry the following morning. If I wanted to I could tag along.

She arrived at my house with her dirty clothes stacked in a neatly folded bundle on her head, accompanied by her daughter, Natalia. As usual she was bare-breasted. Damn! Was I supposed to take my blouse off when I did laundry just because the Maya did? I already felt conspicuous. I'd feel like a freak sauntering down to the river wearing only a bra. But I wasn't about to embrace the totally topless look, either.

I made a quick decision. The Maya might not be civilized—that was still up for grabs. But I was. Dirty clothes tucked under one arm, I walked out the door fully clothed, smiling resolutely.

Nine-year-old Natalia wore a Western-style dress with a Peter Pan collar. In one hand she clutched half a calabash that held a trial-sized box of Tide. With the other hand she clutched the hem of her mother's skirt. She had bright, lively eyes but was very shy.

Lucia took me down the hill where the women got their drinking water, then led me downstream about a quarter of a mile. The river flowed fast here—no telltale soapsuds would remain behind. Near the middle of the river were several flat, greasy-looking rocks set at an angle so one end was higher than the other. Lucia waded out to one and set her laundry on it. The rock she chose had another advantage: a quiet eddy swirled around one end, and without being told, Natalia placed the calabash there. Instead of floating downstream with the current, it bobbed and circled, keeping the Tide within easy reach.

I chose a washing stone a few feet below Lucia's, so I could watch. She positioned herself at the raised end of the rock and reached for the first piece of clothing.

Step 1: Unfold item to be washed and use the calabash to splash water on it.

Step 2: Sprinkle detergent on the item.

Step 3: Use one end of the item to scrub the rest of the item lengthwise.

Step 4: Flip the item over and repeat the process.

Step 5: Dunk the item in the river until the water runs clear.

Step 6: Squeeze every last drop of water out of the item.

Step 7: Refold the item and set aside on a dry rock.

Step 8: Repeat steps 1–7 with every piece of clothing in your pile.

Lucia had three people to wash clothes for while I only had two, but Aaron had brought several new pairs of chinos before we left the States, which were very stiff. The scrubbing part wasn't a problem, even though I didn't have Tide. I had a bar of laundry soap that had been cut from an even longer piece that resembled curbing that Aaron had bought in Punta Gorda.

The tiny, worm-thin fish that lived in the river liked the taste of laundry soap—or else they liked the taste of me. Their "bites" were more like exploratory nibbles, but what if they attracted bigger fish, that *did* bite? What if they attracted crocodiles?

I couldn't squeeze the water out of Aaron's chinos. My hands were accustomed to typing, not wringing water out of clothes. No matter how hard I tried, the chinos continued to leak, wetting all the clothes underneath and on top of them.

As we headed back to the village, I saw the same expression on Lucia's face that I'd seen on Cirila's when I flunked *Tortilla* Making 101. I carried my clean clothes on my head, the way she did, but I could barely see where I was going because of the water dribbling down my face.

"Lucia, how much would you charge to wash our clothes once a week?"

"How much you pay Dolores for *tortillas*?" Lucia parried.

Small-town life, I thought. *Just like Verona*. I was surprised she didn't already know. "Fifty cents a week."

"Two dollar."

"But that's over four times what we pay Dolores!"

"*Pues*, but she going make *tortilla* anyway. Me, I only got to wash for three peoples. Now I got to wash for five."

I didn't like bargaining; it made me feel petty. We compromised on two dollars BH a week.

As I draped my clothes over a makeshift clothesline, half a dozen kids ran over, pointing at my bra. "Teacher! What this could be?" an adolescent boy demanded. I made another snap decision: I wasn't going to wear bras in the rainforest.

By the time I walked into the house, I was feeling pretty cocky. Twenty years old and I'd hired a washwoman. Maybe I could hire a cook, too.

But Bear-Bear was aghast. "You promised her two bucks a week when we hardly have money to buy food?"

"What are you talking about? As soon as I start teaching we'll have plenty of money!" Money was rapidly overtaking cigarettes and skirts as the sore point between us. Aaron had applied for a grant from the anthropology department at Michigan, which had funded only part of it, which meant we depended heavily on my teaching salary. Father Cull had agreed to pay me sixty-three dollars BH a month. The money would finance Aaron's enrollment in the Universidad de San Carlos and cover our living expenses.

"Did Lucia agree to do it?" Aaron demanded.

"Yes."

"Then I won't renege on a promise. But I want to reevaluate the situation in a few months."

I didn't like what I heard. The Answer Man was turning into Mr. We'll-Do-It-My-Way.

"And promise me you won't hire anybody else to do anything." Aaron stared into my face, his eyes hard. "Squirrel, did you hear me?"

I stared back. "I heard you."

"Well?"

"Well what? I *heard* you!"

"Promise me you won't hire anybody else."

"Oh, come *on*! Okay—I promise not to hire anybody else. Happy?"

"No, to be honest. Why didn't you talk to me about it before you asked Lucia?"

Because it hadn't occurred to me? Because he had accepted an invitation without consulting me, and then defended his decision? "I'm an only child," I snapped. "I'm used to making my own decisions."

"Well, you're not an only child anymore," Aaron snapped back. "You're my wife. So let's start thinking about 'us' for a change."

Wrong, I thought. I was *still* an only child. As for thinking about "us," I wasn't sure there *was* an "us" yet.

I walked out the door fuming, my empty water bucket on my head. We couldn't live on rice, *tortillas*, and instant oatmeal for the next year. I *had* to learn to cook.

xxxxxxxxxxxxxxxxxxxxxxxxxxxxxxxxxxxxxxxxxxxxxxxxxxxxxxxxxxxxx

TRADITIONAL MAYA RICE . . .

> rice
> water

However much rice you cook, add twice that amount of water. If you use a cup of rice, pour the rice in a pot and add two cups of water.

Bring to a boil, uncovered. When the mixture reaches a rolling boil, stir, cover, and lower the heat. Simmer about 15 minutes. If it's crisp on the bottom, check after 10 minutes next time. If it's still runny, recover and simmer another 5 minutes. When the rice is done, it will look as though somebody drilled holes in it.

A cup of uncooked rice feeds 2 people.

xxxxxxxxxxxxxxxxxxxxxxxxxxxxxxxxxxxxxxxxxxxxxxxxxxxxxxxxxxxxx

. . . AND BEANS

These are old-fashioned beans, the way Cirila Chub used to make them—well done, with a lot of bean gravy.

> 2 cups dried beans—pink, red, pinto, or kidney
> 8 cups water
> 2 dried *chile arbol* peppers or to taste (see the caution that follows)

    1 large onion, diced
    2 teaspoons dried thyme leaves
    ½ teaspoon ground black pepper
    salt to taste

Wash the beans by putting them in the cooking pot and adding water. Pick out pebbles and discard any beans that float. Drain and rinse.

Return beans to pot and add water. Do not cover. As the beans come to a boil, dice the onion and add it to the pot. Add *chile* peppers by tearing them into small pieces, seeds included. Add thyme and black pepper.

When beans come to a boil, lower the heat and cook, uncovered, about 2 hours. If they get too thick, add more water. If you want extra fire, add cayenne in very small increments.

Do not add salt until the beans have finished cooking; it retards the cooking process.

Feeds 6–8 people.

Caution: Wash your hands with soap and water immediately after handling peppers, and do not rub your eyes. If you do, you'll be half blind the rest of the day. Some cooks find *chiles*, fresh or dried, so irritating to their skin that they wear rubber gloves.

xxxxxxxxxxxxxxxxxxxxxxxxxxxxxxxxxxxxxxxxxxxxxxxxxxxxxxx

MODERN MAYA BEANS

Contemporary cooks prefer this method. It doesn't yield as much gravy, but the taste and texture are more appealing because the beans don't cook as long. I combined two recipes, one from Don Owen-Lewis's daughter, Francisca Bardalez of Big Falls, the second from her Kekchi neighbor, Juana Tut.

    2 cups dried beans
    6 cups water
    2 whole dried *chile arbol* peppers or to taste, or use fresh *chile*
        pepper (see the note that follows)

1 teaspoon dried cumin

1 teaspoon dried thyme, or 1 tablespoon fresh

1 teaspoon dried oregano

¼ teaspoon ground black pepper

2 tablespoons lard

½ large onion, diced

2 large cloves garlic, pressed or minced

1 or 2 teaspoons salt

Cook the first seven ingredients (up to lard) as in the preceding recipe, but simmer gently just until beans are tender, about 45 minutes. As they cook, heat the lard and sauté the onions. At the last minute add the garlic; you don't want it to brown. Add the mixture to the cooked beans along with salt to taste and simmer about 15 minutes more to blend the flavors.

Also feeds 6–8 people.

Note: A *chile arbol* looks like a skinny red string bean. A *chile pequin* is a small, raisin-shaped *chile* much hotter than a *jalapeño*, a.k.a. "bird pepper." Both are available dried in most American supermarkets. Use sparingly until you know your tolerance for heat. Fresh *chiles* can usually be found in the produce section. Follow the same precautions you would for dried *chiles* and, if necessary, wear rubber gloves.

FIVE

No Lips or Eyelids

Before class started Aaron and I went up to the schoolhouse to see if
anything needed fixing. Outside the door a heavy metal pipe hung like
a pendulum, threaded through the top with tie-tie vines and fastened
to a roof beam. "What's that?" I asked.

After examining it Aaron picked up a thin metal rod lying in the dirt
beneath it. "I bet the former teacher used it for a school bell." He swung
the rod against the pipe like a baseball bat. The result was a deep, vibrant
hum I felt in the marrow of my bones. Even my sinuses resonated. People
all around us swarmed out of their houses toward us. Something must
have happened. Why else had Teacher summoned a meeting?

Teacher hadn't. In fact Teacher was so alarmed by this sudden on-
slaught of people that she almost bolted again. But this time there was
no safe haven.

Aaron decided it would be the perfect opportunity to tell people
when school would start. "Go ahead, Squirrel."

I squirmed. I hated public speaking. "*You* tell them."

Newcomers kept arriving, panting and out of breath—people who
lived down by the river crossing, as well as people from the Tux clan

(as Aaron called them), who lived in the opposite direction. In limping Kekchi Aaron told the crowd that school would start tomorrow at nine o'clock. There would be an hour-long break for lunch, and school would begin again at one o'clock and go until three. "At eight o'clock Teacher will ring the school bell three times, to let you know that school will start in one hour. At nine o'clock she will ring the bell once, to announce the start of school."

The villagers continued to stare at us. "Teacher will ring the bell again at one o'clock," Aaron continued, and then talked about supplies the kids would need. After his brief speech he looked around at the villagers to see if they had questions. It appeared that they didn't. I asked him if he was sure they understood what he'd said. Aaron looked surprised. Of course they understood. What made me think they hadn't?

"Then why are they still standing here?"

"They're intrigued by us," he said patiently. "You know that, Squirrel. Let's take a look inside the school."

It was twice as big as our house but otherwise just like it, with a dirt floor and a thatched roof. All it lacked was hammocks and a fireplace. Two minutes later we walked back out. The villagers were still there. Aaron and I looked at one another. Aaron shrugged, and we walked home. To my consternation the entire crowd followed us. People pushed through both doors and made themselves comfortable on the benches, picking up magazines, sometimes upside down, to look at the pictures. A few people leafed through J. Eric Thompson's book, which happened to be on the table. Others simply stared, either at our belongings or at us. It was exactly what had happened the first day, except now they apparently felt they knew us well enough to ask questions.

"How much this could cost?" Dolores wanted to know, pointing to my typewriter. Like most Maya, she had trouble with the *th* sound, and "this" came out "dis." I told her. Martín Ical pointed at Aaron's machete, an English-made Collins exactly like his own, and asked the same question in Kekchi: how much had it cost? Topless women leaned against the door frame, nursing babies and gossiping. Everybody seemed relaxed and at ease, as though they planned to spend the rest of the morning here.

I lay in my hammock trying to read, wondering if they'd leave as it got closer to lunchtime. Half a dozen giggling little girls surrounded me, all of them stroking my hair the way the kids in Crique Sarco had. Suddenly one grabbed a few of the scraggly short hairs on the back of my neck and pulled. Hard.

"Hey, that hurt!"

"Ayiii!" she shrieked, stepping backward to look at the strands of hair in her hand. "*Coma ik'e!*"

Laughter erupted. Even the nursing infants giggled and cooed. "She says your hair is like henequen—what they use to make hammocks," Aaron said loudly, so I could hear him. He was laughing, too.

I clenched my teeth and stared resolutely at my book, but the print blurred. Living in a bush house in the middle of the jungle wasn't nearly the adventure I'd thought it would be. This was worse than Crique Sarco, where I could leave after three weeks. This felt like doing prison time.

I hated it. I hated how strange everything was. I hated the poverty—the kids with their big, wormy bellies, the starving dogs. I hated the people, who were constantly underfoot and couldn't get enough of watching me. I hated that they felt free to touch me. I hated this house, the humidity, the rain, the heat, the tarantulas I knew were out there somewhere, the sand flies, the toad that lived under my flour sack, the cockroaches, the smells, and the *tortillas* I didn't know how to make. Most of all I hated the Maya's idea of food. Chicken feet in *tamales*? Soup made with deer the size of dogs? Soup made with rodents the size of dogs? How did I know the Maya didn't make dog soup?

I snuffled back tears. "That wasn't funny," I told Aaron, my voice shaky.

"They're just having some fun at your expense." He grinned at me. He was growing a beard, and I was fascinated that it was coming in red. With his green eyes, he looked very handsome. But not at that exact moment.

"Would it be as funny if somebody pulled *your* hair?" I rolled out of my hammock and walked purposefully toward his. "Let's give your beard a try."

"Okay, you lot," he yelled to the assembled villagers. "*Elen*. Out of the house! Visiting hours are over."

I retreated to my hammock and picked up my book, refusing to look at anybody. Gradually, with muted laughter, the adults left, the children straggling after them, until just a few remained on the benches, thumbing through the magazines.

"Thank you," I said, without looking up.

"You're welcome."

I waited for him to ask me if I wanted to go home, but he didn't.

When I rang the school bell at eight the following morning, the "downtown" kids raced out of their houses and followed me into mine, where they amused themselves until school started by watching Aaron and me eat breakfast. By the time I walked to the schoolhouse, teaching materials tucked under my arm, I had an escort of two dozen kids.

Maybe it was the formality of being "in school," but the kids refrained from touching me here. But I still moved away whenever someone brushed against me, especially the little girls—all potential hair-pullers.

The schoolhouse was furnished with a portable blackboard, a wooden desk, and a stool—which was about as comfortable to sit on as perching on a rock. The students sat facing me in rows of wooden desks attached to wooden chairs. Each row accommodated three students. To judge from the amount of squirming that went on, the seats weren't any more comfortable than my stool.

I didn't have a formal lesson plan. I didn't have textbooks. I didn't have anything except stage fright and a respectful group of kids who seemed excited to be here. It was years before I appreciated the fact that their attitude might have been more important than mine.

Before leaving the States, I had tried to prepare myself for living and teaching in the bush. A doctor at Michigan's student clinic gave me the shots I needed, but when I asked him about first-aid supplies for the

Maya, he was appalled. How old was I? (Twenty.) Did I know anything about medicine? (Yes—I was allergic to ether.) Was I pre-med? (Why? I wanted to be a writer.) Well, then. Sorry, Miss, but that's totally out of the question. If we suggest an antibacterial ointment to put on cuts, give you pills to treat malaria, teach you how to give a penicillin shot, or explain what to do for burns or stomachaches—teach you the basics of field medicine, in other words—we would be violating the Hippocratic Oath. And *you* would be practicing medicine without a license.

"Help" from Michigan's English Language Institute, briefly famous a couple of years later for admitting Marina Oswald as a student, was more of the same. To my dismay even the English department declined to help, with the exception of one professor who gave me a grammar book. It came in handy—not for the kids but for me, when I went back to college the following year.

My mother was my savior. She worked for the Verona Board of Education and had introduced me to Dr. Sydney Grant, who was teaching English as a second language to Puerto Rican kids in New York. He gave me something much more useful than a grammar book: he gave me ideas. As a result I arrived in British Honduras armed with pencils, a year's supply of chalk, half a dozen white poster boards, a couple of black marking pens, and a box of gold stars.

The night before school started, by the smoky orange flare of a kerosene lamp, I drew a woman wearing a Kekchi-style blouse and a Mopan-style skirt on one poster. On the second I drew a man, a much easier project because Maya men all wore the same kind of clothes. I drew the woman barefoot and put boots on the man.

That first day the kids and I spent about an hour rearranging the desks so I could divide the students into three groups—beginner, intermediate, and advanced. At first the "beginners" were the little kids and the "advanced" students were the teenagers. Placing kids in the "intermediate" group was harder. I shuffled a few kids back and forth a few times, although since I had recently been a teenager myself, I was careful not to move a teen, no matter how dense, from the intermediate group into the "baby" group with Aprimo Tux and his uncle Crisantos.

I taught the kids English the same way I had learned French in high school: I spoke only English to them. It was not a decision driven by current pedagogical ideology—for one thing, I'd never taken an education course (they specialize in terms like "pedagogical ideology"). The real reason was because I spoke nine words of Kekchi and no Mopan. There was no other way *to* teach them English.

Once the children were seated and waiting, bright-eyed, for whatever I might do next, I picked up one of my posters, took a deep breath, and tried to pretend my knees didn't feel like Jell-O. "This," I announced in a quavering voice, "is a man."

Thirty-four blank faces stared back at me. Nobody said a word.

I cleared my throat. "Man," I repeated, trying to indicate his hair, face, body, legs, and boots. Then I made the beckoning gesture that, to Americans, means, "Come on—your turn. Say something." More blank looks. The gesture obviously meant nothing to the Maya. Time to shift tactics.

I put the poster down and scrutinized faces until I found Aprimo Tux, one of the few children I knew by name. With his pale, scrubbed face, slicked-back hair, and brand-new shorts, he was the picture of eager innocence. "My name is Joan," I said, pointing at myself. Then I pointed at Aprimo. "What is *your* name?"

He parted his lips and blinked. Somebody hissed at him. In a barely audible voice, Aprimo bleated, "MynameisAprimoTux."

"Good!" I glanced around to see who had coached him. My gaze locked on Maxiana Choc's. She was Lucia's younger sister, quiet and soft-spoken. Like many girls, she wore a homemade Western-style dress with a frilly little collar and two strings at her waist that tied in back, like an apron. I stared at her, willing her to understand me. "My name is Joan," I said. "What is your name?"

Maxiana stared back. "My name is Maxiana Choc," she said finally, in perfect, unaccented English. For the next few minutes I went around the class, introducing myself to each student and marking each one "present" in my ledger book when they told me their name. Paulina Tux. Julian

Choc. Andrea Boh. Natalia Bah. Adelaida Garcia. Estevan Choc. And so on until I had everybody accounted for—by name, at least.

I held up my poster again, looking at Maxiana. "This is a man."

"This is a man," she repeated dubiously.

"What is this?"

She hesitated. I bit my lip, afraid she would simply parrot my own words back to me. Finally she blurted out, "This is a man?"

"Good! *Very* good! Paulina—what is this?"

The two girls were almost the same age, but Paulina clearly wished to be someplace else. But whatever she wished for—a husband, probably (I suspected Dolores was right about that)—she'd been paying attention. "This is a man," she said, her voice soft and suggestive, as though she were waiting for an excuse to laugh at me. She seemed to know I was faking my way through this—that I was an imposter. But my lack of confidence didn't make her sympathetic. In spite of the difference in our ages, she clearly considered me a potential rival.

I ignored her tone and called on Arcenio Garcia. He knew the answer. I called on Luis Choc. He knew. Hilario Ical knew. Sylvario Boh knew. Teodora Tux knew.

I switched to the poster of the woman. "This is a woman," I said, emphasizing the last word. I looked at Natalia Bah. Since Lucia was her mother and Maxiana was her aunt, I was pretty sure she spoke English. "What is this?"

Natalia stared at me in terror. "This is a wu-man?" she whispered.

"Very good! Adelaida?" Adelaida knew. So did Cresencio and Teodora and Epijenia. I felt as limp as lettuce and called recess while I was still on a roll.

Aaron and I hadn't eaten meat since our arrival. Several families raised pigs but butchered them only on special occasions, or if the owner needed money. Planting corn was a special occasion. So was a dance. But the Maya wouldn't plant corn until December, and September was the wrong time of year for dances.

Every family kept a few chickens, but nobody was selling those, either. Most chickens had died of fowl pox just before our arrival, and we couldn't even buy eggs. According to Aaron, the few remaining hens were setting on nests woven from dried corn husks in their owners' kitchens, hatching the next generation.

Thanks to our parents, we had freeze-dried packets of meat mixes like beef Stroganoff—just add water and simmer till done. They didn't taste *bad*, but they didn't particularly taste like meat. Neither did the various tinned meats, like sardines and Vienna sausage, that we'd bought in San Antonio. At first they were a treat. But Aaron wasn't as crazy about canned salmon as I was, and he liked Twello more than I did. Twello reminded me too much of Spam.

One night while I was eating salmon and rice and Aaron was eating *tortillas* wrapped around fried crumbled Twello, I read the label. "Oh, hey—listen to this. After it lists the ingredients, know what it says?"

Aaron, his mouth full, shook his head.

"'No lips or eyelids.' Doesn't that make you wonder what's in it that *isn't* lips or eyelids?"

Aaron stopped chewing and shot me a dirty look. So much for Twello. The next time we shopped in San Antonio, I discovered canned Danish bacon—pricier, but I knew what was in it.

But we couldn't live on canned goods. For one thing they were too expensive. For another we didn't like them—except the bacon. What we liked was the food the Maya ate. Although most of it tasted like nothing I'd ever eaten before—and the women cooked with far too much *chile* pepper—I thought that if I could get my hands on the raw ingredients, I could cook something edible.

Aaron put the word out: Teacher and her husband liked the food the villagers ate. The very next day Adelaida Garcia brought over half a pint of sugarcane juice. It had a slight molasses tang and was a welcome addition to our breakfast oatmeal. The day after that Lucia came over with fried plantains to accompany our lunch.

The following weekend, Crispino, her husband, went hunting. When he came back Lucia brought us some *watusi*, bush rabbit, cooked with ground *chile* pepper and *samat*, a highly flavored herb that grew profusely all over the village. Aaron told me that a "bush rabbit" was really a paca. He didn't elaborate. I didn't ask for details.

Lucia was the one I turned to for help the next morning. Her house was the same size as ours but had only one entranceway, and the door stood open. I stopped in front of it, unsure of protocol, but as soon as Lucia saw me she waved me in.

I had seen the inside of only one Maya house—the one I'd fled from in Crique Sarco. The first thing that struck me about Lucia's was how neat it was, like Lucia herself. Dried corn was stacked neatly in a corner, the hammocks had been carefully folded over the rafters, and all her cooking utensils had been put away. A small fire was still burning, and the room smelled pleasantly of corn and wood smoke. The second thing I noticed was her floor. Unlike mine, it was pale gray and smooth as cement, and had the effect of making her small house seem airy and inviting.

"Do you have any vegetables I could buy?" I asked nervously.

Lucia—dressed in a shiny, violet-colored skirt that looked brand new—conferred with Natalia. Then she went into the kitchen area—her *comal* was built into its own clay fireplace; I'd have to tell Aaron—and handed me a pear-shaped green thing that looked hinged, like a clam shell. I asked her what it was.

"*Chocho.*"

I asked her how much it cost.

She shrugged.

I asked her how much she wanted for it.

She shrugged.

I asked her how to cook it.

"Bile it."

"Excuse me?"

"In *caldo*. When you make it *caldo*—" She stopped. "Soup. When you make it soup, you put in the *chocho* and bile it."

"Oh." *Boil* it—of course. "Do I cut it up first?"

To Lucia's credit she didn't laugh. "Yes, you could cut it."

Back in my own house, I put the *chocho* on the top shelf of my "pantry," grabbed an onion to repay Lucia, and ran to her house. Natalia, at her mother's urging, wrapped a few pieces of uncooked *watusi* in a banana leaf. As I accepted it, she clapped both hands over her mouth. She had her mother's lively dark eyes, and underneath her hands I could see she was smiling.

For dinner that night, Aaron and I ate fresh *tortillas*—courtesy of another neighbor, Silvaria Choc, an elderly, haggard-looking woman with too many children—and *watusi* stew made from Knorr's instant vegetable soup, water, diced *chocho*, and a little chopped onion. Impatiently I waited until Aaron had eaten a few mouthfuls. "Do you like it?"

He deliberated. "It's . . . okay."

The meat was gamey and I'd overcooked the *chocho*. "No," I said sadly. "It's just different."

The next time I cooked *watusi*, I'd use *chile* powder. A *lot* of *chile* powder.

"Arcenio, what is that?"

Arcenio Garcia slid me a guilty, sideways look. "I don't know the English, Teacher." He elbowed his neighbor, Luis Choc, who elbowed *his* neighbor, until the object Arcenio had been handing around to show the other boys was returned to him.

"May I see it?" I wasn't sure what I expected—Playgirl of the Month?

Wordlessly Arcenio handed it over.

The object resembled the head of a tomahawk, fashioned from some fine-grained stone and smooth to the touch.

"Where did you get this?"

"My father find like so in his *milpa*."

"Is call it thunder stone," put in Luis excitedly. "When it rain, with lightning, Li Mama C'a throw like so into the *milpa*. Make it big noise—BAM!

It could stay in the ground seven rains—seven *years*—before somebody find it." In the background I heard a few faint, astonished gasps.

"Hmm." I juggled the artifact in my hand. For its size it was surprisingly heavy. "May I take it home to show my husband? I'll give it back to you tomorrow, okay?"

Arcenio grinned, relieved to find he wasn't in trouble. "Okay."

He usually *was* in trouble. To keep the big kids occupied while I taught the little kids (and vice versa), I'd give them something to do—write the alphabet in script, answer a list of questions I'd written on the board, solve a few math problems. Arcenio was very bright. As a result he always finished his assignment before anybody else did, and got into trouble because he was bored.

"It's a celt, a ceremonial stone ax head," Aaron said when I showed him the object. "Usually they're jade. I'm surprised Luis told you the name of the god—they're usually pretty cagey about that. Are you sure he said *C'a* and not *Chac*?"

"Some of the kids acted surprised when he said it, so he might have meant *Chac*, but I heard *C'a*. Why?"

"Chac is the rain god. He's usually the one associated with these celts. Most Maya think they're petrified lightning."

I was horrified. "They think this is what lightning looks like? That it's *solid*?"

"They don't know their ancestors made these, Squirrel. So they made up a story to explain them."

"But—are you *sure*? I mean—all those ruins! Xunantunich, Lubaantun, Tikal—who do they think built them?"

The Answer Man leaned back in his hammock. "None of the Maya here have seen the ruins. Even if they did, they wouldn't understand any of the glyphs or what's written on the stelae—those big slabs of rock. They don't speak that language. They don't *know* who built the ruins."

His words made me immeasurably sad. So Arcenio and Luis didn't understand that a human being had made this little ax head, possibly a human being they were related to. They didn't understand that over two thousand years ago, their ancestors had developed a highly sophisticated civilization unique in the world, and that for all we knew, Rio Blanco was sitting on a Maya ruin the size of Athens.

I put the ax head on top of my schoolwork, and the following day I gave it back to Arcenio.

"Good evening, Mr. World," Evaristo called from outside our closed front door. The Mayas' last names all meant something. *Choc*, Evaristo's last name, was Mopan for "cloud." *Bah*—Lucia's married name—was Kekchi for "ground mole." When Evaristo heard "Ward," he had apparently decided our last name was "World." We were just pronouncing it wrong.

Aaron rose from his hammock and opened the door. Evaristo liked to stop in after dinner and drink coffee with us, complaining that people in Rio Blanco went to bed too early—the village was usually dark by eight thirty. I looked forward to his visits. Like my grandfather, he had been places and had stories to tell about them. He also liked to chew on the Big Questions that most contemplative humans ponder at some point in their lives. But the first time I asked him a question, the Answer Man shook his head in warning. Now what had I done? As soon as Evaristo left, Aaron told me. He and Evaristo had been talking together, man to man. Maya women kept to themselves, making sure their guests had coffee and tending the fire. They did not participate in the conversation.

So whenever Evaristo visited, I lay down in my hammock with a book, listening when I was interested and reading when I wasn't. Since I loved a good story, I didn't get much reading done. Reading at night was hard anyway, since our only light source was a smoky kerosene lamp behind me on the table.

Evaristo's expressions were unusually animated for a Maya. He smiled a lot, and in profile, with his jutting cheekbones and high, sloped forehead, he reminded me of the kings' faces I'd seen on monuments. He told us (maybe I was imagining things, but he *seemed* to be including me in the conversation) that he'd run away from San Antonio at an early age and worked in the outside world until last year, when he came to visit his family in Rio Blanco. Aleja, one of José Tux's daughters, caught his eye, and when she got pregnant, he married her. Now they lived in the same house with José, his wife Ana, and their three youngest children. But Evaristo was openly disdainful of these know-nothing Indians and their peculiar, rigid beliefs. *He* knew what a haircut was. *He* knew that shirts were supposed to be white, not some improbable Easter egg color. *He* knew that trousers were supposed to be dark, with a crease in them, and should be worn with a belt and shoes and socks, not rubber boots.

His first job had been up north, in Cayo District, working in the lumber camps. After that he smuggled *chicle* out of the Petén for a few years, where he'd been in and out of knife fights and jail. Although he never finished school, he taught himself to speak, read, and write English and Spanish. Once, stiff with rum and fright, he took a plane to Guatemala City, where he squandered almost seven hundred U.S. dollars in two weeks. He swore—Manuel Xi in Crique Sarco had told us the same thing, and nobody believed him, either—that he had seen a *sisimito* in the zoo there, a creature out of Maya folklore that was large, hairy, and humanlike, except the Spanish called it a *gorila*.

Evaristo was telling Aaron about an eclipse of the moon he had seen once when he was a kid in San Antonio. The people there had beaten on drums and fired their guns to scare away the animal that was gobbling up the moon. That was tonight's Big Question: what held the moon up? And all those stars—if the sky was nothing but empty space, like the air we breathed, what kept *them* up?

I peeked over the top of my book and watched as Aaron took his knife out of his pocket. "Have you ever wondered why, when you let go of things, they fall?" He dropped the knife. It hit the dirt floor with a soft thud.

Evaristo frowned.

"Gravity." The Answer Man leaned down to pick up his knife. "Come on outside. I'll show you."

I remained where I was, swinging in my hammock with one foot on the floor to rock myself. *Aaron* should be teaching, I thought. He was a natural at it. When other little boys his age had been playing doctor with little girls, he had probably been explaining trigonometry to them.

"See that bright star? It's not really a star. It's the planet Saturn." I could hear Aaron's voice plainly through the open door. "The earth is another planet. All the planets circle the sun, just like in that drawing you saw. If we were standing on Saturn having this conversation, that's what the earth would look like to us—a pinpoint of light. The pull of gravity is what keeps all the planets in their orbits around the sun. But the earth has its own gravitational pull. It—I'll simplify. *That's* what holds the moon and stars up."

After a long silence, Evaristo cursed softly in English. Earlier he and Aaron had been looking at pictures of the planets orbiting the sun in *Life* magazine, and to judge from the awe in his voice, he had just made the connection between the drawing and the night sky arching overhead.

"The ancient Maya thought the world was a *milpa*, with a god holding up each of the four corners," Aaron continued, his voice tentative.

There was a long pause. "Yes," Evaristo admitted finally.

"Is that what you were taught?" Aaron tried to pretend he was asking an innocent question.

I shook my head. Although Aaron had many skills, acting wasn't one of them.

"I heard stories like so," Evaristo said cautiously. "Some of the old people, they still pray to those gods."

"You mean the gods of the four directions? The Chac?"

I could almost hear Evaristo's reluctant nod. "Yes."

"And Tzultak'a?" Aaron's voice quickened. "Do the people here still pray to him when they plant their *milpas*?"

"Maybe some people."

"How about José Tux?"

This time Evaristo's pause was even longer. "Well, I don't know."

"But you helped him make plantation, didn't you?" Aaron persisted.

"*Pues*—I'm going now," Evaristo said abruptly. "It's late. Thank you for the coffee, Missus."

"You're welcome." I glanced at the clock. It was just past midnight, that magical hour when Cinderella turned into a waif in a dirty apron and Evaristo remembered he was talking to white people.

Aaron came inside, looking troubled. "Manuel Xi told me about Tzultak'a, but he knew me pretty well by then. I shouldn't have pushed Evaristo so hard."

His words surprised me. Bear-Bear seldom admitted to being wrong, or doubting himself. "I'm sure you'll have other opportunities," I said.

"Maybe not with Evaristo, though."

Again I was surprised, but this time by an intense desire to comfort Bear-Bear in bed. To me the Maya were a job, but they were Aaron's future—he planned to write his dissertation on them. He *had* to succeed here. And I had to help him.

"I'll blow out the lamp," I said softly. "Make room for me in your hammock."

xxxxxxxxxxxxxxxxxxxxxxxxxxxxxxxxxxxxxxxxxxxxxxxxxxxxxxxxxx

CHAYOTE AND TOMATOES

Chocho, better known by its Spanish name, *chayote*, has a slightly sweet, nutty flavor. It grows on a vine—technically it's a fruit—but you can prepare it the same way you would summer squash. Because of its mild flavor, it can readily be combined with a variety of other foods. *Chocho* is so versatile that Creole cooks often use it, with the appropriate spices, to make apple pie. Here's a vegetable dish I never ate in Rio Blanco but could have made easily using local produce—if I'd known what I was doing and had been willing to experiment.

1 *chayote*

2 garlic cloves, pressed or minced

1 teaspoon oil, preferably olive oil

½ teaspoon thyme
½ medium onion, diced
salt to taste
a pinch of ground white pepper, or to taste (optional)
½ small onion, diced
1 medium tomato, diced, or a handful of halved cherry
    tomatoes

Since the skin of the *chayote* is edible, don't remove it. Slice in half horizontally. The pit is also edible; don't remove that, either. Cut each half into thin slices.

Heat the oil over medium heat in a heavy frying pan. Add garlic and cook until it starts to turn color. Add remaining ingredients except the tomato. Cover the pan, turn heat to low, and simmer 10 minutes. Remove the cover and stir—the *chayote* should be lightly browned. Add the tomatoes and cook down until most of the liquid has evaporated, another minute or two.

Serves 2 people.

xxxxxxxxxxxxxxxxxxxxxxxxxxxxxxxxxxxxxxxxxxxxxxxxxxxxxxx

FRIED PLANTAINS

Lucia taught me how to cook these, and I still enjoy them. I use butter and I don't drain the plantains, which all Belizeans pronounce PLAN-tins, not—as Americans do—plan-TAYNES.

The Maya often deep-fry plantains when they render the fat from pork skin to make lard. The crisp pieces of skin are called by their Spanish name, *chicharrones* (cracklings, in English). The two foods in combination will probably clog every artery in your body, but they taste so good you won't care.

    2 large, very ripe plantains
    butter or canola oil

A plantain is ripe when the fruit yields to thumb pressure and the yellow skin is heavily streaked with black. If it were a banana, you'd throw it out. Peel the plantain and cut it in half horizontally, then vertically. Lower the strips carefully into melted butter. Turn once. Cook until golden brown. If using oil, drain.

Serves 2–3 people.

Variation: Fry the plantain strips in butter. Just before removing them from the pan, add a splash of balsamic vinegar. Cook till the vinegar stops spitting, transfer the plantains to a serving plate, and pour the sauce over them. Use a rubber spatula to get all the sauce out of the frying pan. Yes, it's that good.

"HERON H" - 1971

1. The *Heron H*, which piloted me and my husband safely through a hurricane on our way from Belize City to Punta Gorda. Photographer unknown. Part of the Maritime Museum Collection of the Museum of Belize. Used with permission of Lita Hunter Krohn, museum director.

2. Don Owen-Lewis with Cirila Chub, Don's
goddaughter, Gloria, and Cirila's son, Huni.
Courtesy Terry Rambo.

3. Petrona Xi in Crique Sarco, rinsing off her
youngest son while housebreaking him. She
wears a traditional Kekchi Maya skirt. Courtesy
Terry Rambo.

4. A Kekchi man in Crique Sarco shows off his
corn crop. Courtesy Terry Rambo.

5. Petrona cooks her *tortillas* on a handmade clay *comal*. Courtesy Terry Rambo.

6. A Kekchi woman in Crique Sarco weaving with a waist loom. This skill, along with basket weaving and pot making, has largely disappeared. Courtesy Terry Rambo.

7. My boss, Father John Paul Cull, S.J., smiling.
Photo taken in Raton, New Mexico, by Joan Fry.

8. Evaristo Choc and his wife, Aleja, holding
Fidel, the couple's firstborn child. Courtesy Terry
Rambo.

9. José and Ana Tux, far right in the back row.
Front row, right to left: Nicasio, Crisantos, two
children too young for school, and Crisantos's
nephew Aprimo, with his finger up his nose.
Courtesy Terry Rambo.

10. Dolores Choc, (*front right*), tries to scoop up
hail with a calabash. Photo by Joan Fry.

11. Crispino and Lucia Bah and their daughter,
Natalia. Lucia has dressed up by wearing a
traditional Mopan Maya *huipil* in addition
to her traditional Mopan skirt. Courtesy Terry
Rambo.

12. Maxiana Choc and I, standing in front of my house. Although most of the women wore traditional clothing, they tended to dress their daughters in Western clothing. Courtesy Terry Rambo.

13. Natalia Bah, wearing a Western-style dress in shades of pink and turquoise, and Paulina Tux, wearing an old-fashioned dress-length *huipil*. Courtesy Terry Rambo.

14. Standing with most of my students in Rio Blanco. Maxiana Choc stands directly in front of me, with Paulina Choc on the far right, wearing clips in her hair. (The two girls are not related.) Courtesy Terry Rambo.

15. Silvaria Choc and her youngest, another boy.

SIX

Kinship

A board groaned. I raised my head, squinting into the darkness. Damn horse, I thought. There goes Don's fence again. I shifted position; my back hurt.

A series of grunts followed. Sleep vaporized like fog and I sat up and blinked, trying to unscramble my brain. This was Rio Blanco—not Crique Sarco, where a neighbor's horse had broken through Don's fence one night.

A beam from Aaron's flashlight pinpointed the clock. "It's four thirty in the damn morning," he grumbled. "Whose pig is scratching his back against our house?"

Pig?

More grunts and groaning boards. If this pig scratched any harder, the wall would collapse.

Swearing, Aaron got up and exited the back door, flashlight under one arm so he could flap his hands. As he disappeared behind the puddle of light he yelled, "Hoooch! H-O-O-cha!" It was how the Maya shooed pigs away, just as Americans called their cats with "Heeere, kitty-kitty-kitty!" The cats always came, and the pigs always fled.

Aaron padded back inside, pulling the back door closed behind him. But it hadn't been made as carefully as our front door, and as the tie-tie vines stretched, the door had begun to sag.

Still muttering about inconsiderate people who didn't secure their pigs at night—he meant the two Boh families, our nearest and least-loved neighbors—Aaron clicked his flashlight off and climbed into his hammock. I lay down again, too, on my back this time, with my legs stretched out. The ideal way to sleep in a hammock is to wedge yourself in sideways, straight as a stalk of celery. Wishing for the dozenth time that my hammock were longer, I dozed off again.

The next sound I heard was the scrape of wood on dirt as somebody pushed our back door open. I opened my eyes to see Jesús Boh framed in the doorway, mouth ajar, shirttail flapping. It was barely light outside.

"What do you want?" Aaron had lit the kerosene lamp and was seated at the table, writing up his field notes from the previous day. Maybe I'd pretend I was still asleep.

A brief discussion in Kekchi and Spanish ensued. Jesús had scratched his foot and wanted *ban*, medicine. I heard the word "iodine." I opened one eye and watched Aaron paint Jesús's big toe an ostentatious red that made it look like the bull's-eye of an archery target. "There. Off you go," Aaron said in a loud, hearty voice.

Jesús stared at him, jaw still agape, then at the clock, then into the rafters. "You stupid bastard," Aaron muttered. Still facing Jesús, he moved a step closer to him. Jesús took a step back, his eyes widening.

I stopped pretending to be asleep. This was much too interesting. Although the kids tackled, hit, held hands, and slung their arms around each other's necks all the time, adults never stood as close to one another, face-to-face, as Aaron was standing to Jesús. What followed resembled a dance. One step at a time, Aaron backed Jesús away from the table, around the fireplace, and out the back door.

"*Pues*," Aaron said curtly, as soon as Jesús was outside. *Pues* was an all-purpose Spanish word that usually meant the speaker was stalling for time until he figured out what he wanted to say next. "*Hasta mas tarde*," Aaron concluded, closing the door in Jesús's face. See you later.

"I thought we weren't supposed to be rude!" I said.

"They're not supposed to be, either. Do Lucia and Crispino just walk in on us? No. Does Dolores? No."

"But Don doesn't . . ."

"He tells them to get out when they just barge in unannounced the way this oaf just did."

"But when he lived in Crique Sarco he never closed his door!"

"He does now. We are too—and from now on we're going to lock it."

Aaron lifted one of the boxes from our wooden platform and rummaged around until he found some rope. When I spied magazines in the box, I climbed out of my hammock and grabbed an armload to distribute on the benches. If our visitors had enough pictures to look at, they might not spend so much time watching us.

While Aaron looped three feet of rope around the end post of the door and the door frame, Jesús remained just outside, peering in at us. He and his family were what the other Maya derogatorily called "bush Indians," new arrivals who spoke only their own language, didn't know local customs, and didn't want to participate in village affairs. Jesús had agreed to send his son Silvario to school only after I threatened to fine him—as Father Cull had instructed me to—a nickel each day the boy was absent.

I waited until Jesús finally shuffled home before wrestling my clothes on underneath my floral cotton nightgown. Then I lit the fire.

The parts of my day I hated the most were the most necessary. I was trying to master balancing a bucket on my head the way the Maya women did. But the first time I attempted to climb the riverbank with it, the bucket slid off sideways and nearly sliced my ear off. It was still tender and inflamed. Even though I didn't fill the bucket so full anymore, I still sloshed water every step of the way, trying to ignore the women hissing their disapproval. In their eyes I was wasting water, and to the Maya waste was a sin—worse than having two wives. Their disapproval made me feel even worse.

The second job I dreaded was making a fire. As long as I had paper for tinder, lighting one was easy. But since Aaron gathered firewood only as we needed it—every three or four days—I was always burning green wood, and green wood would rather sputter and die than keep burning. Whenever I cooked, I spent most of my time on my hands and knees, babying the fire along by hand-feeding it, tears running down my face from the smoke.

I kept this fire alive long enough to boil water and make oatmeal. Afterward, as I sat in my hammock drinking coffee and mentally going over what I planned to teach that day, I heard Lucia's murmured "Good morning, Teacher" outside the back door. Nobody called me by my first name. I was "Teacher" to everybody except Evaristo, who preferred "Missus" or "Missus World."

I untied the rope and opened the door. Wordlessly Lucia handed me some okra neatly wrapped in *mox*, a big, pliable green leaf that resembled a banana leaf. I thanked her even though I'd never eaten it before and had no idea what to do with it.

Lucia looked at me questioningly, a crumpled BH dollar bill in her outstretched hand. "I could buy two pound flour?"

"No. You and Crispino are our friends," Aaron interrupted from the table. That was a surprise, since I'd heard Aaron and Don discussing the fact that there *was* no word for "friendship" in Kekchi. "I'll *give* you two pounds of flour, but I won't take any money."

Lucia had given up trying to maintain her neutral expression around us. We *sac li gwink*—white people—did and said too many outrageous things. She frowned at Aaron as if she could discern his motive better that way. "Okay," she said finally.

How to measure two pounds of flour without a scale? All I could remember was the old saying "A pint's a pound the world around," so I nudged the toad aside with my bare foot, plunged a measuring cup into the flour sack, and emptied two cups into a bowl. I handed it to Lucia, who accepted it with a brief nod and walked out the door.

I turned to Aaron. "Friends?"

"Crispino came over the other afternoon while you were teaching and sat here for half an hour, trying to talk to me. My Kekchi's still pretty limited so we didn't get very far. But he seems like a nice guy. And you and Lucia get along."

"She accepts me without making me feel like I'm on exhibit in a zoo, but that's not being 'friends.' And how can you be 'friends' with Crispino if you can't understand a word he says?"

"But Lucia speaks English."

"So it's *Lucia* you want to be friends with."

"I need Kekchi informants," Aaron said. His tone suggested that I go back to planning today's lesson.

"Then why don't you talk to José Tux? Lucia is Mopan."

"No, she's not. She's married to Crispino, who doesn't speak word one of Mopan. And I *do* talk to José. But I can't rely on a single informant."

"There are a lot of Kekchi-Mopan marriages in the village. Look at Evaristo—he's married to Aleja Tux."

"That's the problem with using *him* as an informant. He's Mopan."

"He's Lucia's brother."

Aaron gave me an indulgent smile. "You misunderstood, Squirrel. Or somebody gave you bogus information."

"Look. Maxiana is one of my students, and she's their younger sister." I was getting mad. Couldn't the Answer Man credit me with *some* intelligence? "Their father is Marto Choc, the old man who limps. He's Mopan. But Candelaria, their mother, is Kekchi. I asked Maxiana," I said, anticipating Aaron's next question. "I asked all the kids who their parents are."

"They must have been humbugging you."

"Then there's no point in continuing this conversation, is there?" I snapped. Aaron would have to figure out for himself that Marto and Candelaria's sons spoke Mopan, their father's language, while the girls spoke Kekchi, their mother's—except for Lucia, who spoke both. "May I get past you, please? I have to ring the school bell."

As I stalked out the door, fuming, Aaron picked up his pen and went back to his field notes. He took notes on everything—what birds and animals he saw, who said what about whom, who was related to whom, what the Kekchi planted, hunted, ate, believed in, prayed to.

Why had I let the discussion deteriorate into an argument? Because being the Answer Man was different from being a dictator? Because arguing, even though painful, was at least familiar?

As I started back to the house after ringing the school bell, half a dozen barefoot children ran to catch up with me. My day had officially begun.

The following afternoon, since it wasn't raining—it had rained off and on ever since our arrival—Aaron decided to dig a ditch around the house. The water that dripped off the thatch was seeping in under the wallboards. Using a hoe he had borrowed from Dolores's husband, Joaquin, he dug a runoff channel to divert the water.

Half a dozen little boys were "helping" him.

Then Cresencio, one of the not-so-little boys, pointed at two large blackbirds strutting back and forth over the ridgepole of the schoolhouse. "You shoot like so?" he asked. Aaron was one of the few men in Rio Blanco who owned a rifle, and since our arrival hardly anything exciting had happened in the village. People were starved for entertainment.

Aaron straightened and looked at them. "Yes, I do, Julian."

The other kids tittered, and when Aaron came inside for his gun I murmured to him, "That was Cresencio. Julian's his little brother."

Without answering Aaron strode out the door with his rifle. A few seconds later I heard a shot. And, following so close behind that it sounded like an echo, I heard a second shot.

I glanced out the door again. The boys were racing toward the school, yelling, "*Ki kam! Ki kam!*" Dead.

I put down the papers I was grading, stood up, and stretched. The table was too low. Or maybe my hammock was responsible for my nearly chronic backaches. From the doorway I saw Dolores step out of her house, probably wondering who'd been shot.

Triumphantly Aaron returned carrying the two dead blackbirds. He nodded to Dolores and came inside.

"What are you going to do with them?" I asked dubiously.

"Eat them. We haven't had fresh meat in two weeks."

As if I hadn't noticed. "If you're through with the hoe, I'll take it back to Dolores and ask how she cooks them," I offered.

"Yeah, and then she'll want one as payment. I know what to do. Whenever we went camping, Dad always shot quail or pheasant for dinner. Here. You pluck these and I'll cut some green sticks. We need green ones because . . ."

". . . otherwise they burn. I was a Girl Scout, remember? Wait!" I yelled, as Aaron headed for the door again. Hot dogs didn't have feathers. "How do I pluck them?"

"I don't know. My mother always did that."

"*Bear . . .*"

"Boil a pot of water and dunk the birds in it a few seconds," Aaron said, clearly enjoying himself. "*Then* pull the feathers out."

I crumpled up paper and struck a match against one of the rocks. The paper burst into flame. I was carefully adding sticks to it, teepee fashion, when Aaron returned, whittling the bark off two long, sturdy sticks.

Aaron helped me pluck the blackbirds, then chopped their heads off and slid a peeled stick through each naked body. Stripped of their feathers, the birds looked ridiculously small. Two per person might have made a meal—one would be an appetizer. As a backup, I put some beans over the fire to reheat and made a pot of rice. By the time I lowered the tiny carcasses over the coals, I was so hungry I was drooling. "Is this how your mother did it? Just held the birds over the fire? Did she rub oil on them first or anything like that?"

"I don't know. I wasn't watching."

How long would it take before the blackbirds turned a golden, glowing brown from the heat, looking like preshrunk Colonel Sanders's "finger-lickin' good" chicken?

The birds were done in less than twenty minutes, but they somehow passed from raw to soot-colored without any intermediate browning stage. What we had on our sticks were two charred bird carcasses. Aaron and I sat down at the table and regarded "dinner."

Nothing I did to mine—cut it into miniscule pieces, add margarine, add salt, add ground *chile* pepper, mix it with rice—rendered it edible. After the third bite, I remembered that blackbirds liked to follow the horses around, waiting for them to drop a load of manure. The birds squabbled with one another over the undigested corn.

Pushing my plate away, I told Aaron. He turned pale and put his fork down. "That's kind of what they taste like. I should have let you ask Dolores."

"You know what she'd have told me—make soup."

"They might have tasted better that way," he admitted.

Reluctantly we abandoned the blackbirds and ate another rice and bean dinner. It was still October, but after washing the dishes I took down the wall calendar and checked off the days that remained until Christmas vacation.

I felt more relaxed around the kids now—especially the girls, and especially early in the morning when they were still docile from sleep and breakfast. It was their parents who got on my nerves.

Part of my change of heart was due to something Aaron figured out. The usual age span between one child and the next was two years. The Maya doted on babies, and parents spoiled their newborns silly. Even their fathers would tickle them and kiss their naked bellies while the babies squealed in delight. But these same parents completely ignored the next-youngest child—the same two-year-old they'd been spoiling until the day the new baby arrived. If these kids tried to sit on their mother's laps and cuddle, their mother—preoccupied with the newborn—would shove them away. Every mother I knew treated her children like that. But the little boys didn't seem to mind it as much as the girls, who edged up to anything remotely female, including me, their small faces alight with joy at simply *touching* me.

This morning, as on all other mornings, kids of all ages sprawled against one another on the benches while they looked through the magazines, carefully licking their thumbs before turning a page. The magazines had been handled so often they were the consistency of cloth. For the most part the children sat quietly, but every so often one would blurt out a question.

"Teacher, look! Is a man?"

"Yes, Adelaida." Wearing a suit and carrying a briefcase.

"Teacher, what you call like so?"

"That's a bulldozer, Nicasio."

"Bull-dosser. Bull-dosser? *Pues*, Teacher—*no esta vacax!*"

He was right—it wasn't a cow. "Bulldozer," I said firmly, trying to unite the two words. Like all the Tux children, Nicasio looked as though his mother had just scrubbed him. His hair was clean, he was clean, his clothes were clean and brand new—a long-sleeved white shirt rolled up nearly to the elbows, and tan shorts.

"Bulldoser."

"Good, Nicasio!"

"Bulldoser," he repeated under his breath. "Bulldoser."

Then Hilario stuck a magazine under the nose of the kid sitting next to him. It was one of the magazines I had just put out the other morning. A sibilant whisper traveled up and down the bench, igniting the children's expressions like a struck match. A few of the little girls covered their mouths as though embarrassed or frightened. Hilario ran up to show me the picture—three gorillas in a zoo. "Teacher! How you call like so?"

"Those are gorillas."

Half the children repeated what I'd said. The other half, in lowered voices, repeated what they'd said earlier: "*sisimito*."

"Really? A *sisimito*? Let me see that." Aaron had agreed to help José Tux and Evaristo build a hog pen and was getting ready to leave. After scanning the magazine, he handed it back to me. "Keep your eye on this, okay?"

"Okay. Wait a minute—what's a *sisimito*?" I remembered hearing the word, but I couldn't remember what it meant.

"A Maya gorilla," Aaron said, deadpan, and walked out the door.

Promptly at nine o'clock a.m.—I carried the clock to school with me—I took roll. Then we sang "God Save the Queen," and, in a quick spiritual curtsey to Father Cull, I helped the kids recite a Hail Mary. I had developed a teaching style that closely resembled the way I cooked: a little of this, a little of that, and let's see what happens.

The novelty of "This is a man" was wearing thin, so I told the kids we were going on a field trip to learn some new words. The younger ones gaped open-mouthed at the older ones, waiting to be enlightened, but the older ones didn't know what a "field trip" was either.

"It means we'll go outside," I said. "We'll still have school, but we'll walk around the village and I'll tell you the names of things in English."

They weren't sure exactly what made this "school," but they all liked the idea of spending time outdoors, even though it would probably rain again before long. The air was so humid it felt like trying to breathe through beaten egg whites.

We started at Mateo and Micalia's house.

"What is that?" I asked.

"House, Teacher!" three dozen voices chanted. Micalia stuck her head out the door.

Arcenio jutted his chin toward her. "Woman, Teacher!"

Everybody laughed. Micalia scowled at us and disappeared inside.

"What's that?" I called, pointing at the thatched pen in Micalia's yard where she and Mateo closed up their chickens at night.

"A house for the chickens, Teacher," Lute yelled. Everybody called him that. "Elutario" was too long.

"Good, Lute." I pointed at Nene, the Icals' dog. In Kekchi her name meant "too small." "And that?"

"*Tzi*, Teacher!" cried Crisantos Tux, Nicasio's youngest brother. Today he wore new brown shorts held up by straps over each shoulder. Built-in suspenders.

A dozen voices corrected him. "Is a dog, Teacher! *Dog!*" Nene took one look at us and fled behind the house.

"Yes. Dog. Good, Crisantos."

I led the way to the Bohs' yard, wondering if we'd see Jesús and his red toe. Instead we saw his wife, Gregoria, topless, stringing wet clothes over bushes as the family pigs foraged nearby. She stopped what she was doing to watch us.

"Teacher—pig!" Luis jerked his chin at a sixty-pound porker with a gray spot on his side that looked like a map of Texas.

"Good, Luis! Yes, that's a pig." Probably the same one that had woken us up the other morning.

Estevan scooped up a hen. She squawked in indignation, struggled briefly, then lay limp in his arms. "Chicken, Teacher?"

"Good, Estevan! Yes, that's a chicken."

Gregoria yelled something at him, and he carefully set the hen back down. Shaking herself to rearrange her feathers, she ran off. Gregoria was still yelling.

Maybe this hadn't been such a good idea. Maybe I ought to skip pointing out items of interest in the village and take the kids down to the river instead. We wouldn't have my neighbors to contend with, and we'd see insects and animals I could identify.

I started walking, the children fanning out behind me. We were almost out of the Bohs' yard when I spied a corncob. Even though it had been completely stripped of kernels and had apparently been tossed away as trash, I knew they'd recognize it.

I picked it up and faced them. "What is this?"

But instead of answering they shuffled their feet and looked uneasily at one another. Paulina giggled.

I shook the corncob at her. "What is this?"

She backed up, her face wiped clean of expression. I heard a few more muffled giggles, and snatches of Kekchi flew back and forth. I scowled at them and the giggles subsided.

But then Gregoria started to laugh.

"It's corn!" I wanted to strangle all of them, especially Gregoria. What was so hilarious about a naked corncob?

"Kern, Teacher," a few dutiful voices repeated. But most of the kids covered their mouths with their hands, trying to stifle their laugher.

I ditched the corncob and marched out of Gregoria's yard, the kids running to keep up. Living here wasn't going to be a year-long replay of Crique Sarco, was it? Where between the Maya and my own husband I couldn't do one damn thing right?

I stopped at the first tree we came to and smacked it with my open palm so hard my hand stung. "What is this?"

"Tree, Teacher," the kids chanted, grinning in obvious relief that I'd dropped the silly corn business.

It wasn't until I told Aaron about the incident later that afternoon that I found out the Maya used corncobs for the same purpose we used toilet paper.

José Tux—short, solid as a river rock, physically unimpressive—was Aaron's self-appointed mentor in all things Kekchi. I could stretch the point and say José adopted Aaron, and it wouldn't have been far from the truth. As though José and Ana didn't have enough children of their own (nine), they had also raised an orphan boy, Alejandro Mijangre—no kin to them—who lived with his wife not far from them. Evaristo and Aleja lived in the elder Tuxes' house. And now the Tux siblings, natural and adopted, had another, temporary brother—Aaron, who watched them doing it, whatever "it" was, then tried his hand at it himself, an anthropological technique known as participant observation.

Today he'd gone hunting with José and Alejandro. Aaron was an experienced outdoorsman who had spent summers camping with his parents and older sister, and he wasn't afraid of hiking long distances through unfamiliar terrain. He was good with a knife—he'd carved a pancake turner for me out of wood, with a corncob handle. He was also a very good shot—he'd drilled both of those blackbirds through the head. I fervently hoped that he'd come home with something for dinner that was edible.

It was almost dark when Aaron pushed through the front door of our house, sweaty but triumphant, to grab his camera.

"Did you catch anything?"

"No, but I shot something. Come take a look."

The three men had bagged an iguana and two gibnuts. Except for the spots on their backs, the gibnuts resembled twenty-pound guinea pigs. Aaron informed me that they were some of the world's largest rodents. Fleetingly I thought about Pixie, the hamster I'd had as a kid. But after seeing the iguana—it looked like a miniature dragon—I prayed that our portion would be the rodent.

To my immense relief we got a gibnut haunch. Back home I stretched it out on my makeshift cutting board and cut off the feet—so I wouldn't have to look at its little curled Pixie toes—and skinned it. Aaron sat at the table, cheerfully cleaning his rifle. I reviewed my cooking options. I had only two: (1) fry it; or (2) boil it. Since I had okra, *chayote*, and an onion, I decided to throw everything in a pot and make

XXXXXXXXXXXXXXXXXXXXXXXXXXXXXXXXXXXXXXXXXXXXXXXXXXXXXXXXXXX

GIBNUT GUMBO

approximately 2 pounds skinned gibnut haunch (you can use venison or other game meat, or lean pork)

> 1 tablespoon lard or canola oil
> 8 cups water
> 2 cups sliced okra
> 1 medium zucchini or *chayote*
> 1 medium onion, diced
> 2 cups shredded *callaloo* (see chapter 16) or spinach
> 1½ teaspoons dried oregano
> 1 teaspoon salt
> 2 dried *arbol chiles*, crumbled
> 2 cups hot cooked rice

Heat the water in a large pot. While you wait for it to boil, dice the meat into bite-sized pieces, leaving the bones in for flavor. Brown the meat in oil in a hot frying pan. Add onion and okra and stir until the onion turns color. Drain the fat. (Like humans, gibnuts store fat under their skin.) Add remaining ingredients to the stew pot and return to a simmer. Cover and simmer about 1 hour.

Cooked this way, the dish will thicken because of the okra's sticky sap. If you don't want the gumbo texture, leave the okra whole. (Some cooks sauté it separately in a little oil and add it during the last 10 minutes of cooking time.) To serve, scoop a few spoonfuls of hot rice into a dish and ladle some stew over it. The exact ratio of stew to rice is up to you. Remember—you're eating a rodent.

Feeds 3–5 people.

xxxxxxxxxxxxxxxxxxxxxxxxxxxxxxxxxxxxxxxxxxxxxxxxxxxxxxxxxxxxxxx

GREEN CORN DUMPLINGS

If I'd known about green corn dumplings, and if suet (raw beef fat) and green corn (fresh, uncooked corn on the cob) had been available, I would have omitted the rice and added dumplings to my stew.

This recipe comes from Rita G. Springer's *Caribbean Cookbook*, first published by Evans Brothers in 1968. Don't substitute any other kind of fat for the suet—it won't work. If you can't find suet, buy a standing rib roast or tri-tip and cut out the hard white fat. And don't expect these dumplings to be light as milkweed puffs. Green corn dumplings taste like a smooth, sweet pudding and are delicious in stew.

Cook the dumplings separately after the stew is done. I modified the original recipe to serve 2 people.

½ up fresh corn (about 2 large ears)
½ cup flour
¼ teaspoon salt
2 tablespoons shredded suet, lightly packed

Fill a wide, deep pot halfway to the top with water and bring to a boil. Husk the corn and remove the silk. Using a large bowl and the next-to-coarsest blades on a hand grater, strip the kernels off the cob so you get all the liquid. If you don't have a grater, use a sharp knife to remove the corn and the blunt edge of a table knife to extract the liquid.

Measure flour and add salt. Add both to the grated corn.

Grate suet over a paper towel and add to the corn mixture. Using a large spoon, mix the ingredients. If mixture is too dry, carefully add a small amount of milk or water.

Use the spoon to cut apricot-sized balls out of the mixture. Drop one at a time into boiling water—they will sink. Do not cover pot. The dumplings will cook very quickly, in less than 5 minutes. When they're done they will rise to the top.

Remove with a slotted spoon. Ladle out your stew and lay the dumplings on top.

SEVEN

Home Brew

"When Arcenio is bad you must lash him."

I stared at Sebastian Garcia, hoping I had misunderstood. He stared back without smiling. I hadn't misunderstood.

While Sebastian's mother was Kekchi, his father had been a "Spanish man" from Guatemala. Sebastian looked Spanish—his skin was pale and his dark hair was slightly curly. But his first language was Kekchi, and he lived like the Maya and considered himself Maya. He was a very hard worker. Although he had never gone to school, he spoke good English, and along with Evaristo was one of the few Maya men who insisted on wearing a *white* shirt.

"I want it Arcenio learn English and do sums, make he don't get cheated when he sell he rice in Punta Gorda," Sebastian said earnestly. "You must lash him, Teacher."

"*Pues*," I murmured. I couldn't see myself lashing anybody, and if I did, it wouldn't be the smartest kid in school.

But it was true that the storekeepers in Punta Gorda cheated the Maya unmercifully whenever they could—raising the prices of popular items like machetes when the Maya sold their hogs and rice, or not giving them the full amount they were owed. The villagers weren't accustomed to handling large sums of money, and the first thing most of them did after selling their produce was to turn back to the storekeeper and buy rum from him. If they couldn't keep track of their money sober, they did an even worse job reeling drunk.

Sebastian was still looking at me.

"Okay," I said weakly.

He smiled, looking relieved. "*Uss.*" Good.

I had just agreed to beat his son.

Aaron kept a close eye on the magazine with the gorilla pictures because most of the Maya who saw them believed they were *sisimitos*, fearsome creatures that lurked in the bush and attacked lone travelers. Men met a quick death. Women were carried off for sex in the creature's lair, a nearby cave. Bullets "melted" in the *sisimito*'s thick, reddish fur—the only way to kill one was to set fire to it. It had one other unusual trait: its feet pointed backward.

Aaron wanted the photograph as a conversation starter to use with his "informants."

"What is this?" he asked Dolores, showing her the photo. Dolores, who had stopped in to buy some sugar, was probably in her early thirties. In spite of nursing four children, her breasts were still shapely. Her youngest baby, a squint-eyed, cranky boy she often foisted off on Paulina, was in the process of being weaned. I wondered why Aaron was questioning *her*—she was Mopan. But this time I kept my mouth shut.

Sitting across the table from Aaron, Dolores examined the magazine warily. Although she considered herself "just another poor Indian living out here in the bush," a phrase the Maya used about themselves in a variety of contexts, she was related to Tommy Salam. He owned a store in San Antonio and by Maya standards was a rich man. Dolores had his dignity to protect as well as her own. "*Pues*, I don't know."

It was another overcast day, and instead of her usual faded pink skirt, Dolores was wearing a dingy white one that made me glad Lucia was doing our laundry.

"Have you ever seen anything like this before?" Aaron persisted, pointing at the photographs.

"No. I never see like so."

"But you've heard people talk about them. They live in the bush, don't they?"

"Maybe."

Aaron fiddled with his pen and tried another approach. "You come from San Antonio, isn't that right?"

"Yes. I live there all my life until I marry Joaquin."

"And Joaquin is Silvaria and Enriques Choc's son."

Now you're on the right track, I thought. The only Kekchi in Dolores's family were her in-laws.

"Yes."

"Have any of *them* talked about seeing a *sisimito*?"

She shifted in her seat. "I hear like so, yes." Finally her desire to gossip won out over her concerns about acting like an ignorant bush Indian. "People say they see them near the Rock Patch. Joaquin, he see one when he go hunting. He shoot it and it run. He going follow it, but when he see it go to one cave, he don't follow it no more."

"Why? What's in the cave?"

Looking unhappy, Dolores—who had just realized she'd been tricked into talking about some of her most deeply felt beliefs—shifted in her seat again. The ancient Maya had used caves for ceremonial purposes, including human sacrifice. Today's Maya viewed them with suspicion and dread. "*Pues*, I don't know."

To put her at ease again, Aaron backed away from *sisimitos* and caves and asked instead who her parents were, where they had been born, and so on.

Drowsing in my hammock, I was the only one who noticed the rain had started again. I wondered if Paulina, who had been walking around looking moonstruck for the last couple of weeks—a state that probably had to do with the arrival of Juan Oh and his handsome young son in the village—would remember to bring in her mother's laundry.

It rained all night and most of the morning. By noon the sky had cleared enough to allow a few watery rays of sunlight to filter through. As soon as the rain stopped, the bugs rose up in waves. Mothers ordered their sons to the family *milpa*, and they returned bent in half under a double load of dried corn and firewood. The men had cut the wood the previous year and stacked it to dry in a field house.

Meanwhile the women rushed to the river to bathe and wash clothes. As soon as they got back, they spread wet laundry over bushes and chicken pens until just before dark, then sent their daughters to snatch the clothes up and drape them inside the house. Eventually the fire would generate enough heat to dry them.

By late afternoon the thunderheads massed again. The air was completely still. When it was this quiet, I could hear the rain coming from very far away. I liked to stand outside the front door and wait for it, anticipating the rush of coolness that always preceded a storm. At first all I could hear was a vague, whispery sound, like a distant wind. Slowly the sound gained in strength and intensity. Seconds before the storm hit, the sound shattered into millions of raindrops hitting every surface of the already saturated jungle—every leaf, weed, rock, and granule of soil. The noise was frightening but strangely exhilarating. I ran inside, and for the rest of the night I listened to the rain pounding on the thatch roof.

Except for necessary trips to "go bush," I had given up on shoes. As Petrona had demonstrated in Crique Sarco, there were benefits to going barefoot. First, it saved wear and tear on my shoes. But even more important, it allowed me to *use* my feet. Petrona walked downhill heels first, so her weight stayed over her center of gravity. She could walk downhill carrying a full bucket of water on her head, her youngest son astride one hip. If the slope was particularly steep, she walked down sideways. Whenever she crossed a log, she walked pigeon-toed, her toes gripping the slippery wood. She could even cross a log carrying a bucket and her baby, whereas I—who wasn't carrying anything—could barely teeter across without falling. But she hadn't taught me how to climb *uphill* with a bucket of water on my head.

The following afternoon I joined the women at the river to bathe and get water. The bank was slippery, and one woman carried an old machete blade to scrape out toeholds. With my bucket on my head, I started up the hill, telling myself I'd be happy if even a third of the water was left by the time I reached the top. As usual, I was the first person to climb the bank—nobody had carved out steps yet. I had taken only two or three steps before I slipped. The bucket bounced off my shoulder and rolled down the hill, water spilling everywhere.

"Ayiii," the women chorused in dismay. I stared at the slope, belatedly realizing why they got so upset when I spilled water: I was forcing the rest of them to climb up a bank that was slick as lard with mud.

Doggedly I retrieved my bucket, rinsed the mud off myself, filled the bucket half full, borrowed the machete to gouge out steps, and struggled up the hill with the bucket on my head, curling my toes as I scrabbled for traction. I was *not* going to spill any water. And this time I made it—bruised shoulder, two skinned knees, and no pride left whatsoever. Or, as I wrote to Barbara that night, "I'm fine but fly-bitten, and my ego is in shreds. Yeah, I did it, but why did it take me so long to discover what I was doing wrong?"

Some evenings after dinner, while I lay in my hammock with homework or a book and Aaron wrote up his field notes, we shared the high and low points of our day. He especially liked hearing the gossip—that according to Lucia, for example, a man in San Pedro Columbia had two wives.

But Aaron's main interest was the men and their work. During the winter months, the Maya often planted a second corn crop along river-banks that flooded every year—a crop most of them called by its Spanish name, *matahambre*, "kills hunger." He was intrigued by the possibility that agriculture had begun in the New World the same way it had in the Fertile Crescent of the Middle East—by farmers planting crops in the mineral-rich topsoil of flooded riverbanks.

I was less interested in *matahambre* than in figuring out why I was having so much trouble teaching the kids how to tell time. There were quite a few clocks in the village, but after listening to alarms go off at odd hours of the day and night, I concluded that people didn't know how to use them. It wasn't uncommon for somebody to stop by, thumb through magazines for a while, look at the clock, and ask me what time it was.

"They don't understand that the number 'twelve' signifies a shift from morning to afternoon, and from one day and the next," I told Aaron. "They're fine with 'one o'clock' all the way through 'eleven o'clock,' but there's something about 'twelve' they just don't get."

"Their system of counting is based on twenty. The idea that 'twelve' indicates the start of a new day is probably too abstract."

"Twenty? That's interesting."

"Why?"

"Because whenever I give the kids a math problem that involves numbers over ten, they count on their fingers first, then their toes."

"Hmm." Aaron bent over his notes, pen in hand.

"How can I explain that the number 'twelve' is an arbitrary cutoff point between one day and the next?" I asked.

"So you think they have a hard time conceptualizing numbers."

Since *I* had a hard time conceptualizing numbers, I wasn't quite sure how to respond. "If you mean the ability to add or subtract numbers in their heads . . ."

"Yes."

"Then that's what I mean."

Aaron tended to draw sharp lines of differentiation between Maya behavior and American behavior. He told me he'd seen a little girl slip in the mud on her way to school. After examining her knees and elbows for scrapes, she looked at the mud on her dress and ran home to clean off. "She wasn't bawling, the way most American girls would have," Aaron concluded. "Very matter-of-fact—she just headed home to change clothes."

"I don't think *all* little girls in America would cry in that situation," I protested. "That's a pretty big generalization."

"I have a sister," he reminded me.

"And I'm a girl. This is firsthand information, straight from the horse's mouth, untainted by cultural bias: *not all little American girls cry if they get dirt on their clothes.*"

Aaron rolled his eyes.

I on the other hand tended to draw parallels. "Silvaria Choc reminds me of our neighbor in Verona, Mrs. Bonnelli. She had only two children, but some of her teeth were missing and she looked old and worn out the way Silvaria does. Her husband was usually drunk and they didn't have much money—not to say that's the case with Enriques. But she was a nice person. She didn't mind this little kid tagging around after her, showing off the necklace I'd just bought at the five and ten. She even told me I could take a shortcut through her backyard if I wanted to . . ."

"Don't do that."

"Do what?"

"Try to make the Kekchi into people you know."

Oh, crap, I thought. "I'm not trying to 'make' Silvaria into anything. I'm just saying she reminds me of Mrs. Bonnelli."

Aaron stopped writing. "How people behave isn't a foolproof guide to how they *are*," he said, as serious as I'd ever seen him. "José Tux is a kind, patient man—a good man. He's certainly been kind to me. He works hard to provide for his family. He doesn't beat his wife. But when we're hunting, he doesn't care if the animal he shoots is dead or not before he stuffs it in his *champa*. Sometimes they whimper for a long time, yet he does nothing. In his culture people don't think animals feel pain, or else they don't care."

"But I'm not *interested* in their culture! Well, I am. But . . ."

"You're trying to Americanize them so you feel more comfortable with them. I know—I did it myself the summer I stayed in Crique Sarco with Manuel and Petrona. But it's not a good idea."

I ground my teeth and wished for a cigarette. Aaron was right about how the Maya treated animals, their dogs in particular. But conceding that just made me angrier. If he wanted to be a neutral observer, fine.

As for me, I would continue to consider Silvaria as a tolerant, motherly neighbor with too many children and not enough money who seemed to take things as they came, one day—one child, one meal, one misfortune—at a time.

I taught the children "The Alphabet Song." I taught them "Row, Row, Row Your Boat," and after they'd learned the words I taught them three-part harmony. One day I tried to teach them "The Star-Spangled Banner," but I misjudged the key and couldn't reach the high notes at the end. Paulina giggled, her eyes sly, and I went back to "Row, Row, Row Your Boat."

From their former teacher they'd learned "London Bridge Is Falling Down," and during recess I showed them how to play the game. The boys loved it. Even the older ones would grab some unsuspecting youngster under the armpits and swing him around until his feet cleared the ground, yelling, "Take the keys and lock her up, my fair lady!"

One rainy morning I wrote some math problems on the board for the advanced group and sat down with the little kids for a lesson in addition. I counted out three black beans on Lute's desk. "How many beans does Lute have?"

"Three, Teacher!" they chorused.

"Very good." I added two more to the pile. "*Now* how many beans does he have?"

But before anybody could answer, Luis Choc let out a yell. The next minute my entire class stood raptly in the doorway watching José Ical's stallion breed José Tux's mule mare.

I was probably more interested than they were because I'd been a horse-crazy kid and had ridden since I was five. I knew mules were sterile and assumed that meant female mules didn't come in season. But this one obviously had, even though her long ears were pinned back against her sparse, upright mane and she didn't look the least bit lovelorn, standing in the rain as the stud raked her shoulders with his front hooves to keep his balance while he thrust himself inside her.

While we watched I thought, *American kids would be snickering and talking dirty by now.* Then I thought, *Not if they were farm kids.* And these were farms kids. Their *culture* didn't matter.

With a grunt the stallion slid off the mule mare. She swung her head around, big yellow teeth bared, before deciding payback might not be in her best interests and trotting off. The stallion raised his head suddenly and neighed, both ears pricked forward.

We all turned to see what he was looking at. A strange horse and two strange mules approached us from the trail—animals none of us had noticed earlier because of the impromptu biology lesson. A Maya man, a stranger, rode one mule and led the other. The second rider, the tattered hem of his cassock crusted with mud, was my boss.

Father Cull's face looked stern, but that was his habitual expression. I hoped fervently that the rain dripping down his glasses had prevented him from seeing Teacher and her class gawking at an act of fornication that he would surely consider immoral, since it was not for purposes of procreation.

He had ridden from San José without rain gear of any kind, and his clothes were sodden. Since it was almost lunchtime, I dismissed class early and asked him to have lunch with us. He refused, saying he wanted to visit with the children. They crowded around him in the open area in front of the school.

From the house I watched him show the boys how to do calisthenics. He must have looked very strange to them—a white man with thinning hair wearing a black dress doing deep knee bends in the rain—but the boys mimicked every movement he made. They looked mesmerized.

In the afternoon Father Cull watched me teach awhile, then wrote in my attendance ledger that I was "making excellent progress." Elation spiked through my body like an electrical charge. Hallelujah! Maybe I *was* a good teacher! This must be how my kids felt when I handed back a "correct" paper. I couldn't stop smiling.

The following morning the entire village showed up for Mass. Even very small children not yet housebroken wore their Sunday best. (They usually ran around naked—much easier to rinse off "accidents.") Father Cull preached about the Ecumenical Council and how nobody should work on Sunday because it was the Lord's day.

Most Maya men *didn't* work on Sunday. To them work meant farming, and they used Sunday for miscellaneous labor, like gathering firewood or hunting. For the women Sunday was no different from any other day. They still got up at four in the morning to grind corn for *tortillas*.

After promoting the concept of leisure time on the Lord's day, Father Cull cautioned young girls against dropping out of school before they were of legal age. Since I hadn't asked him about Paulina, Dolores must have. If so, she had her answer.

As Father Cull waited for José Tux to bring mules and a horse to take him to Pueblo Viejo, he told me he'd be back the following month with schoolbooks.

My day typically began about six o'clock, even on weekends. By the time I'd lit the fire and cooked breakfast, it wasn't unusual to have half a dozen Maya in our house. The children were mainly interested in the magazines, but the adults still preferred to watch us eat. I always offered them instant coffee. Even though theirs tasted much better because they grew and ground their own, nobody ever refused.

Early one Sunday while Aaron and I were eating breakfast, Julian Jimenez stopped by. Three little girls had sidled in earlier and were sitting on a bench, sharing the same magazine. Every once in a while I heard a whispered "House!" "Boy!" "Road!" "Ayiii—that lady has red hair!"

Julian, a tall, thin, stooped man with a deferential manner, had been a *chiclero* for most of his life, which meant he'd made his living bleeding sapodilla trees for the raw latex that was the basis of chewing gum. He spoke Kekchi, Spanish, and English, and had recently moved in with his sister Silvaria and her family. To judge by his clothes, he was as poor as they were. After finishing his coffee, he wanted to know if he could borrow our mousetrap. Even though they were cheap and for sale in all the shops, we owned the only one in Rio Blanco. Dolores had borrowed it twice, Lucia had borrowed it, and now Silvaria wanted to borrow it.

I poured Julian more coffee and Aaron gave him the mousetrap. Julian thanked us. His English was so strangely inflected that even Aaron, who was tone-deaf, asked him where he had learned to speak it. Julian replied that he'd worked in a lumber mill in Scotland during the Second World War. He was telling us about his introduction to oatmeal—*real* oatmeal—when a soft "*Caba nu*" outside the door brought the conversation to a halt.

It was the *alcalde* of Aguacate, a Kekchi man Aaron knew but I didn't. Dutifully I rekindled the fire and heated more water for coffee. Half an hour later, after an exchange of pleasantries, Julian translating, the *alcalde* finally got around to the reason for his visit. Would Aaron and I consent to be *padrinos*, godparents, at his son's wedding?

Aaron and I exchanged glances. This was quite an honor. Don had been a *padrino* many times, but only after he'd lived here a few years. But Don was Catholic, a difference both of us failed to take into consideration when we accepted.

Proudly the *alcalde* pulled a bottle of rum out of his pocket, uncorked it, and passed it around the table. It was typical Maya rum that came in a green bottle without a label, 180 proof—almost pure alcohol. Since it had no taste *except* the alcohol (I could see why American Indians called it firewater), it was very easy to drink yourself stupid in ten minutes flat—which Aaron and I proceeded to do.

It couldn't have been much later than seven thirty. I'd never had a drink this early in the morning, but I didn't want to hurt the *alcalde*'s feelings, especially since he was already calling us *compadre* (godfather) and *comadre* (godmother).

Either rum is unusually potent in the early morning, or I hadn't eaten enough instant oatmeal. Either way, the alcohol bypassed my stomach and went straight to my brain. As we made small talk in three languages, we swapped the bottle—the common denominator, the great social equalizer—back and forth. In a matter of minutes the children had disappeared, along with everything else in my peripheral vision.

The level of rum dipped by a quarter, then a third, then half, and I shook my head the next time the bottle came my way. Looking upset, the *alcalde* questioned Julian. Was something wrong with his rum? Didn't I like it? Didn't I like *him*?

Of course I liked him. At least I did right now. So I smiled contritely and downed a few more swallows.

The bottle made one more trip around the table. I noticed Julian clutching the mousetrap firmly, his arm fully extended, as though it had tried to bite his leg.

Abruptly everybody except the *alcalde* turned black, as though I were seeing him through a tunnel. He was outlined in a shimmery white light and looked ready to levitate. Without warning he struggled to his feet, knocked the chair over, and lurched out the door, holding the empty bottle by the neck. Julian disappeared. Then Aaron disappeared. I staggered to my hammock and lost consciousness.

Father Cull refused to let us sponsor the *alcalde*'s son's wedding because we weren't Catholic. Privately, I thought somebody had told him that Teacher and her husband liked to get drunk before noon on the Lord's day.

xxxxxxxxxxxxxxxxxxxxxxxxxxxxxxxxxxxxxxxxxxxxxxxxxxxxxxx

CHICHA

Chicha is home-brewed moonshine made with corn and fermented sugarcane juice. This recipe comes from Pedro Choco, formerly of Crique Sarco. It differs from the *chicha* I would help Lucia make for the *fiesta* in that it calls for yeast. I haven't tried this recipe because I'm not that crazy about *chicha*. Before you mix up a batch in your bathtub, you might want to find out whether making it is legal where you live.

> 3 quarts dry, crushed corn (corn chewed by weevils, unsuitable for making *tortillas*, is preferred. As Lucia put it, don't use "pretty" corn)

5 pounds raw sugar (also called *turbinado* sugar)
5 gallons water
1 tablespoon dried yeast
1 tablespoon ground black pepper
5 allspice seeds
cheesecloth or other thin cotton cloth

In a container with a tight lid, soak the corn, 2 pounds of sugar, and 2 gallons of water for 3 days with at least 6 inches of space above the mixture. On day 4, discard the liquid. To the corn mixture add the remaining sugar, water, and yeast. Wrap the pepper and allspice in cheesecloth. Stir thoroughly with hands or a long spoon. Allow to soak another 3 days. Using more cheesecloth, strain the *chicha* into bottles.

The longer the brew ferments, the stronger it becomes. You can continue to add water and sugar in equal amounts and strain off the *chicha* every 3 days.

Will make enough to get an entire village drunk.

EIGHT

Walking with the Dead

Contrary to my expectations, our thatched roof turned out to be snug and waterproof. But it did have one drawback: creatures lived in it. As soon as the sun went down and I lit the kerosene lamp, they woke up. We very seldom saw them, but we heard them all night long—rustling, scuffling, scratching like cats in a litter box. It was like listening to static with no way to turn down the volume.

"Mice?" Aaron suggested. Since most families kept a supply of dried corn inside their houses, mice were rampant. "Or maybe vampire bats? That's why people burn candles at night."

"I thought they burned candles to keep mischief-minded spirits away," I said.

"Who told you that?"

"You did. You said José Tux told you the Kekchi burn candles on the Days of the Dead to keep the 'shadows of the ancients' at a distance. The ones that might hurt you." The Days of the Dead—the Maya celebrated two of them, the first two days of November—were less than a week away.

Aaron gazed thoughtfully at the thatch. "Or it could be scorpions."

"You can lay off the humbug any time you want," I said, returning to my book, a Somerset Maugham novel Don had loaned me.

"Or cockroaches." Every night the cockroaches held a dance in our house. When they got intolerable, Aaron went outside, a sandal in one hand. I stayed inside, similarly armed. We took turns—first he would bang on a plank with his sandal. To escape, the cockroaches ran around the plank to the inside of the house, where I whacked them. I would hit the next board, and Aaron would squash the cockroaches that scurried outside. On a good night, working our way around the entire house, we could easily kill three dozen cockroaches in ten minutes.

I was in my hammock, immersed in Maugham, and Aaron was at the table cleaning his rifle when he yelled, "Jesus Christ!" and scrambled to his feet. I looked up to see what was so perturbing. The next second I was on the other side of the room with him, wrapped around his neck. A tarantula, black as velvet and the size of a skillet, crouched on the table.

"Sonofabitch fell out of the thatch and landed on my hand," Aaron said, his voice shaking. "Look at the size of him!"

"Where's your sandal? Flatten him!"

"*You* flatten him. I'm not going near the damn thing."

I wasn't either.

After agreeing we'd be happier knowing the tarantula was dead and not roaming around the house somewhere, Aaron gingerly picked up his machete, intending to smash it with the flat side, but we'd waited too long. As he approached the table, the tarantula slid between the planks and disappeared.

That night I lay crosswise and sleepless in my hammock, looking up into the rustling thatch. I wondered how many other tarantulas lived there and what I would do if one fell on me.

At least once a month Joaquin Choc lashed Dolores with his belt. Once he beat her because she knocked over the kerosene lamp. She told me the story without shame or bravado. The lamp hadn't broken, that wasn't the problem. But the dirt floor soaked up all the spilled kerosene, and kerosene was expensive. When I realized she was giving Joaquin an excuse for beating her, I felt sick.

He usually lashed her at night, and Aaron and I gritted our teeth as we listened to her scream. The next morning her back would be striped with welts. I didn't understand why she never tried to conceal them by wearing a blouse or *huipil*. Was she proud of having a husband who beat her? Or did Joaquin forbid her to cover herself, so everybody in the village would know how *macho* he was?

Just before Aaron left for Punta Gorda to pick up the mail and stock up on supplies, Joaquin beat Dolores so badly that she ran out of the house to get away from him. She didn't go to the Bohs for refuge, or come to us, but we heard her sobbing in the darkness between our two houses.

I set my book down. "I'm going out there."

"Oh, no, you're not," Aaron said.

"Please don't give me another lecture about cultural relativity. *Listen* to her, for God's sake! She's crying—she's in pain!"

Aaron shook his head, clearly agitated. He usually wasn't at a loss for words. "We can't do anything," he said finally. "It's none of our business. Do you see anybody else running to help her?"

"She has no relatives in this village! And her worthless goddam husband has three grown brothers! Who's willing to risk getting the entire Choc family pissed off at them?"

"Which is one reason you shouldn't get involved."

"If you're telling me it'll jeopardize your work—"

"Do you think I *like* listening to Dolores scream? But if we intervene, where do we draw the line? I guarantee you that every parent in Rio Blanco has lashed their child for disobedience at least once."

The old slippery slope argument. But I had to admit that I didn't really *want* to go to Dolores. What would I do after that? Tell her, "It's okay, sweetie. Want a Band-Aid?" Or, "How about a shoulder to cry on?" Better yet, "Why don't you just brain the bastard with your *comal*?" Nobody had elected me to office, I wasn't British, and I wasn't Father

Cull. It was also very possible that anything I did to help might backfire and make her situation even worse.

About five minutes later—Dolores was still sniffling outside the house—Joaquin began playing his violin. The people of Santa Cruz planned to dance the *Moro* in a couple of weeks, and Joaquin had been invited to play. He was practicing. To my dismay he was a very capable musician. The music he coaxed from a rough, handmade instrument was on key and moving. I tried to reconcile those two things—a man beating a woman so brutally that she ran away from him in tears, and that same man then picking up a musical instrument and playing it with skill and refinement. I couldn't.

At noon the following day I was home, eating lunch, when Lucia came in with the laundry. "I don't like that man," she announced.

"What man?"

"Joaquin. He get vexed too easy—he lash Dolores, he lash all he children. No good."

I was astounded. It was the first time I'd heard a Maya pass judgment on somebody's behavior, and I didn't know what to say.

Silently Lucia placed the wet clothes and my bar of soap on the table and walked out. I pondered. Before I could talk myself back into neutrality, I ran to her house. "Lucia?"

She was sitting in her hammock smoking a *puro*. Her skirt—this one was a deep shade of pink—was still tucked into her waistband, and her feet stuck out in front of her, crossed at the ankles. Wordlessly she gestured me inside and pointed at a wooden *banco*.

I sat down. "Why doesn't Dolores leave him?"

"She have it too many childrens. She leave Joaquin, who going make plantation for she?"

That particular question had never crossed my mind. Without Joaquin, who *would* plant corn for her—or grow beans, or chop firewood? Lute, her oldest son, was only eight. "Why doesn't anybody help her?"

"If we have it *alcalde*, he could make Joaquin stop. But Rio Blanco don't have it *alcalde*."

Jurisdictionally, Rio Blanco was part of Pueblo Viejo, where the *alcalde*, the mayor, lived. If Dolores wanted to file a complaint against Joaquin, she'd have had to walk to Pueblo Viejo to do it—right past the houses of both of his brothers.

It struck me suddenly that I was on lunch break and had to go back to school. I started to get up, then noticed the expression on Lucia's face. She was looking over my shoulder, grimacing. "That man no good neither."

I turned around. Martín Ical was walking directly toward us. But as soon as he saw me he shifted course and tried to look as though he was heading for his brother Mateo's house.

"Why not?"

Lucia smoked contemplatively. "He humbug me when Crispino not here. No good, one man in the house one-one with a married lady." One-one meant "alone."

Hmm. So the Maya sometimes cheated on their spouses, or tried to. Wait till I told Aaron! "Lucia, I have to go teach. *Pues*—maybe I'll come back later?"

Lucia puffed on her cigar and nodded. I really wanted to know why she wore that damn safety pin on her necklace.

Martín Ical was the youngest of three brothers and the wildest. He was Kekchi, but Fernanda, his wife, was Mopan. He beat her so often that she and her son went back to her family in San Antonio periodically, leaving Martín to mope around by himself. Once while she was gone, he took up with one of José Tux's daughters and had a baby with her. As soon as Fernanda found out, she came back and chased the girl out of the house and back to José and Ana.

I didn't much like Martín, but he shattered a preconception about the Maya that even Aaron had bought into. In spite of his adventurous love life, Martín was a hard worker and had amassed enough money to buy a strapping young mule. It had cost him 160 dollars BH less than a year ago, and he was very proud of it. When the mule died one day,

Martín was in Santa Cruz. Half the village gathered on the hill by his house to talk about it and look at the mule. Aaron and I joined them. Fernanda stood by herself, wiping her eyes. She wasn't feeling sorry for the mule. Martín had a slight harelip, which gave him a raffish look, and an unstable temper, and she was crying because of what he might do to her when he found out about the mule.

The animal lay on its side, and even though the sun was hardly up, its stomach had already bloated. Martín didn't come back until late that afternoon. By then the mule had begun to smell. Martín just stood there and looked at it, tears streaming down his face that he made no attempt to hide. "Shet," he groaned again and again. "Shet."

So much for the stoic Indian.

Contrary to what I'd been taught in home economics, fresh eggs do not require refrigeration. The setting hens had hatched their chicks, which meant people had eggs for sale again. Now and then a neighbor would bring me some. In cool weather—dry season was approaching, and the daytime temperature had dropped to the midseventies—eggs lasted a week without refrigeration. Maybe they lasted longer, but they were still scarce enough that I didn't want to risk spoiling the ones I had.

The weather continued to get progressively cooler, and I woke up one sunny Saturday in a bread-making mood. I was by myself—Aaron had left the day before for Punta Gorda. After breakfast I consulted Cirila's recipe for Creole bread, which I had dutifully written down. She had an oven and I didn't, but I thought I could improvise one by setting my *comal* on top of the fireplace, building a fire beneath it, and putting one of my big pots upside down to make an enclosure.

First I cleared a space on the table and laid down a clean cotton skirt, so I'd have someplace to knead the dough. Although I wasn't sure of the proportions, I made milk using powdered KILM ("milk" spelled backward—distributed free throughout the colony by one of the international health organizations) and heated it while I assembled the rest of my ingredients. The iffy part was the yeast. Cirila had told me that conditions had to be just right or the dough wouldn't rise. Her kitchen was usually warm and sunny because it faced south. But even in hot weather she shut both doors to keep the drafts out when she baked bread.

As per her instructions, I stirred and kneaded until I had bread dough. Then I covered the bowl with a damp towel and set it next to the fire, for warmth. There was nothing I could do about drafts.

Ten minutes later the sun disappeared behind a cloud. When it didn't reemerge, I peeked anxiously at the bread dough. It was rising, but very slowly. I rotated the bowl so the other side would be close to the fire. While I waited I typed a letter to Aaron's sister. The rains had lasted so long that nearly everything we owned had mildewed, including my typewriter ribbon.

October 28, 1962

Dear Ginger,

It's a chilly Saturday morning. Aaron left early yesterday for Punta Gorda—PG, as everybody calls it. He planned to spend last night with Don, so he should be home today.

Yesterday afternoon Dolores Choc, our *tortilla* lady, wanted to know where he was and when he was coming back. When I told her, she sent her two oldest kids—Paulina and Lute—over here after dinner to spend the night, so I wouldn't be by myself. Maxiana just walked in to see if Aaron had come back yet.

I stopped writing and checked the bread dough, leaving Maxiana to stare at the sheet of paper in my typewriter. She had watched me type dozens of letters, but she still suspected the process was magical.

The bread dough had risen enough that it looked twice its original size—or so I told myself—so I sprinkled more flour over the skirt I'd spread on the table, punched down the dough, and kneaded it again. I made two slightly curved, oblong loaves, checking to be sure I could fit the pot over both of them. Belatedly I thought I should probably have heated the pot *before* putting the bread on my *comal*.

Maxiana watched me dubiously. "What is like that, Teacher?"

"Creole bread. Do you eat it?"

She made a face. Some of the Maya liked Creole bread—she obviously didn't. It was hideously expensive to buy and had the taste and consistency of a sponge. But it would be a pleasant change from *tortillas*, and I knew Aaron would appreciate it.

I added more wood to the fire and sat down to finish my letter. After watching for a few more minutes, Maxiana left.

The bread was supposed to bake about half an hour, but when I lifted the pot to check, the crust still looked pale. I added a few more sticks of wood to the fire and gave the bread another fifteen minutes. Lute and his younger sister Valeria sidled through the door. Valeria, one of the little girls who loved to snuggle up against me, flashed me a shy smile before heading for the magazines.

The next time I checked, the crusts looked a little darker. I removed the pot and used my wooden pancake turner to slide the loaves onto a plate. At least the bread *smelled* good, I thought, although it was too hot to eat right this minute.

"Teacher?"

"Yes, Lute?"

"What is that?"

"That is Creole bread."

"Is good?"

"I hope so."

They hung around for a few more minutes and then left. After shaking the flour out of my skirt, I wadded it up into a potholder and used it to hold the bread in place while I cut a slice. Maybe I shouldn't have built such a hot fire—the bottom of the loaf was scorched. But the smell of freshly baked bread made me hungry, and I was eager to taste my creation. I cut the bottom crust off and slathered margarine and peanut butter on the bread. It was chewy but satisfyingly warm and filling. I sighed in contentment. Nothing like home-baked bread.

I cut off another slice. This one was firmer and chewier, but still delicious.

I was debating whether to go to the river or take a nap when Evaristo sauntered in. He'd heard that I had taught the schoolkids "The Star-Spangled Banner," and he wanted to learn it. He was fascinated with anything American and had applied for a job picking grapefruit in Florida. But so far he hadn't heard anything. Aaron and I wondered what would happen if he were accepted. Would he leave, like the Maya Buster Hunter had talked about, only to come back to Rio Blanco when it was time to plant corn? Or—given his past behavior—would he leave and not come back?

I told him I'd type out the words to "The Star-Spangled Banner" and go over them with him later. Then I grabbed some clean clothes and my water bucket and headed for the river.

I had been home less than five minutes, wet hair dripping down my back, when Crispino and Lucia came over. Maxiana had told them about the Creole bread. Could they buy a loaf?

"I didn't make very much," I said truthfully. "But I'll give you some. Would you like to taste it first?"

They both nodded, so I cut off two more slices. The bread had gotten so firm it was hard to cut. After spreading margarine on each piece, I handed one to Lucia and the other to Crispino. Lucia pointed at the peanut butter. "I want it like so."

I grinned. She and I apparently agreed that small talk was unrewarding in any language. After smearing peanut butter over her bread, I handed it back.

Crispino's jaw muscles were working so hard it looked as though he was trying to gnaw through a pair of Aaron's chinos. Lucia nibbled at hers, and from the expression on her face I could tell she didn't like the peanut butter. Finally she bit off a piece of crust and started to chew.

His expression kind, Crispino handed me his half-eaten slice of bread. "*Coma li pek,*" he said regretfully. Like a stone.

I blushed in mortification. Lucia stepped outside to spit out the remaining peanut butter. When she returned, she handed me her uneaten bread, too. "When you husband going come back?"

"Tonight, I hope." I wanted to cry.

They left. After tossing the crusts of my Creole rock-bread to Micalia's chickens, I sat down dejectedly to type out the lyrics of "The Star-Spangled Banner."

By the time I finished I was hungry again. I checked the bread. It was so hard the loaves barely yielded to hand pressure. The next time I made bread I'd chose a warmer day, so the bread would rise properly. I would preheat the pot, keep the fire at a consistent . . . Who was I kidding? There wouldn't *be* a next time. I wasn't a baker. I wasn't even a cook. More like a warmer-upper, and even then I could barely keep a fire lit. Maybe I should just resign myself to the inevitable and stop trying. Everything I did here seemed to end in disaster, especially if it involved cooking.

The fire. *Damn!* I jumped up and poked hopefully at the ashes. But the fire was dead. It was almost dark outside, and I had only a few sticks of wood left. I was beginning to doubt that Aaron would make it home tonight. He didn't like walking in the bush by himself after dark any more than the Maya did. But he wasn't worried about *sisimitos*. He was worried about jaguars. One had already "escorted" him out of its territory when he walked back from Santa Cruz.

I decided to use half the wood to boil water—dinner was going to be oatmeal and a cup of coffee. I'd save the *tortillas* for Aaron, and if he did come back tonight I'd use the remaining wood to make a pot of Knorr's soup.

I was on my hands and knees, holding a match under a few crumpled sheets of paper, when Andrea Ical came in, holding her baby brother by the hand. All he had on was a thin, patched shirt, a hand-me-down that was already too small for him.

Andrea's arrival drew Cresencio and little Julian. All four children stood directly behind me and watched while I placed splinters of kindling over the burning paper, willing them to catch fire and swearing when they didn't.

When Evaristo came in I sat back on my heels. "The words are on the table. Why don't you sit down and have a look? Once I get the fire started I'll teach you the melody."

Nodding, Evaristo sat down on the bench holding the song lyrics. I bent forward again, swearing silently this time.

"Oh, say can you see, by the down's . . ."

"Dawn's," I shouted over my shoulder.

". . . dawn's early light, what so proud—proudly we hell as . . ."

"*Hail!*"

". . . hail as the twilight's last glim . . ."

"Just let me get the fire lit, okay? Then I'll come help you."

Evaristo continued to read under his breath, but I could still hear him. The kindling finally caught. Carefully I fed twigs to the flame, then bigger twigs, then sticks, until I had a small but decent fire. As I got up, wiping my tears away with my knuckles, Lucia walked in the back door. I caught the unmistakable fragrance of her stewed chicken, made with so much *cilantro* the broth resembled seaweed.

"For you," she said, handing me the bowl. She had correctly deduced that with Aaron gone and the bread being inedible, I had nothing to eat for dinner.

"*To ho cre!*" I told her fervently. Thank you! It was a big bowl. She nodded, then said a few words to my assembled guests. Reluctantly Andrea and her brother and the Choc boys eased out the door, leaving only Evaristo. He and Lucia had a brief discussion in Mopan. Then Lucia left, muttering.

I frowned. Why had she told the kids to get out? Did she think I was going to be attacked by the ghosts of dead ancestors? Whose? Hers or mine?

"I'm going to eat dinner," I told Evaristo. "Want some?"

"No, thank you."

"How about a cup of coffee?"

"No, thank you."

Then why don't you go home? I thought, setting Lucia's stewed chicken over the fire. When it was hot I'd reheat a couple of *tortillas*.

"Lucia and Maxiana, they worry for you," Evaristo said abruptly.

"They do?" I didn't believe him. "Why?"

"No good, a lady in her house by herself."

"I'm fine. I have trouble lighting a fire sometimes because the wood is so green, but that's all."

"*Pues*," Evaristo said, climbing to his feet. "I'm going, Missus." He stuck the lyrics to "The Star-Spangled Banner," which he had folded into neat fourths, into his back pocket.

"Oh no—the song!" I had completely forgotten my promise to help him. "Evaristo, I'm sorry. Please sit down and I'll go over the words with you."

"I come back some other time."

He doesn't want to be alone with me, I thought. That's what his conversation with Lucia had been about—she had *told* him not to stay here alone with me. Were so many evil spirits gathering around me that she didn't want to expose her big, brawny brother to them?

Shortly after I finished eating, Maxiana and Natalia came over and announced they were here to spend the night. "I give up," I said in exasperation. "Are you two ghost-proof or something?" The girls regarded me gravely and didn't answer. I sank into my hammock and waved them into Aaron's big one. The kids all loved to sleep in his—each additional kid jumping into it caused the rest to tumble around, giggling, as though they were in a mixing bowl.

I had no idea why the Maya did anything. Their behavior was a complete mystery to me. Why had Lucia chased the Ical and Choc children out of my house only to substitute her own? If she seriously thought the spirits of the dead might hurt me, why had she put the lives of her sister and her only daughter in danger?

Early the next morning—the sun wasn't even up yet—Luis, her younger brother, silently stacked three days' worth of dry firewood outside my back door.

xx

LUCIA'S *CILANTRO* STEWED CHICKEN

The best way to make any kind of soup is in a slow cooker. The contents stay at the same steady simmer, which means the broth remains clear and the soup develops a deep, full-bodied flavor.

This recipe can also be made the old-fashioned way, in a large pot over the stove. I call it a stew because of the amount of *cilantro* Lucia put in it.

> 1 heavy, free-range broiler/fryer cut into parts (or one skin-on, bone-in chicken breast per person)
>
> chicken feet (optional—peeled and with the toenails removed, they add flavor and texture to the soup, as well as enabling the cook to feed more people)
>
> 1 medium white onion, diced
>
> 1½ teaspoons salt
>
> 2 teaspoons dried thyme
>
> 1 teaspoon dried oregano
>
> 2 dried *arbol chiles*, washed and broken into small pieces (include the seeds). If you're a real *chile* fanatic, use the smaller, hotter *pequin chiles* (see the caution in the rice and beans recipe, chap. 4.)
>
> 6 cups chicken broth or water
>
> 1 cup packed *cilantro* (fresh coriander), washed and drained. (See the note below.)
>
> additional *cilantro* for taste and garnish

Add chicken pieces to a pot of cold water, then add remaining ingredients. Bring to a boil and simmer, uncovered, 1½ to 2 hours (4–7 hours in the crock pot), depending on how tender you like your chicken. If you like a strong *cilantro* taste, add more about 10 minutes before you eat (20 minutes in a crock pot).

Adjust seasonings.

Serves 4–8 people, depending on how you cut up the chicken.

Note: the dish will be quite robust if you use this much *cilantro*. You may want to experiment using a few sprigs before you throw in an entire cup. Alternatively, use fresh parsley. Although the two taste nothing alike, you'll still have the visual appeal of the bright red *chile* peppers and a leafy green vegetable.

NINE

The Essential Nature of the Rainforest

According to the Maya, it should have been dry season, and finally, in mid-November, the rain stopped. The sun came out. No more darting between raindrops using both hands to hold a *mox*-leaf umbrella over our heads. The road was still muddy, but people began making arrangements to haul their rice to San Antonio.

The sunny weather brightened everybody's outlook, even mine. One Saturday around noon, when I figured everybody else would be relaxing over a midday meal, I lured Aaron to the pool below the falls where the women bathed. The men bathed downstream—I saw them occasionally in the late afternoon, when I was on my way to get water. They would stop soaping themselves and stand motionless, hands crossed over their genitals. Eyes averted, we solemnly wished each other a good day, which for some reason—a Mopan custom—had been shortened to the Deity's name. "*Dios*," we murmured in subdued tones.

But today nobody else was around. Even the kids had gotten tired of following us to watch us bathe. Aaron and I had the waterfall and the clear green water of the pool all to ourselves.

I washed my hair first, then held my nose and dove underwater. Once my hair was rinsed clean, I swam for the sheer pleasure of being in such a pretty spot on such a beautiful day. As though by invitation, a cloud of blue Morpho butterflies, their six-inch iridescent wings flashing in the sunlight, swooped over our heads.

Aaron quickly grew bored with a pursuit as mundane as swimming and decided to climb the thirty-foot falls above the pool instead.

Must be a guy thing, I mused—wanting to climb waterfalls, glaciers, Mt. Everest, for no reason other than *because they're there*. "Careful," I called. "The current's still pretty strong."

Aaron looked at me over his shoulder. "Stop trying to baby me."

I tried to splash him, but he was too far away.

Floating lazily on my back so I could monitor his progress, my arms crossed under my head, I kicked every once in a while to stay afloat. I didn't get to see Aaron naked very often. His arms and a scallop on the back of his neck where his T-shirt ended were heavily tanned. But his upper body, from biceps to waist, was white as flour. So was his entire lower body. What four months ago had been scholarly flab was now muscle, and I admired him with half-closed eyes as he climbed cautiously through the foam and tumbling water. My handsome, adventurous, romantic husband, doing his Ernest Hemingway thing.

Halfway up the falls, Aaron slipped.

But instead of falling backward into the pool, he slid down the falls feet first, as though he had weights tied to each leg. On his descent he hit ledge after ledge of limestone. Sometimes the foaming water completely submerged him. The next second he bobbed up again, still facing the falls.

In horror I righted myself, treading water. As soon as Aaron hit the pool he sank. The water that closed over his head was pink.

"Aaron! Where are you? *Aaron!*"

When he finally surfaced his face was streaming blood. "I can't see," he said fretfully.

"You're hurt!" I heard myself scream as I paddled toward him. I was aware that I sounded more panicked than he did, and wondered if he was in shock. Then I wondered if I was. "Come on, let's get you back to the house."

We swam to shore, where Aaron knelt in the shallows and splashed water over his face. For a second I saw his features plainly. Blood ran from a dozen different places: on his forehead, eyebrows, the bridge of his nose, both cheeks, and his chin.

I'd left a towel on the shore to dry my hair. When I stepped out of the water to get it, I heard a horrified gasp. Three women and their kids were walking toward us, obviously intending to spend a leisurely afternoon at the pool. But the sight of Teacher and her husband, both butt naked, stopped them in their tracks.

I turned my back to them, stepped into my skirt, and yanked it up to my waist. Then I grabbed the towel and held it against Aaron's face, trying to stop the bleeding. "Pull your pants on and let's go," I whispered.

For once he didn't argue. I tugged my blouse on and helped him past the women. As soon as they saw his face and upper body—the damage to his face was much more dramatic—I heard another quick, collective intake of breath and "Ayiii, *Dios!*" All of them, even the kids, stepped back two paces as if they'd rehearsed it and wordlessly watched us go by.

As soon as we were home, Aaron sank into his hammock, pressing the towel against his face. Blood seeped out around the edges. Frantically I dug through our medicine box for peroxide and some cotton swabs—and, as an afterthought, a mirror. As the peroxide frothed and bubbled on his face, Aaron examined himself. "I don't like the looks of that one under my right eyebrow. Damn near got my eye. I'm not crazy about the one on my nose, either," he said, as though commenting on somebody else's face.

"How about your chest?"

"Banged up. My knees, too. But for some reason my face is the worst. Hurts like bloody hell."

He's been spending too much time with Don, I thought. No Yankee said "bloody," although under the circumstances it was the perfect word. "Do you want to go to San Antonio and see the nurse? Or to Punta Gorda?" There was a doctor in PG.

"I don't think I can walk that far."

A tiny prickle, as though my skin were freezing, ran down my spine. "You mean you can't walk as far as San Antonio?"

"No. I can't."

I took a deep breath. "Then we'll borrow somebody's horse," I said, struggling to keep the panic out of my voice.

"You won't find one. Everybody's taking rice to San Antonio tomorrow."

His nonchalance was more frightening than his injuries. "Then what do you want to do?" I asked helplessly.

Aaron scrutinized his face again. "Let's wait. If I still feel like shit in the morning, we'll see if we can find a horse."

I decided to fix an early dinner—Convict Soup for Aaron, because soup was my grandmother's remedy for anything that ailed you. Then I fried some cherry tomatoes with enough *chile* pepper to make my eyes water and Aaron to forget his banged-up face, and scrambled some eggs with them.

Not five minutes later, Mateo sauntered in, followed shortly by Lucia and Crispino. News travels fast in a small village, and bad news travels even faster. Don called it bush telegraph.

All three agreed that the cuts on Aaron's face didn't look good. Although there was a *curandera* in Pueblo Viejo, nobody here practiced bush medicine. If the Maya hurt themselves, they usually came to us. (Unlike the *curandera*, we didn't charge.)

When Lucia and Crispino got up to leave, I followed them to the doorway. "Is José Tux taking his rice to market tomorrow?" I asked Lucia.

"I don't know. Make I ask Evaristo. You going take you husband to PG?" She pronounced "husband" the same way Dolores did—"whosban."

"He said he'd decide in the morning. I want to be sure that we have a horse if we need one."

When I came back inside, Aaron was shivering violently in spite of the *chile* pepper and the blanket he had wrapped himself in. I tucked another blanket around him and kissed his forehead. His skin was clammy with sweat.

I blew out the kerosene lamp, prepared to call it a night. In the sudden darkness I saw a flash of lightning followed by a long growl of thunder. Good. If it rained tomorrow, nobody would risk getting their rice wet. I'd be able to borrow a horse.

The sound of the Rio Blanco roaring over the falls woke me up, and the first thing I did was look at Aaron. In the dim, predawn light, his breathing was so shallow that at first I wasn't sure he was breathing at all. When I saw his lips move, I struggled out of my hammock. "What did you say? I can't hear you." The white noise of the river and the rain pounding on the thatch were louder than human speech.

"I said babies have been born since we moved here. People have gotten married. But nobody . . ." Aaron paused to breathe. "Nobody has died."

"Stop it. I'm going to make breakfast," I said, trying to imagine the smell of bacon sizzling in the pan, the taste of smooth, sweet egg yolks on my tongue. "Maybe you'll feel better after a good—"

"I'm not hungry."

I wasn't either, but I made breakfast anyway, just to keep myself occupied. At daybreak I peeked outside. We had a moat around the house. According to Aaron's rain gauge, it had rained four inches since we'd gone to bed.

Evaristo, leading José's mule, showed up in time for coffee. Lucia and Crispino must have walked to José's last night to ask about borrowing a horse—a two-mile round trip.

While Aaron got dressed, I threw clothes, toothbrushes, my birth control pills, and other essentials into his rucksack. None of us had rain protection, not even a *mox* leaf, and as soon as we walked out the door we were wet to the skin. Evaristo held the mule's lead rope while Aaron—who didn't like horses and didn't trust mules—cautiously hauled himself into the saddle. Once he was settled, Evaristo handed up his rucksack.

Sometime during the night the Rio Blanco had flooded its banks. That's why José had sent the mule, I realized. They're smarter than horses about where they put their feet. If the mule refused to cross the river, the river could not be crossed. Nobody was going anyplace.

Evaristo stopped by the edge of the water. The current was stronger and faster than I'd ever seen it, and so loud conversation was practically impossible. "You go first, Mr. World," Evaristo yelled. "If the mule crosses, Missus and me going to cross below." About twenty feet downstream the riverbed was rockier, but the water wasn't as deep.

Aaron kicked the mule. She had no bit, just a henequen rope halter with a lead rope. No reins, either. Cautiously she stepped into the churning water, edging upstream. Aaron tried to move her back to the crossing. "No!" Evaristo shouted. "Let *her* choose how she go."

Aaron relinquished the lead rope and the mule, step by hesitant step, walked deeper into the water until all I could see was her head and ears and Aaron's upper body as he held the rucksack over his head to keep it dry. My heart dropped to the bottom of my soggy sneakers. Was *all* of him going to disappear? What if this mule was stupid?

Without warning she launched herself and started to swim. "My *God* it's cold!" Aaron howled. After a few yards the mule heaved herself out of the river and plodded to the opposite shore.

Evaristo and I had already moved to the crossing downstream. As soon as Aaron and the mule reached the other side, Evaristo said brusquely, "Take off your skirt."

I stared at him.

"It could catch in the current," he added in a softer tone. "Pull you off balance."

That made sense. I stepped out of my skirt and tied it around my waist. "Okay." Ready or not.

Evaristo took my hand and in we went. The water felt refrigerated— I almost howled myself. Gripping my arms with both hands, Evaristo moved me in front of him until we had traded places. Now he took the full brunt of the current and I was on his left, the downstream side.

The water was up to my knees. By the time we reached the middle of the river, it was up to my hips. The current was so strong I could hardly move. Evaristo pulled me against him and used his left leg to kick my right leg forward. With an effort I dragged my other leg up underneath me. Had I come all this way just to drown in a river? I could have done that in New Jersey.

Finally the current released us into shallow water. After we caught our breath, Evaristo and I grinned at each other like a couple of kids who had just pulled off some cool, death-defying stunt.

Aaron and the mule took the lead because if Evaristo and I had, we would have left the mule behind in no time. Evaristo suggested cutting a switch to make her go faster, but Aaron vetoed that idea.

"How do you feel?" I asked.

"Thinking you're going to drown is a better pick-me-up than coffee," he said tersely. His skin color looked better—almost normal.

The mule's pace was infuriatingly slow; we had come only as far as the turnoff to Santa Cruz when Aaron stopped her.

I ran up to him. "What's wrong?"

He was dripping wet and looked miserable. "I can't ride this thing all the way to San Antonio. It's too damn uncomfortable."

He didn't mean the mule. He meant the saddle, which looked like a hand-carved copy of a McClellan saddle, an American cavalry saddle. No seat, simply a rim of wood. The middle was empty space, designed to protect the horse's backbone. If necessary it could double as a packsaddle.

Aaron slid off and handed me the lead rope. "Here. You like horses. *You* ride."

I hesitated. I'd never ridden in a skirt before. On the other hand, Evaristo had gone through a lot of trouble—to say nothing of risking his neck—to get us safely across the river. *Somebody* ought to ride the damn mule.

I eased my foot into the loop of bark that doubled as a stirrup and swung my leg over the mule's back. Aaron handed me his rucksack, which I balanced in front of me.

The saddle was worse than uncomfortable. It was like riding a toilet seat.

I didn't like being in the lead. All I could see was wet rainforest, although it had stopped raining. Gradually the sun came out, and that was even worse because the bugs came out, too, eager and voracious. But the sunshine—maybe in conjunction with the shockingly cold river water—seemed to revive Aaron. Behind me I could hear him talking to Evaristo about the *chol gwink*, the "little people" who, according to Kekchi folklore, lived in the bush. Compared to the *sisimito* they were harmless mischief-makers about the size of five-year-old children. All they wanted from humans was to trade their cacao for salt. If Aaron was asking anthropology-type questions, he couldn't be *that* sick.

The mule and I stayed in the lead until we reached San Antonio. We were so close to town the trail had widened, and I had just started around a turn when a flatbed truck crammed with passengers made the same turn from the opposite direction, mud flying from its tires. Mules don't usually startle the way horses do. But this mule did a very horselike thing—she shied at the sight of the overloaded truck and bolted.

It's hard to stop a runaway horse, even one with a bit in its mouth, and mules are notoriously less cooperative than the average horse. I did the only thing I could do—I pulled back on the lead rope so she was forced to bend her neck around until her muzzle touched my toes. The rucksack gouged me in the stomach. The saddle was big enough for me or the rucksack. Not both. I shoved the rucksack off, braced my free hand against the wooden pommel, and concentrated on circling the mule.

The passengers were a bunch of Maya headed for San José, and to judge from their laughter the mule and I were putting on a great show. Here was Teacher, her wet skirt hiked halfway to her waist, trying to stop a runaway mule. Even Evaristo and Aaron were laughing.

Finally the mule got tired of tripping herself and slowed down. Aaron, looking considerably more chipper than he had at the start of our journey, caught up with me, his rucksack slung over one shoulder.

"Not funny," I mumbled, shrill Maya laughter echoing in my ears.

Aaron smiled up at me. "Not as funny as a *Roadrunner* cartoon, but close."

Because the accident had happened nearly twenty-four hours earlier, the Belgian doctor, a man of few words, refused to stitch Aaron's face. But he cleaned Aaron's wounds, bandaged the worst ones, and gave him a penicillin shot. Next?

Punta Gorda was a Garifuna town. About twenty people stood patiently alongside the dirt thoroughfare that was its main street, awaiting their turn with the doctor. They were tall, dark-skinned, and very friendly, and spoke a rapid slang that was even harder to understand than Creole. Whites were still enough of a novelty here that they had insisted that Aaron go straight to the front of the line, even though I suspected most of them were sicker than he was.

Since Evaristo and the mule had left us at San Antonio, Aaron and I caught a ride with a Forestry Department worker to Machaca Creek. After Don stopped teasing Aaron about the scars he was going to sport for the rest of his life, he invited us to stay the night—just what we'd been hoping for. As soon as dinner was over, Cirila shooed the kids off to bed and went with them.

Don, Aaron, and I sat around the living room, drinking rum and lime juice in the white glare of the Coleman lantern, listening to the *ping* of the moths as they hit the glass.

"Well, now. You've lived in it, walked through it, seen it up close," Don said. "What d'you think about the bush?"

"Do you mean high bush?" Aaron demanded, ever the academic.

Don shrugged. "High bush, *wamil*, doesn't matter." High bush was virgin rainforest—canopy—and I'd seen it only once. *Wamil* was second and all subsequent growth. "It follows its own logic, you know. Has its own nature. What d'you think its nature *is*?"

I inhaled one of Don's Colonials and instantly pictured Punta Gorda town—a pretty little seaside village that smelled like fish and ripe mangos.

Unpainted wooden shacks the salt air had bleached silver. Hibiscus, red flamboyant trees, orchid trees, and bougainvillea everywhere you looked. Mangos, yes, but also oranges, grapefruit, papaya, bananas, plantains, all with brilliantly colored birds flashing in and out of the foliage. But as soon as the land began to rise, this lush profusion of color simply— stopped. On one side of an invisible line was civilization. On the other was the rainforest, green, vast, unbroken. In PG the jungle *surrounded* me. It was a felt presence, much more so than the leafy green woods of New Jersey. It was what took over at the edge of downtown Rio Blanco, inexorable as a wall, and it had accustomed the Maya to living in small cleared spaces they constantly had to reclaim. Even the women knew how to handle a machete.

"Its nature is malevolent," Aaron said, probably thinking of his recent encounter with the waterfall.

"Benign," Don retorted.

"Indifferent," I said. Were we really talking about the jungle? Given our respective religious beliefs—Don was a lapsed Catholic, Aaron considered himself an atheist, and I was an agnostic—we were probably talking about the essential nature of God.

Aaron started to argue his point, but then announced that thinking made his head hurt. He was going to bed. Reluctantly I got up to follow him. It was an interesting topic, one I would have liked to pursue. Don stopped me. "You're all right, are you?"

"I'm fine. What's the matter, do I look sick?"

He squinted at me. "No, but you don't look—*settled*. You have to make a home for yourself here. D'you know what I mean? You take your books and tea things and whatnot and put them on a shelf where you're accustomed to seeing them, and there you are."

I blinked.

"As you know, I'm Catholic," Don said, his tone uncharacteristically serious. "And for all my ranting, I *do* attend Mass occasionally. It's a comfort. I can go to any Catholic church in the world—Burma, London, Guatemala City—and celebrate Mass. And because it's always in Latin, no matter where I am, I feel instantly at home. D'you see what I'm getting at?"

I did. He was telling me, don't pretend it's a camping trip, or a vacation, or in any way temporary. Live here.

I said good night to him and walked slowly to our bedroom. Don had chosen to live here. Was it possible for me to do the same? Did I *want* to for an entire year?

The next morning Don drove us as far as San Antonio. Before heading back, Aaron and I stopped at Tommy Salam's store to buy supplies, plus two lemonades for the road. A "lemonade" was Creole slang for anything cold and carbonated that came in a bottle. The bottle rarely had a label. Aaron got a Coke, I got a cream soda. You took what the storekeeper gave you—no guarantees. A little like marriage, I thought.

As soon as Aaron and I crossed the river—it was still more brown than green, but the current had subsided—the Maya greeted us as though we'd been gone for months. By the time we reached our house, two dozen people trailed us, including Mateo and his brother Martín, Dolores and her four kids, and most of my students. Aaron immediately sank into his hammock. I was emotionally wrung out and desperate for a hot cup of coffee. Then I wanted to flop down in Aaron's big hammock with him and take a nap.

More people crowded inside to gawk at his bandages. He'd already removed the one over his nose, claiming it made him cross-eyed. The kids, after assuaging their curiosity, hunkered down with the *sisimito* pictures. The women, some with children on their laps, sat on benches to gossip. One man made himself at home in my hammock. The other men squatted by the back door. If I was going to make coffee for myself, I had to offer it to my visitors, too, but I didn't have enough cups. They were going to have to drink coffee in shifts.

I knelt to make a fire. What I felt like doing was flapping my arms like an angry hen and squawking, "*Elen re li rochoch!*" Get out of my house! Couldn't they understand that I might want to be *alone* with my husband? Probably not. Privacy was a Western invention. I sighed and put a pot of water over the fire.

"How you husband could be?" Lucia stood in front of me holding half a dozen eggs.

"*Su esposo—como está?*" Silvaria withdrew a bunch of plantains from the folds of her grimy skirt. Her year-old baby, another boy, lay big-eyed and silent in her arms, wrapped in what looked like a flour sack.

Maxiana approached me shyly. "My mother send you this." She held out a plate of *lancha—chile*-scented fish wrapped in *mox* leaves.

Could half of Rio Blanco really be in my kitchen? Or did it just seem that way?

xxxxxxxxxxxxxxxxxxxxxxxxxxxxxxxxxxxxxxxxxxxxxxxxxxxxxxxxxxxx

KEKCHI SCRAMBLED EGGS

Sauté a handful of halved cherry tomatoes in a little canola oil or bacon drippings (the bacon drippings will give them more flavor) with a few pinches of dried red *chile* powder until the tomato skins split.

Crack 5 or 6 eggs into a bowl; stir with a fork until well mixed. Pour mixture into the frying pan with the tomatoes. Cook slowly, turning the mixture over with your fork to increase the volume. When the eggs have set to your satisfaction (most Kekchi prefer their scrambled eggs moist), slide the eggs onto a serving dish. Tuck a spoonful or two into a hot corn *tortilla*.

Serves 2 people.

xxxxxxxxxxxxxxxxxxxxxxxxxxxxxxxxxxxxxxxxxxxxxxxxxxxxxxxxxxxx

LANCHA

Lancha is one of the few Kekchi dishes I know of that's not boiled or fried. This recipe comes from Juana Tut of Big Falls, who used fresh snook fillets. First she washed them in lime juice (the fruit) and water, then wrapped them in *mox* leaves after rubbing each fillet with salt and ground red *chile* pepper in nearly equal amounts. For additional flavor, some cooks include a bush green or two.

This is the perfect dish for grilling over indirect heat on an outdoor barbecue. I reduced the amount of salt and *chile* pepper in Juana's recipe and added a few ingredients. When you turn the fish over, add plantains and baby zucchini to the grill, both sliced lengthwise and brushed with olive oil. Add salt and a scattering of fresh herbs to the zucchini—thyme or marjoram are good choices.

> 2 pounds snook, tilapia, catfish, grouper, perch, or red snapper,
>   filleted
> juice of 1 lime
> 1 tablespoon olive oil
> 2 cloves garlic, minced
> salt to taste
> ground cayenne to taste
> 4 *mox* leaves (banana leaves you buy in the market will usually
>   work if they're very fresh and you soak them first—otherwise they'll snap. Or, use heavy aluminum foil)

Wash fillets and pat dry with paper towels. Pour the lime juice into a flat, square-sided casserole dish and add olive oil and garlic. Add the fish, one piece at a time, being sure to soak both sides.

Place one fillet in the center of one *mox* leaf. Salt it. Sprinkle cayenne over it—carefully, until you know your tolerance for heat. Add a second and possibly a third fillet (depending on size) until you have about ½ pound of fish.

Drizzle a fourth of the remaining marinade over the fish.

If using banana leaves, tear off a few strips to use instead of string—string burns. Fold the first leaf around the fish to form a rectangular packet. Wrap tightly with the strips to secure it. Turn the packet over and wrap with the second leaf. Tie that. (If using aluminum foil, you need only one piece. Fold it once, lengthwise, and fold the edges under twice to seal the packet.) Whichever method you use, make sure the fish is securely wrapped in a tight bundle so the juices don't leak out. Repeat the process with the remaining fish. Grill over hot coals 10 minutes. Turn packets and grill another 10 minutes.

Serves 4 people.

TEN

Everybody and
Her Brother

I woke up feeling listless and not up to doing much. Aaron obviously felt much the same way, but he had reason to. My lethargy persisted throughout the week. But in spite of the fact that we could barely manage a conversation, we were never alone. *Somebody* was always in the house with us.

Short of deadbolts and a KEEP OUT sign, I couldn't do anything about our visitors. But would having "my things" to look at make me feel better about being here? The only possessions I had that carried any emotional significance were my typewriter and a heavy glass ashtray the color of grape jelly that a friend had given to me as a high school graduation present. I had packed it before Aaron banned smoking.

On impulse I dug it out of a clothes box and positioned it next to my typewriter. It was gently triangular with smooth, soothing curves. Purple was an uncommon color in the rainforest, and even though I didn't have any cigarettes, I *did* feel better when I looked at it.

But the constant presence of uninvited guests drained me. I decided to keep track of everybody who stopped by over the next few days—who they were, what they wanted, and how long they stayed. Maybe the act of getting it down on paper would help me put things in perspective.

SATURDAY, NOVEMBER 17, 1962

Cold last night. Got up at 5:05 a.m., pissed at the Bohs for making so much noise. Why did they have to build their house five feet away from ours? They've been up for hours, probably because it's too cold to sleep.

5:45   Couldn't go back to sleep so got up and lit a fire. Aaron up too.

6:03   Two men stopped outside the partially opened front door to peer inside, trying to see what time it is. Don't know them. Stayed a few minutes and left. I'm cold!

6:10   Maxiana in to borrow *sisimito* pictures to show her mother and father. Stays to watch me make breakfast.

6:34   Breakfast—pancakes with margarine and syrup, and half a can of Danish bacon. Gave Maxiana some of each. She apparently liked it—she finished everything on her plate. Aaron too. Definitely has his appetite back.

7:18   Isabella Choc, my student Estevan's mother, came in for *ban* for the baby, who had poked a twig into her cheek. I cleaned it with peroxide, rubbed in a little boric acid ointment, and put a Band-Aid over it for looks. Accompanied by a girl about sixteen from Pueblo Viejo who won't leave. She's still here, staring at me.

7:55   Paulina Choc came in for no apparent reason. She and the girl from Pueblo Viejo left together about five minutes later, then Maxiana left. Aaron left to help somebody build a hog shed. Finally! Alone at last!

8:16   But not for long. Cresencio and little Julian Choc, Silvaria's two kids, came in. Cresencio wanted medicine for a sore on his foot. Painted it with iodine. The excitement attracted Ilegorio Ical. They hung around about ten minutes, then left.

8:28   Hilario Ical's mother came in to see what time it is.

By noon I'd had twenty-eight visitors and had stopped taking notes. Counting Maxiana, I'd fed one, doctored three, told seven what time it was, and accepted four gifts of food. I had admired Lute's new kid-sized machete and the kid-sized leather sheath his father—Joaquin the wife beater—had made for him. "A house for my machete," Lute said proudly, in English. I had watched Adelaida Garcia's little brother crap on my floor—Adelaida cleaned it up using corncobs. Everybody else came in to see the *sisimito* pictures. Half of Rio Blanco really *had* been in our house the day we came back.

After lunch Micalia Ical delivered a quart of rice, as promised, and I paid her, as promised. Aaron was making an effort to spread our money around. Whenever he visited somebody, he bought eggs or bananas from them. But if people came to our house with food, it was a gift—unless they wanted their kid excused from school. Then it was a bribe.

When Maxiana came back with the *sisimito* pictures, she gave me some okra, with cooking instructions from her mother: slice them and fry them in lard. Later, when I went to get water, I met Goyita Boh, one of our noisy neighbors. Goyita was Mopan and married to Jesús's brother Francisco—which meant there were four adults and at least as many children crammed into that tiny house. I couldn't really talk to Goyita but I liked her—she was a pretty, effervescent woman who loved ruffles. Today she flashed me a smile and gestured at the bucket she was carrying. Freshwater snails—did I want any? No, thank you, since I had no idea how to prepare them and no desire to find out. I gave Crispino the same answer later that afternoon when he asked if we ate monkey meat.

Silvaria came in with a sweet potato, followed by Cresencio and little Julian—their third visit for the day. In addition to her sickly looking baby, who nursed when he had the energy, she had seven living children, all sons. Three—the baby, Cresencio, and little Julian—still lived at home, along with Silvaria's husband and big Julian, her brother the *chiclero*. Belatedly I realized why their clothes always looked dirty. Doing laundry was a chore most women foisted off on a daughter, but Silveria was the only female in a household of six people. She didn't have *time* to wash clothes.

My heart went out to Cresencio. He was only twelve, but his father was an old man, which meant that Cresencio and big Julian did most of the planting and harvesting. In school Cresencio was so slow I constantly shuffled him back and forth between the oldest group and the intermediate group. No matter what seat I assigned him to, he always ended up sitting next to little Julian.

I felt even sorrier for little Julian. He was seven, a small, sickly kid whose nose was always running. He was the only child in school who came to class dressed only in short pants—no shirt, no matter how cold it was. The straps of his shorts were always sliding down one skinny, naked shoulder. When I tried to explain something, he looked up at me so earnestly and tried so hard to understand that none of the other kids ever laughed at him. While most of them had at least one blue copybook, little Julian made do with a slate and a piece of chalk. But whenever he printed a lopsided A, or added two plus two and got four, Cresencio held up his brother's slate, calling, "Teacher, Teacher! Look!" while little Julian squirmed with pleasure and picked his nose.

Late that afternoon Lucia brought over some chicken *caldo* cooked with *samat* instead of *cilantro*.

"Lucia," I blurted out, "why do you wear a safety pin on your necklace?" The women all bought rosary beads from Father Cull and restrung them, minus the crucifix, into necklaces. I was certain the safety pin had some profound religious significance. I just wasn't sure which religion.

Lucia looked down at hers. "You know what is prickle grass?"

"Of course!" Everybody who went barefoot—in other words, everybody in the village except Aaron—knew that prickle grass was a small, mean, low-growing weed covered with thorns.

"Is to dig prickles from out you foot."

Oh.

By dinnertime twenty more people had come and gone, a rough total of forty visitors on a day that was in no way unusual—Aaron hadn't hurt himself, no strangers had come through town, it wasn't a feast day, and Father Cull hadn't arrived.

Evaristo stopped by to visit just as I was washing dishes. He'd been coming earlier and earlier—which probably meant he was going to bed earlier and earlier. He was turning into a bush Indian.

He told us that Aleja was due to have their baby soon, and he was sure it would be a boy. (Translation: he *hoped* it would be a boy.) But tonight he had religion on his mind, not fatherhood. "What do the Nazarenes believe?" he asked Aaron.

Aaron, looking surprised, said he didn't know. Why was Evaristo interested?

Evaristo said that one of the Tux brothers had been visiting in San Pedro Columbia, and a neighbor showed him a plastic record player that the Nazarenes had given him, accompanied by a 45 RPM record. By cranking a handle, the man could hear the Lord's Prayer in Kekchi. "What do you know about them?" Evaristo demanded.

Aaron shook his head. "Nothing. I know there are missionaries around, but I hadn't heard about the record player. Pretty slick idea."

"Maybe I go to San Pedro Columbia and see for myself what the Nazarenes could be doing," Evaristo said. "You come too?"

"I don't think so," Aaron said.

Evaristo wanted to know why. When Aaron told him he just wasn't interested, Evaristo wanted to know which god Aaron believed in, the god of the Catholics or some other god. I was glad that Aaron took him seriously enough to tell him the truth.

"José, he pray to Tzultak'a before he make plantation," Evaristo said abruptly. Aaron glanced at his field notes, which lay just out of reach on the other end of the table. "He ask Tzultak'a to forgive him for scarring the face of the land. When he goes hunting, he ask Tzultak'a to protect him from the bad things in the bush."

"Bad things like what?"

"Snake. Jaguar."

"Is he a bush doctor? A *curandero*? " Even I knew that Aaron was taking a big chance here, but this time Evaristo seemed eager to talk.

"Yes. Aleja told me that long time ago he cure an old lady with the shakes. But he don't do that no more. Only for his family."

"Does he ever talk about any of the other old gods? The Chac?"

"Last night he tell me about two boys that are brothers, but born the same time. I don't know the English."

"Twins?" Aaron couldn't keep the excitement out of his voice.

"Twins, just so. The mother of *their* mother, she take one next man into her bed and the twins kill him."

Aaron leaped out of his chair. "That's in Thompson's book!" He pushed aside my ashtray—which he hadn't noticed yet—to get at Thompson's *Ethnology of the Mayas of Southern and Central British Honduras.* Impatiently he flipped through pages until he came to the myth of the hero twins. (Other of their exploits appear in the *Popol Vuh*, the so-called Maya Bible.) When he found it, he read it aloud to Evaristo and asked if it was the same story José had told him.

Evaristo got excited too. Yes. It was the same story.

I got goose bumps. After Evaristo left, Aaron and I talked about the implications of José's second, secret identity as a *curandero*, brushed our teeth, and went to bed.

I was just dozing off when Lucia called softly at the back door. Crispino had a stomachache bad-bad, she said. Did we have *ban*? Aaron gave her a codeine tablet and commented to me that Crispino must be in a lot of pain for her to come over so late.

November 19 was Garifuna Settlement Day, a school holiday. Arcenio came to the door just as Aaron and I were enjoying our second cup of coffee. "My father is going hunting and wants me to ask if Teacher's husband like it—likes—wants—to go with him."

"Yes, I *would* like to go hunting. When does your father want to leave?"

"*Pues*, I don't know. Now?"

"Let's go." Aaron jumped up, grabbed his gun, and took off without a kiss or a backward glance, Arcenio close behind him.

The two were still within shouting distance when Lucia came over, wondering why he had left in such a hurry. I told her, then asked how Crispino was.

"He feel good. Last night I dig out the dirt under he hammock, make I put coals from the fire there. Keep he warm." She patted her stomach. "No more pain."

"I'm glad to hear that," I said. Damn! Lucia had dug up her *Good Housekeeping* floor to keep Crispino warm? She must really love the guy! This was a subject Aaron and I returned to often, whether couples married for love, as Americans defined the word, or if they married for other reasons, such as wealth and social position. The evidence so far favored love—or at least lust. Wealth was a dim concept to subsistence farmers, and a couple's social position seemed to depend on how successfully the man provided for his family and how hard the woman worked to keep her house and children clean and well fed. The Maya could *create* their own social position, but since so much depended on personal effort, it was hard to marry into it.

José Ical's kids came in, ready for school. When I explained that today was a holiday, they actually looked disappointed. All three sat down on the bench and leafed through magazines.

Five minutes later Nicasio and Crisantos Tux arrived. Ambrosia Ical told them, in English, that there was no school today. To my surprise the two boys also sat down and started reading.

But when I decided to type a letter to my parents, they all leaped to their feet to stand behind me and watch. They were so close to me I could feel their *tortilla*-scented breath on the back of my neck. Determined to ignore them, I was typing up our the-real-nature-of-the-rainforest conversation with Don when Isabella Choc and her daughter came in for more *ban*. Isabella's daughter was the one who had stabbed herself in the cheek with a stick.

I tried to explain to Isabella that the little girl didn't *need* more medicine, that the scratch was healing nicely all by itself. But Isabella didn't move. She looked at my fireplace, the kids ranged around my typewriter, our clothes, the pots and pans hanging from my corner post as though she had never seen them before. My corner post had leafed out, and I had to admit I enjoyed cooking in a kitchen that resembled a tree house.

"Does she understand what I'm telling her?" I asked the kids in exasperation.

They assured me that she had.

Grumbling, I went back to my letter and tried to pretend Isabella wasn't there. When Cresencio and little Julian arrived, the boys all left to play together in the schoolyard, and the girls went home. Only Isabella and her daughter stayed behind.

"I'm going for water," I announced abruptly, picking my bucket up and holding the door open until Isabella reluctantly stepped outside. I never got water in the morning. But I couldn't get any work done with Isabella gawking at me.

Midafternoon Aaron came back, jubilant. He and Sebastian had shot a gibnut and a brocket deer. "Would you help me with something?" he asked.

"I don't trust you when you act innocent. Help you with what?"

"I'm going to pull my shirt off. I have some hitchhikers I'd like to get rid of. I'd do it, but I can't see them."

I eyed him speculatively. "How many legs do they have?"

"They're not spiders. But they do have mouthparts."

"If you can't see them, how do you know?"

Aaron hiked up one pant leg and beckoned me over. Three brown sluglike things clung to the calf of his leg.

"Yuk! What *are* they?"

"If I tell you will you help me get them off?"

"Maybe."

"I thought you'd say that. Here—I brought you something." Aaron reached into his shirt pocket and pulled out a *puro* the size and shape of a cigarillo. "Compliments of Sebastian. He made it. Go ahead—light it."

My last smoke had been one of Don's Colonials, and that was days ago. I ran for the matches, licked the end of the cigar to moisten it as I'd seen my grandfather do, lit the other end, and inhaled deeply. The *puro* was so strong I doubled over coughing.

"To answer your question," Aaron said, pulling his shirt off and trying to pretend he didn't enjoy watching my choking fit, "they're leeches. And since they have teeth, you don't want to just pull them off. You don't want to burn me, either. Just the leeches."

"That was . . . a con," I gasped, wiping my eyes.

"Yup," he agreed cheerfully.

When I could see again, I examined one of the leeches on his back. "So I jab them with the lit end of the *puro* and they squirm and unclench their teeth and then I pull them off?"

"That's the idea."

I took another drag, coughed, and went to work. By the time the cigar had burned down to a stub, I had pulled over twenty leeches off Aaron's bloody back and tossed them into the fireplace.

Later that afternoon Arcenio came by with deer ribs and part of a thigh. Dinner was going to be venison stew with okra.

At the last minute I decided to try making flour *tortillas*. I'd watched Lucia make them, and they were a lot less work than making corn *tortillas*. How hard could it be to cook something that had only four ingredients? Not very, as it turned out. Even though the finished product was a little thick, the *tortillas* tasted okay—they had cooked all the way through and didn't taste like raw dough, which I'd been worried about. Better than okay. They tasted *good*.

Maybe I was finally getting the hang of cooking over an open fire?

XXXXXXXXXXXXXXXXXXXXXXXXXXXXXXXXXXXXXXXXXXXXXXXXXXXXXXXXXX

FLOUR *TORTILLAS*
I never wrote down Lucia's recipe. This one, which tastes very similar, is adapted from *Elena's Secrets of Mexican Cooking*, by Elena Zelayeta (Doubleday, 1968). Special thanks to Francisca Bardalez of Big Falls and Anita Hunter-Ackerman of the Belize Forums for walking me through the process.

  2 cups flour
  ¼ cup (4 tablespoons) lard or shortening (I prefer lard)

½ cup warm water
½ teaspoon salt

Measure flour into a mixing bowl. Add lard, cutting with 2 table knives until mixture is crumbly. Add salt to the warm water and stir. When it's dissolved, add water to the mixture a little at a time. Turn dough out on a lightly floured board and knead only until the lard is incorporated. Dough should be soft but not sticky. Do not overhandle. Divide dough into 6 pieces and roll each one between your hands until it's egg-shaped. Return "eggs" to the bowl, cover with a warm towel, and let the dough rest 20 minutes. (Some people let it rest as long as an hour.)

Sprinkle additional flour on the board. Using the palms of your hands—I fare better with a rolling pin covered with a floured sleeve—flatten each piece into a membrane-thin circle approximately 9 inches in diameter by rolling the dough up from the middle, then down from the middle, then giving the dough a quarter turn and repeating the process.

Meanwhile, heat a heavy, well-seasoned, cast-iron frying pan on low to medium-low. Don't let the pan get too hot, or you'll scorch the *tortillas*. You may need a heat diffuser, a low-budget, low-tech gadget available at any cookware store.

Cook the *tortillas* one at a time, flipping (I use a pancake turner) as soon as the top of the *tortilla* bubbles. The bottom should be light brown in spots. If not, leave your next *tortilla* in the frying pan a little longer before flipping. Keep the cooked *tortillas* warm by stacking them on top of one another wrapped in a towel.

Serves 2 hungry people.

XXXXXXXXXXXXXXXXXXXXXXXXXXXXXXXXXXXXXXXXXXXXXXXXXXXXXXXXX

CHICKEN VEGETABLE *CALDO* WITH *SAMAT*
This recipe comes from Santa Sanchez of Big Falls, who is Petrona Xi's niece. Santa prefers to cook her vegetables separately. One reason

Lucia's *caldos* tasted so good was because she had to feed only three people and used the same amount of meat but less water.

> 1 4-pound free-range chicken, cut into serving pieces
> juice of 1 lime
> 10 cups of boiling water
> 1 tablespoon salt
> 5 large cloves garlic, minced or pressed
> 3 tablespoons chopped fresh thyme (locally called French thyme)
> 30 *samat* leaves or parsley to taste
> ¼ cup chopped *cilantro*, packed
> 1 dozen small green onions, diced
> 3 small green (fresh) *chile* peppers, stemmed and diced, or 4–5 dried *chiles arbol*, torn into small pieces (see the caution in the rice and beans recipe, chap. 4.)

Wash the chicken pieces in lime juice. Add to the boiling water with the salt, garlic, and herbs. Simmer uncovered until meat is tender, about 1 hour.

> 1 *chayote* squash cut into chunks (peeling is optional)
> 1 potato, peeled and cut into chunks
> 2 cassava, peeled and cut into chunks
> ½ teaspoon annatto powder dissolved into a little water (optional—it adds color but very little flavor, and is a fat magnet, which makes cleaning the pot a chore)

Wash the squash, potato, and cassava with lime water, cut into pieces, and cook separately in a medium pot with boiling water. Cook until soft but not mushy, 20 or 30 minutes, depending on how big your chunks are. Adjust seasonings. Serve with the *caldo* or on the side with hot corn *tortillas*.

Serves 7–9 people.

Variation: For additional flavor, add 3–5 *tomatillos*, husked, washed, and diced; 4–5 diced fresh tomatoes, skin and seeds removed; and 1 medium carrot, peeled and cut into thin slices. For an interesting contrast of flavors and textures, add the carrots at the very end and cook only a few minutes, so they're still slightly crunchy.

16. Dinner for two families: two gibnuts and an iguana. The dried corn (upper right) is ready to be shucked, soaked, and ground into *tortillas*.

Courtesy Terry Rambo.

17. Rainy season. I shot this downpour while standing under the thatch overhang of our roof.

Photo by Joan Fry.

18. Valeria Choc (Dolores Choc's youngest daughter), Silvario Boh (with the iguana), and Esteban Choc (one of Silvaria's grandsons).

Courtesy Terry Rambo.

19. In the Monkey Dance the devil is the father of monkeys. Photo taken in San José. Courtesy Terry Rambo.

20. During the dance, villagers dress up in costumes and masks to impersonate the two monkey groups. Courtesy Terry Rambo.

21. The man playing the *marimba* explains the dance to me. With the exception of the Deer Dance, which seems to be indigenous, the masked, ceremonial dances were most likely introduced to the Maya by Spanish priests during the 1700s. Courtesy Terry Rambo.

22. Our nearest neighbor, Goyita Boh, gave birth one night and we never heard a thing. Here she shows off her baby and her daughter, Eva. Courtesy Terry Rambo.

23. Joaquin Choc and his future son-in-law, John Oh, construct a pole platform so they can cut down this tree in order to "make *milpa*" (plant corn). Courtesy Terry Rambo.

24. The dry bush goes up in flames. When the ash cools, the men will plant, a practice known as slash-and-burn agriculture. Courtesy Terry Rambo.

25. Before planting his *milpa*, José Tux, holding
an ear of corn, prays to Tzultak'a. Courtesy Terry
Rambo.

26. José Tux and the male members of his family
plant corn. Courtesy Terry Rambo.

27. José Tux shows off his grandson Fidel after
the baby's *hetz mek* ceremony. Fidel is now old
enough to be held astride an adult's hip. Courtesy
Terry Rambo.

28. Evaristo's kin help him thatch the roof of his
new house. Courtesy Terry Rambo.

29. The procession leads the *santos* to the church.
Laura, the *curandera,* is followed by Lucia and
Crispino Bah. Both women swing *censarios*,
which contain burning incense. Courtesy Terry
Rambo.

30. Musicians welcome the saints to Rio Blanco.
The instruments are all handmade. Courtesy Terry
Rambo.

31. My students and I welcome the *santos* with songs. Here we're taking a food break. Courtesy Terry Rambo.

32. Sebastian Garcia contemplates the recently bulldozed road between Santa Cruz and Rio Blanco. It's rainy season again. Courtesy Terry Rambo.

33. Maxiana Choc and Natalia Bah, photographed
about four years after we left. Courtesy Don Owen-Lewis.

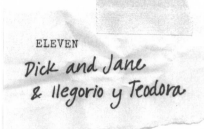

ELEVEN

Dick and Jane
& Ilegorio y Teodora

The inevitable happened—I fell in love with my students. But not until I beat Arcenio Garcia.

In school the kids were lively and responsive and full of laughter—and occasionally (although not for long, and never to me) sullen, angry, and irritable. Most were eager to live up to my expectations and helped other students do the same, a trait that Aaron said mimicked their society at large: they depended on one another to survive.

The first time I noticed it, I was giving them a spelling test. Nicasio Tux, younger but smarter than Cresencio, his seatmate, whispered urgently to him in Kekchi. When Cresencio continued to look mystified, Nicasio grabbed the pencil out of his hand and made the correction himself. He did it so openly that it was clear he didn't consider it cheating. He was just helping Cresencio.

The difference between school and real life was that in school individual effort was never greeted with derision. If somebody volunteered to go to the board and made a mistake, nobody laughed unless the mistake was just silly, like writing a backward "3." In that case everybody laughed, even the kid who'd written the backward "3." When I called on somebody for an answer, if he knew it, he gave it. If he didn't, he said so—and all the kids who *did* know the answer frantically waved their hands in the air, calling "Teacher! Teacher!" If somebody raised her hand who usually didn't participate, her classmates—including those with their hands raised—would call my attention to that fact. "Epijenia, Teacher! Look—Epijenia!"

In addition to pasting a gold star after their name for every "correct" paper (I kept a poster nailed to the wall with everybody's name on it), I praised the kids extravagantly whenever I handed back quizzes. "Good, Esteban!" I exclaimed with the fervor of an evangelical preacher. "*Very* good, Julian!" They grinned and waved their paper at their friends, so pleased with themselves they puffed their chests out and preened like roosters.

Praise was a scarce and precious commodity among a people whose chief social control was ridicule.

Silvaria told me the same thing Sebastian Garcia had, that if her sons were bad I "must lash them." (Her sons were too malnourished to misbehave.) Lucia said I should beat *all* the children who misbehaved because unless they were afraid they wouldn't learn. I didn't believe her. I think she would have sliced off all ten of her fingers, one at a time, rather than hurt Natalia.

Arcenio wasn't afraid of anybody, least of all me. He would glance at me slyly, to see if I was watching him. If he didn't think I was, he would whisper to his seatmate, and they would both break out into smothered giggles. I tried moving him. The same thing happened.

One day, after reprimanding him for the fourth time, I told him I wanted to see him after class. Everybody knew what that meant and a low, musical hum erupted, as though a swarm of bees had taken up residence in my classroom.

As a child I had avoided squabbles with other kids. The single exception, when I was thirteen, was when I attacked a strange girl for mistreating my next-door neighbor's horse. Even though she was older and bigger than I was, I went after her in such a white-hot fury that she was crying by the time she ran off, and I had her blood under my fingernails.

But as I approached Arcenio, holding a length of rope, I felt very calm and purposeful. His father had specifically *asked* me to discipline him. Arcenio had brought the punishment on himself. So I whipped him across the buttocks with only a small pang of conscience: nice girls from New Jersey didn't do things like this. At the time I didn't wonder, although I do now, how wife beaters or child beaters rationalize what they're doing. Probably the same way I did—by telling myself I had permission, and Arcenio had it coming.

Arcenio, perversely, refused to cry. By the time I let him go, I was forced to admit I wasn't beating him to teach him anything. I was beating him because I was mad.

My conscience really let me have it when I found he'd been lashed a second time, by his father, after he got home.

Then little Aprimo Tux, who always wore a crisp white shirt and new brown shorts to school, got in trouble for the same reason—being bored and talking. Aprimo had big, trusting brown eyes, and when I told him I was going to punish him, his eyes filled with tears. I told myself that I couldn't differentiate. If I'd lashed Arcenio for being disruptive, I had to lash everybody who was disruptive. But I couldn't convince myself. My heart shriveled up with guilt and self-loathing. Nice girls from New Jersey *didn't* beat children.

I hit Aprimo only once, feebly. I couldn't stop thinking about how much care his mother took preparing him for school every morning, and how he was always one of the first to arrive, his homework done, his clothes spotless, his face full of eager, open trust.

What kind of monster was I to hurt a defenseless little boy? It didn't matter whether I disciplined the children on principle, by parental request, or out of anger. I vowed never to do it again. The Maya could beat their own kids. But I refused to.

Evaristo arrived just after sunup one morning, his face pale and his eyes puffy with exhaustion. Aaron and I knew better than to ask him what was wrong—bad manners. He'd get around to it in his own time. So I served him coffee and he and Aaron discussed the weather, and we waited.

"Aleja had a baby," Evaristo blurted out. "A boy."

"Congratulations!" I said warmly.

Aaron grinned and stood up, reaching over the table to shake hands with him.

"What's his name?" I asked.

"He doesn't got one yet. I'm afraid Aleja is going to die."

"*What?*" Aaron and I gasped.

Evaristo smoothed his hair back from his face. It had taken this baby two days to be born. Aleja had been in so much pain that he was afraid to fall asleep in case she died giving birth. To his relief the baby had been born alive and healthy, but Aleja was still in agony. The afterbirth hadn't come out.

"I told José I want to take Aleja and the baby to the hospital in PG, but he say no, the road is too bad. He told me he was going to say prayers in Kekchi and give her bush medicine to drink. Me, I want to go to San Pedro Columbia because one lady lives there. She helps other ladies have babies."

"Like a midwife?" Aaron asked.

"Yes, just so. But José, he hang one strap from the ceiling in a loop and say to Aleja to lean back with her head against the strap while he push on her stomach." Evaristo was sweating. "When the afterbirth come out, José took it away to the bush to bury it."

"When did this happen?" Aaron asked.

"Yesterday."

"And Aleja?" I interrupted. "Is she all right?"

"I don't know, Missus." Evaristo looked directly at Aaron. "José said all the afterbirth came out. But Aleja still hurts bad-bad, and I'm afraid for her. You been to the doctor in PG. What you think I should do? Take Aleja to the lady in San Pedro Columbia, or to the doctor?"

I was very glad he was asking Aaron this question and not me. Western medicine versus traditional bush medicine was not a debate I wanted to take sides on. I was having enough trouble being a good teacher. I still despised myself for beating Arcenio. I didn't want anybody's death on my conscience.

"*Pues*, the doctor's expensive." Aaron evidently didn't want to take sides, either.

Evaristo gave a loud, dismissive snort. "Money don't mean nothing. I don't want Aleja to die."

"Then I guess the question is, if *you* got sick—if something happened and *you* were in pain and afraid of dying—what would *you* do?"

The Maya were terrified of hospitals. They would see a doctor reluctantly and only as a last resort, but if he sent them to the hospital—where the doctor would probably send Aleja—they would wait until nightfall and sneak home. As a preventative measure, the nurses in PG took the Maya's clothes away after admitting them. But some left anyway, without their clothes.

Evaristo stood up. "Thank you, Mr. World. I will think about what you say." He shook Aaron's hand again and nodded at me. "Good-bye, Missus. I'm going now."

The next day Father Cull rode in alone on a mule, a lumpy cardboard box strapped behind him on the mule's rump. I excused the children for an early lunch. He usually brought some little treat for them, and today he had an old-fashioned wooden top. As the kids gathered around him, he carefully wound the string around the top and then yanked on the string. The children watched raptly, sucking their breath between their teeth as the top spun around and around, a vivid red blur amid a cloud of dust.

Dolores dashed inside my house, shoved a plate of *tortillas* at me, and joined the neighbors huddled around my front door, watching as Father Cull showed the children how to rewind the string and spin the top again. They would have had a better view if they'd gone to Mateo's house.

After making sure the kids knew what they were doing, Father Cull carried the box over, and, on top of it, our mail.

"Schoolbooks," he told me. "Donated by a ladies' auxiliary in St. Louis. They're ten cents each. Make sure the family pays before you give them a book."

Schoolbooks! I finally had *school*books! "But why do they have to pay for them? Didn't you say the books were donated?"

"Yes, but we have to be careful about giving the Indians handouts. If they pay for the books they'll take better care of them."

I wasn't sure about that—it seemed to me that some people took care of their belongings no matter how much they cost, while others didn't. But since I was no expert on handouts—and since Father Cull was my employer—I accepted his explanation and invited him to stay for lunch. He thanked me but said he had to return to San Antonio.

I cut through the packing tape around the box, ripped the top flap back, grabbed a book, and read the title. *Dick and Jane*? I dug deeper. All the books were *Dick and Jane*. Whose attic had these come out of?

They weren't the schoolbooks I had hoped for, but they were better than nothing. I passed them out so the children could look at them and explained that their parents would have to pay for them—they couldn't take the books home with them. The kids were so excited they were all talking Mayan. I was tempted to just pay for the books myself. But Father Cull had made a decision, and I felt duty-bound to honor it.

Except for one small, square box, the mail was the usual assortment of letters and magazines from home. The box was addressed to me; Father Cull had signed a customs form so the postmaster would release it to him. Half of the return address label was missing—the bottom half said it had been mailed from Ann Arbor, Michigan. Curious, I opened the box.

Father Cull had unwittingly brought me a three-month supply of birth control pills from Planned Parenthood.

Teaching *Dick and Jane* made me want to scream and throw things. The vocabulary was bad enough—the entire book seemed geared for infants. My kids, even the youngest, recognized and could pronounce all the words in the stories. What they had trouble with was content. Dick and Jane had a mother who wore makeup and high heels, her hair in plump, artificial curls. Their father wore a three-piece suit and a tie and carried a briefcase when he "went to work."

But "work" was never defined, and apparently no flowers or vegetables grew in Dick and Jane's world. Almost everything they did happened indoors, except for a story about the time the family went to the zoo and saw a rhinoceros. My kids didn't know what a rhino was—or a zoo, for that matter.

In another story Dick and Jane and Baby Sally helped their mother—still in makeup and high heels but wearing an apron over her dress—bake cookies. What did a "cookie" mean to kids whose only experience with sweets was sucking on a piece of sugarcane? I couldn't improvise a rhinoceros, but I thought I could improvise cookies—resolutely ignoring the fact that the last time I had tried to improvise, I had baked Creole bread and created stones. But in the meantime, I *had* successfully made flour *tortillas*. Cookies, I reasoned, had the same ingredients. All they needed was sugar.

One afternoon while Aaron was out interviewing—his Kekchi had finally gotten fluent enough to do that—I assembled the necessary ingredients. This time I wouldn't try to bake them. If I didn't make them too thick and I *fried* them, they should cook all the way through, right? The way the flour *tortillas* had?

I made a last-minute run to Lucia's to borrow an empty rum bottle—I needed a rolling pin. Natalia followed me back to see what I was up to. Along the way we picked up Maxiana and her brother Luis.

I already had the fire burning, and they watched silently as I rolled the dough out on the table—dough to which I'd added sugar and a smidge of extra lard—and used a narrow tin cup as a cookie cutter. I piled the cutouts on a plate and rolled out more dough. When I had used all the dough, I carried the cookies to the fire. My onlookers moved, too, crowding behind me so they could peer under my arm or over my shoulder.

After holding my hand flat over the *comal* to judge the heat, I added the first batch of cookies, tilting up their edges from time to time with my corncob spatula to inspect them. When the bottoms started to brown, I flipped them. The kids oohed and ahhed—they were accustomed to seeing their mothers flip *tortillas* using their fingers. That's why their mothers left no fingerprints. I wondered why criminals in the States had never figured this out and tried to imagine Al Capone flipping *tortillas*.

When the cookies looked the proper shade of brown, I scooped them up on a plate and cooked the second batch. Natalia tilted her chin in the direction of the cookies. "Are those for to eat, Teacher?"

"When they're cool enough."

"What are this?" Luis wanted to know.

"*These* are cookies."

Just before the second batch turned a sugary brown, I handed each child a cooled cookie from the first batch and took one myself. Natalia licked hers before nibbling off a corner. Like her mother, she was a picky eater. Then her eyes widened and she shoved the whole thing in her mouth. Maxiana and Luis already had their hands out for seconds.

I ate half of one. As a cookie it wasn't anything special—no flavoring, no chopped nuts or chocolate bits, no confectioner's sugar. But for a home-fried cookie, it was pretty damn good.

I didn't believe in the *sisimito*, or the "little people" the Maya called *chol gwink*. But the story that kept me awake at night was about the woman they called *ixtabai*. Evaristo had told us about her. A lone male traveler is returning through the bush to his village when he sees a beautiful woman ahead of him on the trail. She beckons to him and he follows her, even when she leaves the trail and heads into the bush. Looking seductively over her shoulder at him from time to time, she allows him to get closer—but never close enough to touch her—until finally, when he's hopelessly lost, she turns to him. As he hungrily wraps his arms around her, he discovers that her back is rough as tree bark, and hollow. The beautiful woman has vanished. He's embracing a tree.

To me it sounded like a cautionary tale about not traveling alone in the bush—something the Maya didn't like to do even in daylight. But then again, they didn't like to do much of anything alone. When Aaron told me that the ancient Maya in the Yucatan had honored a deity named Ix Tab, the goddess of suicide, I felt the hair on my arms stand up. Suicide didn't have to be intentional, like hanging yourself. It could be a single act of stupidity—like deciding to follow a mysterious woman.

I thought of Ix Tab when Maxiana and I went to get water one afternoon. It had rained so hard the Rio Blanco was in flood again, and Maxiana took me to a different spot because we couldn't get "good" water at the usual place. By that she meant the water wouldn't be fit to drink until the mud had settled.

She led me to a tiny spit of land where we could fill our buckets directly from the deep part of the river, not the muddy shallows. The current ran fast as a riptide, but I didn't even consider that when I swung my bucket into the water.

The force of the current jerked me off my feet. I stumbled, trying desperately to keep my balance, adrenalin spiking through my body like a lightning bolt. I wasn't a strong swimmer, and if I were pulled into the river I would drown. At the last possible second, I grabbed the handle of the bucket with both hands and yanked it out of the water. Maxiana and I exchanged the briefest of glances. I had met Ix Tab face to face, and she had let me go.

I suddenly grasped what Aaron had been trying to tell me about not treating the Maya the way I would my neighbors in Verona. What had just happened was, to me, a terrifying, once-in-a-lifetime experience. To Maxiana it was commonplace. So was the bite of a malaria-infected mosquito. So was a swarm of army ants overrunning her house and consuming every living thing in it. So was a tommygoff, the one-cigarette-and-you're-dead pit viper Don had told me about. (The Kekchi called it *us li xul*, the good animal, because to call it by name was to summon it.) The slightest misstep, the most insignificant miscalculation, could end in death. Life in the bush was dangerous—a single thread with the potential to break in less time than it took to blink.

Did Maxiana think me lucky to have attracted Ix Tab's attention only to wriggle out of her grasp? I had caught the goddess's eye once—did that mean I might again?

Maxiana filled her bucket without speaking, and we walked back to the village. She never said.

One Saturday morning Aaron and I and about a dozen other people walked to San José to see the Monkey Dance. According to Evaristo, who had finally allowed his father-in-law to treat Aleja, she was out of danger and slowly getting better. But he didn't want to leave her so he could attend the dance, and his sisters—except for Lucia—also stayed home.

The trail to San José was still wet in spots. Leonardo Ical shoved his friend Miguel Choc—one of Lucia's brothers—into a puddle, and Miguel inadvertently splashed mud on Lucia's skirt. She hissed angrily at him, a sharp *hssstt* that people used to warn off dogs and misbehaving children, and stopped, dabbing at the mud with the white towel draped over her head—the tropical version of a *rebozo*, or shawl.

I was surprised at how upset she seemed. I hadn't dressed up for the occasion, reasoning that we lived in houses with dirt floors—everything was dirty, including our feet. What was the big deal about getting a few drops of mud on your clothes?

But Lucia was as thoroughly put out as any American woman would have been if she'd splashed mud on her party dress. When she made us stop at the river so she could wet her towel and finish cleaning her skirt, I realized she *had* dressed up. Her magenta skirt looked brand new, and her towel and blouse were so white they made me squint. She looked like a Tide commercial. She even wore her hair in a new style—she had braided a ribbon into it and wound it into a bun that resembled a flower.

I marveled at my stupidity. I'd lived among the Maya for half a year now and had just realized that "clean" was not an absolute.

By the time we got to the village, the Monkey Dance was well under way. If a family wanted the dancers to perform for them, they fed everybody, spectators as well as dancers. At the first house women served us coffee and sweet *tortillas* made with corn, lard, and sugar. They were crisp and delicious, like shortbread.

The man playing the *marimba* recognized Aaron. "Come and sit down," he said to me, elbowing the man who sat next to him on a stool. "I going explain the dance to you."

I would have preferred to watch from the sidelines, but I sat next to him and tugged my skirt down. The dancers all came over so they could hear his explanation, too.

"That man there, in red, with the tail—he could be the devil. The father to all the monkeys." The devil's mask was ferocious, borrowing as much from the ancient Mayan glyphs as from Christianity—tongue lolling, snakes writhing around his head, fangs like boars' teeth. "These here, with red faces, they could be *batz*," he continued. *Batz* were howler monkeys. "And them there could be *max*. In English you say it spider monkeys." There were six of each—twelve dancers in all. When the dance resumed, the devil chased the monkeys from house to house, switching his long tail. The monkeys fled from him, the *max* attacking the *batz*—who retaliated in kind—behind his back. A crowd of over a hundred people watched them perform, the kids goggle-eyed with awe.

After the dance wound down, the villagers planned to hold a second, social dance, that everybody was welcome to participate in. Several people, including the *marimba* player, asked us if we planned to stay.

"*Pues*, we have to go back to Rio Blanco tonight," Aaron said. He had told me earlier that he wanted to leave before the drinking got serious. But a lot of people were already drunk. To the ancient Maya—and to the ancient Romans as well—music and drinking and dancing had been inseparable.

They still were. The present-day Maya lived and worked in very close proximity with each other. If a man couldn't get along with his neighbors, he complained to the *alcalde*. If the *alcalde* didn't rule in his favor, or the situation got worse, he and his family usually moved—sometimes to a completely different village. (But first the villagers had to agree to let them in.) The only other acceptable way to work out grievances was a *fiesta*, because what was a *fiesta* without rum? Nothing—which is why none of the villages celebrated without it.

By law, whenever the Maya bought rum in quantity, they were required to tell the police, so the police could protect them from one another. Two uniformed Garifuna policemen lounged against their truck, just close enough to the dancing to remind people that they were there.

Aaron and I were the only people who returned to Rio Blanco that night. The others didn't show up until the following morning. The first person I saw was Lucia, who looked hungover and disgusted. Behind her was Crispino, who looked even worse—one black eye, limping, and barefoot. He'd been wearing rubber boots when we walked to San José.

Later that afternoon Mateo staggered home, muddy and so drunk he could hardly walk. Micalia and the kids had arrived hours earlier, and as soon as she saw him coming, she barricaded the door. Immediately a crowd of women dashed into my house for front-row seats. Would Mateo chop the door down with an ax? (It had happened.) Would he set fire to his house and burn it down to get even with Micalia for shutting him out? (That had happened, too.) Once inside, would he beat Micalia? (Unlikely. She was a strong, independent-minded woman who could have floored him with a single punch.)

Mateo pounded his fists on his front door, cursing in Spanish. "*Soy hombre! Soy macho! No tengo patron!*" I'm a man, one hell of a stud, and my own boss! *Nobody* tells me what to do!

Micalia, unimpressed, refused to let him in. Mateo lurched from house to house demanding to borrow a machete—presumably to cut his way in. Finally he collapsed against a tree and began to snore. After half an hour of inactivity, the onlookers left our house, muttering in disappointment. Last year at a *fiesta* a man tried to beat his wife up. She stabbed him in the eye with a knife. They were still living together.

After letting Mateo sleep it off for a couple of hours, Micalia helped him inside the house.

"Stupid, stupid, stupid," Aaron murmured.

"You mean her, for letting him back in?"

"No, I mean *him*! That's why I didn't want to stay for the dancing. Mateo might have had a justifiable grievance against somebody, but by the time he got home he was ready to take it out on Micalia. The Kekchi are completely unpredictable when they're drunk. Anybody can be a target."

What Aaron meant was, *we* could be a target. Until he mentioned it, that thought had never crossed my mind.

xxxxxxxxxxxxxxxxxxxxxxxxxxxxxxxxxxxxxxxxxxxxxxxxxxxxxxxxxx

COMAL COOKIES

I was back in the States making piecrust, following the directions in my *Betty Crocker Cookbook*, when I realized that my *comal* cookies were basically just that—piecrust. My mother used to bake small "twists" of leftover dough by adding vanilla to the mixture and dusting each twist with sugar and cinnamon.

⅓ cup lard

¼ cup raw sugar (also called *turbinado* sugar. It gives the cookies a crisp, appealing texture)

1 cup flour

2 tablespoons cold water

Cream lard and sugar in a big mixing bowl. Add flour all at once and add the water very gradually—you may or may not need more than 2 tablespoons. Knead in the bowl until the entire mass adheres. Turn out on a floured surface and roll into a thin sheet of dough using a rolling pin with a cotton sleeve. Cut the dough into small shapes or use a cookie cutter. Fry in a cast-iron skillet over low heat for 5 minutes or until they're golden brown on the bottom. Flip the cookies and cook until done. The thinner they are, the faster they'll cook. You may need a heat diffuser to keep them from burning.

Makes approximately 2 dozen cookies.

Early one December morning I woke up having to pee. Ordinarily this was no big deal. Turn flashlight on. Shine flashlight on floor so you don't step on a scorpion. Use flashlight to find shoes and a sweater. Pick up a roll of toilet paper. Go bush.

I was squatting in the scrub by our house, holding a tree for support, when I saw lights flickering between the plank walls of the schoolhouse. My heart lurched. When my class occupied the building, it was a school. But when Father Cull took it over with his altar cloth and crucifix, it became a church. Even though Father Cull was in San Antonio, nobody would burn candles in school unless they were praying—or casting a spell.

I dashed back to the house. "Aaron!" I panted in his ear. "Somebody's in the schoolhouse, burning candles."

Instantly his eyes opened. "*Obeah?*"

"I don't know—I was afraid to go too close."

"Let's take a look." He rolled out of the hammock, pulled his pants on, grabbed his flashlight and his gun, and headed out the door with me right behind him.

Obeah was black magic. The Garifuna, who traced their ancestry to the "red" Carib Indians of the Caribbean islands and escaped slaves from West Africa, practiced *obeah*. So did the Maya. So did some Creoles. An *obeah* man could make people sick—give them a headache or a stomachache or make them see things that didn't exist. Or he could kill them. If his herbs and spells didn't work, he would slip ground glass into his victims' food. Shortly before our arrival, a Creole man had been convicted of making *obeah* and sentenced to three years in prison.

The authorities preferred to ignore *obeah*'s existence, and most people didn't want to talk about it, especially Father Cull. But under Aaron's prodding, he had admitted to performing exorcisms in San Antonio, and knew from his own experience that an *obeah* man (*ak'tul* in Kekchi) had a sophisticated knowledge of herbs and plants. According to Don, a Guatemalan Maya living in a nearby village was reputedly one of the best *obeah* men in Toledo District. He could make snakes out of pieces of tie-tie and scorpions out of tobacco twists, and because he cast his spells in Pokoman—a dialect not spoken here—no rival *obeah* man could deflect them.

Aaron and I crept to within fifteen feet of the school. I stopped as soon as I could distinguish voices—one male, the other female—but Aaron crawled closer. The rainforest was alive with crickets and cicadas and other insect percussionists, and in the distance I heard the cry of a whippoorwill. Collectively they made enough noise to drown out the conversation going on in the schoolhouse. I wondered whether Aaron could hear anything. After a few minutes, he crept back and gestured toward our house. Once inside, we wrapped ourselves in a blanket and huddled in his hammock.

"Were they burning black candles?" I whispered. Ordinary candles were white. *Obeah* practitioners used black candles to cast a spell.

"I could hardly see. There was a man, tall—I think it was José Ical—and the other was an elderly woman. I didn't recognize her."

"Could it have been José's wife?" I had seen her only a time or two, and always from a distance. "She's supposed to be older than he is."

"Maybe. Or it could have been Laura, the *curandera* from Pueblo Viejo."

"So maybe it was good *obeah*?" I asked hopefully, watching the shimmer of candles in the distance. A *curandero* performed white magic—good magic. *Obeah* practitioners claimed their magic was simply power and could be used to bring about good *or* evil.

"It's possible. Maybe José and his wife are praying for more children. Or maybe he and Laura are praying for somebody's health. If it is Laura."

We lay in the darkness until the candles went out and whoever was inside had left, their shadows mingling with the deeper shadows of the bush.

The next morning I entered the schoolhouse early with a stack of papers under my arm, pretending I was on official business. Whoever had been there had made no effort to conceal what they'd done. The table I used as my desk had been pulled back from the wall so it stood in the center of the building, the way it did when Father Cull said Mass.

When I saw the surface of the table my heart stopped beating. Melted black wax was everywhere.

I sprinted back to the house and told Aaron, who decided we better tell Crispino. The village men had recently held an election, and we had two new *mayordomos*, Enriques Choc and Crispino. Mateo was out of a job.

Aaron asked Crispino, who was taking it easy in his hammock, if he had noticed the unusual activity in school the previous night.

"*Aha*," Crispino answered. Affirmative. He was a little older than Lucia, a big man with a pleasant, open face. Of all the men in the village, he and José Tux would have made the best *alcaldes*. They were both fair-minded, never lost their tempers, and refused to hold a grudge.

"I went up to take a look, and I think the man was José Ical," Aaron continued.

Crispino nodded thoughtfully.

"What are you going to do about it?" Aaron persisted.

After a brief pause, the new *mayordomo* replied in Kekchi. Aaron asked Lucia to translate because he didn't want any misunderstandings. She said Crispino didn't plan to do anything. He hadn't seen who the people were. He didn't know why they'd been there, or what they wanted. They hadn't *done* anything.

"But they were burning black candles!"

Crispino shrugged and said a few short words. "He say," Lucia told us, "that maybe today would be a good day to make *chicha*."

As the rainy season dragged on, Aaron and I went to bed earlier and earlier, fully dressed and wrapped in every blanket we owned. The temperature had sunk to the low fifties every night for the past week. Most of our neighbors kept a fire burning, or a bucket of hot coals under their hammocks. The water was so cold that few people took daily baths anymore, and all the kids had chapped lips and runny noses. So did Teacher.

"What would you like for our last dinner before we leave for Guatemala?" I asked Aaron one night as we lay in our hammocks. "Christmas isn't that far away."

"What were you planning?"

"I'm open to suggestions."

"Beef Stroganoff." It was one of our dehydrated astronaut meals.

"I hope you're not serious."

"I like beef Stroganoff."

"From a *package*?"

"How about fish, then? We haven't had much fish lately."

"That's because nobody's *given* us much lately, and you don't go fishing. Your choices are canned sardines or canned mackerel."

"I wish we had mayonnaise. And pickle relish. And some decent bread. Mustard would be nice, too. Then maybe I could get excited about canned mackerel."

I was surprised at how resentful he sounded. "*I* wish we had steak. Do you realize we've only eaten beef twice the entire time we've been here?"

"I'd rather have a hamburger. Three or four White Castle hamburgers would hit the spot. And some of their French apple pie."

"Remember those half-pound hamburgers at Pal's Cabin? The drippy ones with grilled onions? I still think I'd rather have a steak, though."

We both fell silent. We planned to go to Guatemala City over Christmas so Aaron could sign up for another independent study course at San Carlos and keep his student deferment. After that we planned to spend some time in Cobán, a coffee-growing region in the mountains of Alta Vera Paz where the Kekchi had originally come from. I doubted we'd find our dream meal in either place, but I was really looking forward to a break. From what Aaron had just said, he was, too.

At Evaristo's invitation we went to see Aleja and the baby. I wanted to bring a "congratulations on your new baby" gift, but Aaron said it wasn't customary. So we went empty-handed.

Mother and son lay on a bark bed in a corner of the Tuxes' kitchen while half a dozen women—Aleja's mother Ana and various grown daughters—worked around a fire so big it heated the entire room. Above the fire a side of *waree*, wild boar, lay on a tripod to smoke. Nearby was a lard tin full of empty *pur* shells, waiting to be ground into clay and made into pottery. In another corner stood a *santos* table that held a multitude of candles, a pack of cigarettes, and a few rifle shells. The saint's statue appeared to be a miniature of the full-sized statue of St. Anthony in the church in San Antonio. Ana's floor was like poured concrete—as smooth as Lucia's, even though Ana's house was four or five times bigger.

Like all new mothers, Aleja, a slender, very pretty seventeen-year-old girl, had spent eight days after the birth of her baby doing nothing—the only time in her adult life that would ever happen. On the eighth day new mothers traditionally bathed in the river for the first time and resumed their domestic chores. But I didn't think Aleja had resumed them quite yet. Although her son was almost two weeks old, she still looked pale and tired.

The baby—sturdy, like his father—was wrapped in layers of soft cotton, his arms and ankles bound with rags. Evaristo explained that all new babies were trussed like this so they couldn't kick or hit their mothers. It also prevented them from squirming out of a *lepup*.

"His name is Fidel," Evaristo announced with pride.

I had to smile. It wasn't a name I'd heard before, and I suspected that Evaristo had given it to his son in honor of the guy with the beard and cigar in Cuba, and not—as was customary—a saint. "He's big," I said. For Aleja's benefit I smiled again and added, "*Chabil*."

Aleja smiled back. Yes, her son *was* handsome.

"You think he is too big?" Evaristo demanded, all the gaiety gone from his voice.

"He looks fine to me," I said. "How could he be too big?"

"No good sometimes when a man has good luck, or good things happen to him. People get jealous."

"Jealous how?" Aaron asked. "What do they do?"

"Maybe nothing. Or maybe they try to hex the baby."

"You mean cast a spell on him?"

Aaron was talking about *obeah*. So was Evaristo. Had Aaron and I witnessed jealous parents putting a spell on Fidel that night? But *obeah* wasn't a subject normally discussed in polite conversation, and before Aaron could pursue it, Ana waved us into hammocks.

It was the first time I'd seen the matriarch of the Tux clan. Her physical presence was intimidating. She was a large, efficient woman—not quite as tall as her husband but much broader—with the manner of someone accustomed to ordering people around. Obediently Aaron and I each chose a hammock and sat down. When Ana handed each of us a bowl of *chicharrones*, pork cracklings, we picked up the pieces with our fingers and ate.

"I want you to be *padrinos* for Fidel when he get baptized," Evaristo said. He hadn't been served any food. Neither had anybody else, even Aleja. Aaron and I were the only ones eating. We were guests, and that was the ritual: guests ate first. Although I knew the rest of the family would eat after we left, it still made me uncomfortable.

"We can't do that, Evaristo," Aaron said. "We're not Catholic."

Evidently the cracklings had been an appetizer, because Ana returned almost immediately with a calabash of soup made from pumpkins—*k'um* in Kekchi—in each hand.

"It don't mean nothing that you're not Catholic!" Evaristo said heatedly.

"I know *you* don't care," Aaron answered. "But Father Cull does."

The soup was very good—one of the few foods I'd eaten here that hadn't been fortified with *chile* pepper—and so thick it was like trying to pour pudding into my mouth. But I kept encountering chunks of rind. Trying not to be too obvious about it, I spit them back into the calabash. I hoped Ana didn't expect me to eat them. The Maya had their food preferences; I had mine.

"Then I don't ask Father Cull to baptize Fidel. I take him to the Nazarenes. That way you can be godparents."

Aaron laughed. "*Pues*, if you're sure that's what you want."

I glanced at Aleja, wondering what she thought about letting the Nazarenes baptize her son, and whether her opinion mattered to Evaristo. He was very much the proud papa, but I knew from Maxiana that his application to pick fruit in Florida had been accepted. Would he have gone? I'd never know—neither would Evaristo. Lucia had intercepted the letter and destroyed it.

To my dismay Ana returned yet a third time, bearing steaming bowls of spicy fish *caldo* and *tortillas*. Aaron caught my eye. He had asked for fish and here it was—with a profusion of bones and no mayo or mustard. The fish were *machaca*. One of the Tux sons had caught half a dozen of them using a piece of string, a hook, and some grapefruit rind. On the other side of the fire, I glimpsed nine-year-old Paulina, one of my students, smiling shyly at me. When I smiled back, she hid her mouth behind her hand and ran off.

"José explained to me about a ceremony the Indians make for babies," Evaristo told Aaron. "The boy, they show him everything he uses when he's big—a machete, a rifle, an ax."

Paulina reappeared, her eyes shining. Behind her were Crisantos, her youngest brother, and Nicasio, her older brother, holding his blue copybook. Hesitantly the children edged toward me.

"For a girl, they hold a pot, a calabash—what girls use when they help their mother," Evaristo continued. "They do this ceremony when the baby is three, maybe four months old. José calls it *hetz mek*. Afterward the woman carries the baby on her hip, like so." He grabbed Crisantos, who was trying to sneak past him, and swung the little boy up in the air and astride his hip. Reflexively Crisantos locked his legs around Evaristo's waist. From this sudden new vantage point he grinned down at us before deciding he didn't *like* this new vantage point and turned away, squirming. Evaristo lowered him to the floor.

"So if you don't be godparents when Fidel is baptized, you come to his *hetz mek*?"

"We would be honored," Aaron said.

Nicasio plopped down next to me in the hammock. Gravity immediately took over, and he slid into me butt first. Paulina glowered at him and contented herself with leaning against my legs. Crisantos shot headfirst into my lap, his nose pressed into my sweater. I wrapped my arms around him. He smelled like river water.

"Teacher! I have did my homework already," Nicasio exclaimed.

"I also," whispered Paulina.

"Good for you both! Do you do your homework in the morning? Or at night?"

Nicasio answered. "In the morning, when I don't got something else I should do."

"Chores, you mean?"

"Yes. My mother say, 'Bring firewood,' I bring her firewood. My father say, 'Help me in the *milpa*,' I go."

Paulina nodded. "I, too, teacher."

"And me, Teacher!" Crisantos leaned back to gaze into my face, grinning.

"What are your chores for today?" I asked Nicasio, who hiked his shoulders up in an elaborate shrug. It was still early—he didn't know yet. "Two of my brothers have go hunting, but they don't ask me. I don't have enough years. They want to find—I don't know the English. Big bird, like so." He opened his arms as wide as he could, curving them slightly.

I knew of only one edible bird that size. "Curassow?"

"Maybe. After they shoot it and bring it here, I help . . ." He mimed plucking feathers.

"Paulina, what do you do?" I asked.

"I help with the corn, or to make clay for pots," she whispered.

"If your brothers kill a curassow, will you help your mother cook it?"

She flattened herself against my legs, hiding a smile behind both hands. "Yes, Teacher."

"Who will you help, Crisantos?"

He rocked in my arms. "Nobody!" he crowed.

"Teacher—look." Nicasio held up his copybook. "My name. See? I have wrote here my name." He had printed his name on the cover.

"Good for you, Nicasio! I'm proud of you! *Very* good!"

His face lit up, and he told me he had practiced and practiced to get it right.

Suddenly the house went silent. Evaristo and Aaron stopped talking, and all activity around the fire ceased. Every adult in the room was looking at me.

My stomach did a backflip. "Uh-oh. What did I do wrong? Do I have pumpkin soup on my face?"

"Nicasio and Paulina," Aaron said. "They're carrying on a conversation with you."

"Yes, they are. And?"

"In English."

Even though I was no artist, I thought my students might have fun pretending *they* were. So one afternoon I asked them to draw something they saw every day, either in their house or in the village. A few students drew one or both of their parents. A few more drew their house. But most drew an animal—a pig, chicken, dog, or mule. Regardless of what animal it was, all four feet were always on the same side.

Arcenio drew a very realistic-looking scorpion. When I praised him for it, he looked at me skeptically and didn't say anything. As soon as I turned my back, he leaned over and drew a scorpion in the corner of Luis's paper. I pretended not to notice. By the time I reached the front of the class, he was trying to draw one on Maxiana's paper and she was slapping his hand away.

"Arcenio," I said, "I want to see you after class."

He gave me a tight, grudging smile, as if he'd won a contest—as if he had deliberately manipulated me into giving him another beating.

As soon as I dismissed school, the kids all ran around to the back of the building so they could peek through the chinks and see how many whacks I was going to give Arcenio this time. I sat on the edge of the table so I would be higher than he was. "Come here," I said, patting the seat of my chair.

Reluctantly Arcenio moved from his usual seat and took mine. He kept his face expressionless, something that not even the adults bothered to do anymore.

"Your father talked to me before school started," I told him. "Do you know what he said?"

Arcenio refused to look at me.

"He asked me to lash you if you were bad. When you grow up he doesn't want you to be a farmer like him. He wants you to learn, so you can go out in the world and make money, so you have a good life."

The children outside began muttering. If I was going to let Arcenio have it, what was taking me so long? Finally Arcenio raised his eyes. They were so dark they looked black.

"Do you understand what I'm saying?" I asked.

After a pause he gave a curt nod.

"I'm not going to lash you again. Just remember what your father said. Will you do that?"

He didn't say yes, but he didn't say no. When I excused him, he got up and left without a word. In the following weeks, Arcenio still managed to find new and creative ways to get in trouble when he was bored, but he didn't push the limits anymore. Like me, he had learned when to stop.

Aaron went hunting one Sunday—unaccompanied this time—along the old truck pass, a trail through the bush that had been cleared decades earlier to drag mahogany logs to the river. The only fresh meat we'd had in two weeks was some kind of peppery *caldo* Silvaria had given us that consisted mainly of innards and skin. Our dream-meal conversation hadn't helped.

I hadn't made any progress about "my things." Since I smoked only when I could mooch cigarettes, my grape-colored ashtray had become a place where bugs ended up when they fell out of the thatch. What could I do to make this house more homelike? I was sure I could find something beautiful and unusual in the marketplace in Guatemala City. But for right now all I could think of was to follow Lucia's suggestion and "make my floor pretty," so it would look like hers.

I scooped the fireplace ashes into a bucket and added enough water to make a paste, as she had told me to. I thought I'd start at the fireplace and work my way to the back door. When that patch had dried, I'd work my way from the fireplace to the front door. I had a feeling the process was going to involve more than a onetime effort. As I smoothed the mixture with my palms, I kept encountering bits of charred wood that grated on my skin like sandpaper.

The glaze of ash and water dried quickly, even in the relative coolness of the house, and after working a while longer I sat back and admired my work. Now *my* floor—at least the part around the fireplace that had been pounded flat to begin with—looked like concrete, too. But my hands stung, and I was getting cold. I pulled one of Aaron's flannel shirts on and rolled the sleeves up.

Where *was* Aaron? I hoped he hadn't wounded some animal and followed it into the bush. That had happened to two of José Tux's sons, and they hadn't come home until the next morning.

The floor between the fireplace and my tree-house corner post was crumbled dirt that had never packed, and I wondered if the best policy might be to add water to it until I had mud and then walk on it to smooth it out. *Then* I could cover it with ashes and water.

Since it was getting dark, I lit the kerosene lamp, fumbling with the match because my fingers felt bigger than they usually did. As always, the lamplight drew insects. One was a shiny black beetle that immediately toppled into my purple ashtray. It was over two inches long with hooks on either side of its head that made it look like an armored truck with horns.

I splashed water over the broken clods of earth on the floor and tramped on them with my bare feet until they broke up and the surface was smooth. Then I squatted next to the water bucket and submerged my throbbing hands. Wood ash plus water, I learned later—about the same time I learned that the Cuban missile crisis had come and gone without our knowing anything about it—equals lye.

I had just lit the fire when Aaron stumbled in. His wet clothes clung to him and he was covered with mud. His face looked as gray as my new floor.

"Aaron, what *happened*?"

"I fell. My left leg is so weak it . . . collapses on me," he panted, trembling with exhaustion. I ran to him and he slung one arm over my shoulder. "This is the second time. I didn't tell you about . . . the first time because I didn't want you to worry." He showed me where his pant leg had ripped. His right knee was oozing blood.

I was so scared a roar like a tidal wave pounded in my ears—my own heartbeat. "Let's get you out of those wet clothes so you can lie down."

Aaron raised his arms and I peeled his T-shirt over his head. "You know what this means."

Potentially it could mean a lot of things. "No. Tell me." This was the second time he'd wanted to play guessing games when he had hurt himself.

Aaron wrapped himself in a blanket and crawled into his hammock before answering. "Ever since I slid down the . . . falls I see double sometimes," he admitted, still struggling for breath. "I'm afraid I might have sustained some neurological damage. I want to go to Guatemala City. Roberto Rendón is a neurologist there. He's . . . a Michigan graduate and probably the only neurologist in Central America. It's either that or we go back to the States."

Neurological damage? I forgave Aaron instantly. "Wouldn't it be cheaper to go to Guatemala?"

"Of course," he said impatiently. "It's a lot closer than the States."

But traveling there would be harder, because first we needed visas—and to get them we would have to return to Belize City. After a hasty dinner, we decided to take Christmas vacation early and leave the following morning. As I lay in my hammock, mentally checking off what to pack, a question took shape around the edges of my conscious mind.

Whoever had burned the black candles in school knew that the next person to see them would most likely be me. Had I been *meant* to see them? Were the black candles a warning? The Maya in Cayo District had killed a priest a couple of years ago because he had attempted to suppress some of their most sacred rituals. Aaron wasn't interested in suppressing their rituals, but he was definitely interested in knowing about them.

Was it possible that somebody wanted him to stop asking questions badly enough to make *obeah* against *us*?

xxxxxxxxxxxxxxxxxxxxxxxxxxxxxxxxxxxxxxxxxxxxxxxxxxxxxxxxx

CREAMY PUMPKIN SOUP
Ana Tux made the best pumpkin soup I ever tasted, but no Kekchi cook I've talked to since knows how to make anything like it. My best guess is that she cooked the pumpkin in a small amount of chicken broth and then mashed it.

Here's a contemporary version, but you need a refrigerator, a blender, and sour cream. Even today, almost fifty years after I left Belize, these items are unavailable to many Maya because they still don't have electricity.

    6 cups chicken stock, preferably homemade

    approximately 4 cups fresh pumpkin (buy a medium-sized one)

    1 medium white onion

    1 tablespoon fresh thyme leaves

    2 cloves garlic

    ½ cup sour cream

    ¼ cup watercress (optional)

American pumpkins bought in a supermarket are thin-skinned for easy carving. This means you don't have to spit pumpkin rind back into your soup.

Wash the pumpkin and cut the top off. Remove all seeds and strings. Cut into large chunks, including the skin (I use a meat cleaver). Cut the onion in half, peel and mince the garlic, and add everything except the sour cream and watercress to a large, heavy pot. Simmer, covered, for half an hour.

Remove the pumpkin from the pot. When the pieces are cool enough to handle, dice them and puree in a blender with the other ingredients except sour cream and watercress.

Pour the water out of the pot and pour the puree back in. Simmer another half hour, uncovered. Remove from the heat and stir in sour cream. Just before serving, sprinkle watercress leaves on top as garnish.

Serves 4 people.

THIRTEEN

Strawberry Sunday

More bad news awaited us in Punta Gorda. Included in a letter from Aaron's mother was a note from Uncle Sam. The Universidad de San Carlos in Guatemala City had apparently never forwarded the paperwork proving that Aaron had taken independent study courses during fall semester. Unless he could produce something in writing, he would be reclassified 1A and shipped off to Vietnam.

Now we had two urgent reasons to go to Guatemala City.

But the *Heron* wouldn't arrive until tomorrow, and we had no place to spend the night. Don was in England, saying good-bye to his family. His job was coming to an end, and he planned to move to property he'd bought near the village of Big Falls. Half a dozen families from Crique Sarco had moved there already, including Manuel and Petrona Xi.

PG had no such thing as a hotel. Aaron and I didn't know any locals, but we had met an American anthropologist studying the Garifuna. He was pleasant enough, but he had a wife and three teenage kids. His wife—pale, overweight, and suffering from half a dozen different physical ailments—did nothing but complain about how hard it was to hand wash a load of sheets for five people every week, and to rinse everything they ate with Clorox before cooking it.

I was dumbstruck. Using sheets in a hammock had never occurred to me. Neither had disinfecting our food. I didn't dare confess to her that we drank water right out of the river without boiling it. What did this woman do when the Garifuna gave her gifts of cooked food? Or invited her family into their home for a meal? Did she insist on dunking everything in bleach first? Maybe nobody invited them to dinner—I wouldn't have.

Aaron decided we'd look up another of his acquaintances, an evangelical Christian named Herb who was also living among the Garifuna. Since the Jesuits had a lock on education—Father Cull had built and staffed a high school in Punta Gorda, the only facility for secondary education in Toledo District—Herb's approach was more materialistic. He was teaching the Garifuna how to build hurricane-proof houses and latrines using concrete blocks. By the time we found his house, Aaron was limping, his face pale and dripping sweat. Grudgingly Herb offered us his spare bedroom. He lived in one of his own concrete boxes, and the room felt like a shower stall.

Herb was Aaron's age, unmarried. When he gave us a tour of the house, I commented on his kerosene stove—it looked exactly like the one I'd cooked on in Crique Sarco. Herb apparently mistook my surprise at seeing one as a desire to cook on it, because when it was time for dinner, he took a pot of beans out of the cupboard along with a sack of rice, nodded at me, and went into the front room to talk to Aaron.

I stared at his retreating back. How hard would it be to warm up some beans and cook a pot of rice? Too hard for Herb, apparently. I set the beans on a back burner on low. On the bigger front burner, I poured four cups of water and two cups of rice into a pot. When the mixture boiled, I turned the flame down and joined the guys. They were discussing the drying time of cement—which Herb pronounced "SEE-ment"—under various weather conditions.

Fifteen minutes later, I returned to the kitchen. "Low" on Herb's stove wasn't the same as "low" on my fireplace. The rice had boiled over so violently it had pushed the lid completely off the pot. Rice stuck to the burner in clumps. A river of starch cascaded down the side of the stove and coagulated into a sticky puddle on Herb's SEE-ment floor. The rice still in the pot was scorched.

After bumming a cigarette from Herb, I scoured the pot using a fork and my fingernails, mopped the floor, and cursed him for his quaint idea of hospitality and my seemingly endless string of disasters trying to cook in this god-awful country.

In Belize City we had to wait some more while our visas were processed. We stayed at the same small boardinghouse we had stayed at in July—half a lifetime ago, it seemed. From a distance, or while holding your nose, Belize City was a tropical paradise filled with flowers and palm trees and graceful wooden houses. People spoke a lyrical patois of Jamaican-accented English that I loved to listen to but still had trouble understanding. (Boxes were "cartoons," as though they had Bugs Bunny hiding in them.) There were no sidewalks. Open sewage canals meandered through the city and emptied into the bay, where skeins of garbage and rotting fruit floated gently on the tide.

Aaron wanted to eat at a decent restaurant—one that served beef—and asked for recommendations at the American consulate. We either misunderstood the directions or the man who recommended the restaurant owned it. Hamburgers weren't on the menu. The steaks were long and narrow, and cooked so thoroughly the sides curled up like stalks of celery. But the daiquiris, made with freshly squeezed lime juice, were sublime. After picking at our dinner, Aaron and I gave up and ordered another round of daiquiris. We weren't in a hurry. We had nowhere to go.

The man at the next table, another Yankee, struck up a conversation. One daiquiri led to another, and he invited us to join him. He looked to be in his early thirties, a big, blond Texan who said he worked for Phillips 66, although he never told us exactly what he did. But the more he drank, the more desperately he wanted to talk about something he didn't seem to be allowed to.

"This place is the last frontier," he told Aaron, his tanned face flushed.

Half a dozen empty Heineken bottles stood in front of him. He told us about a man he knew, another American, who owned a small plane he'd named the *Maryjane*. The man used the plane to fly—guess what?— into the States.

Aaron and I stared at him, waiting to be enlightened.

"Tea. Stuff. Weed. You know," the Texan said impatiently. "Marijuana." When the man got caught, his daughter—also named (guess what?) Maryjane—took over and flew the plane for him. "I'm tellin' you—this place is easy money and good times," the Texan said, ordering another round of drinks. "Takes balls"—this with a sideways glance at me, to see whether an apology was necessary—"but long as you know the right people, you got it made. It's go for broke here, boom or bust, 'cause the Limeys aren't runnin' the country. The niggers are."

Whatever fellow feeling I may have had for a countryman evaporated.

"The Limeys are just payin' for it," the Texan continued, oblivious. "Six million a year is what I heard, and that's just to keep the soldier boys in knee socks and mosquito repellent." He meant the British troops stationed along the border to repel a Guatemalan invasion. Guatemala claimed ownership of British Honduras. On some oil company maps British Honduras didn't even exist—it was whatever color Guatemala was.

The Texan licked his lips. "Least the niggers *think* they're runnin' things. You know who really is, don't you?" He leaned forward. "Tell you what. You tell me what you're interested in and lemme introduce you to some people. What do you say?"

He was either CIA or, more likely, running drugs himself. We said good night.

In Guatemala City Aaron and I stayed at a *pensión* Don had recommended. Our room was mustard colored, higher than it was wide, filled with dark, heavy furniture. The first order of business was to figure out the phone system so Aaron could contact Dr. Rendón, his friend from

Michigan. Roberto said he'd be happy to examine Aaron and run the necessary tests. Our only expense would be for the tests and medication; he would donate his time. And please—we *must* join him and his wife for dinner that night. His wife came from Detroit and would enjoy talking to other Americans.

His wife's name was Joanne, and when Roberto introduced her, I felt as though I were looking in a mirror at some other, more expensive version of myself. Like me, Joanne had blue eyes and pale blond hair. And we had something else in common. "I don't believe this!" she exclaimed over dinner. "I was an English major, too!" Impulsively she grasped my hand. "Let's go shopping tomorrow so we can *really* talk!"

I didn't want to go shopping. I wanted to be sure Aaron was all right. "But shouldn't I stay here? In case my husband needs something, or Roberto wants me to—"

"Roberto has a staff," Joanne interrupted me, a remark that made her husband laugh.

"Women," he said to Aaron, shaking his head. "Guatemalan, American—it doesn't matter. They all love shopping."

Roberto and Joanne seemed like genuinely nice people, but they intimidated me. A week earlier there *I'd* been, walking around barefoot and without a bra in my bush house in the jungle, eating what they would have considered table scraps. And here *they* were—rich, beautifully dressed, eating a sumptuous dinner off bone china. Everything in their house was an antique—their dinner table reminded me of something that medieval Spanish royalty would have dined on. It had been a long time since I'd smelled furniture wax. In addition Joanne collected eighteenth-century triptychs the size of room dividers—oils of the Christian saints painted on wood or copper panels by "indigenous" artists, meaning the Maya. Joanne had her own staff—a cook, housekeeper, and a nanny for Patrick, their little boy.

Early the next morning, she walked me to the city's teeming central marketplace while Roberto drove Aaron to the hospital. Her cook followed us at a discreet distance in order to carry Joanne's food purchases.

When Joanne was finished with the day's grocery shopping, she steered me to a different part of the market. "So what do you plan to do with your English degree?"

"Teach, probably. Or work in publishing," I told her, eyeing a hammered silver *quetzal* pin I thought Barbara might like for Christmas. I had already opened—and read—her present to me, a copy of D. H. Lawrence's novel about Mexico, *The Plumed Serpent.* "I really want to be a writer." It felt funny to admit that out loud. Aaron didn't want a writer wife. He wanted a faculty wife.

"Oh, that's exciting! Have you taken any writing courses?"

I bought the pin and picked out some handwoven fabric for my mother and grandmother, and a clay pipe for my grandfather. "I want to take Allan Seager's course when we get back." Seager, a novelist and short story writer, taught fiction.

"Take anything Donald Hall is teaching. He's wonderful—that accent and all. You know he went to Cambridge."

I knew that. And I knew that Allan Seager had gone to Oxford on a Rhodes Scholarship. "Do they sell candles here?"

"Yes, candles, baskets, pottery, clothing, all kinds of things. I'll show you. Have you had anything published?"

"Three book reviews."

"Where?"

"The *Denver Quarterly*. How about books? Do they sell books here? My father loves to read, but he's hard to buy for. Or should I go to a bookstore?"

Joanne finally took the hint. I didn't want to talk about my writing; I was afraid it would never happen. So we talked about the United Fruit Company and its effect on Central American politics for the rest of the morning. By the time I walked back to the *pensión*, I was carrying newspaper-wrapped parcels that contained some tapered green candles, in honor of the season, socks and underwear for Aaron—at his request—and some Guatemalan coffee. For myself I had bought a traditional Guatemalan skirt with a black background, embroidered with white and tan stitching. At the last minute I'd bought something else: a piece of cloth embroidered with tiny, diamond-shaped white figures, surrounded by identical diamonds of purple, blue, and green. It was an intricate and very beautiful piece of material, and some Maya woman had worked on it for a long time.

On a street corner I stopped to buy a Christmas tree—a dead yucca plant about two feet tall that had been spray-painted silver. Aaron was in our room when I walked in. "Now we have something to put our presents under on Christmas morning," I announced as I placed it on the bureau by the window.

I could read his response on his face: why are you imposing your materialistic American values on a culture that doesn't want them?

"Oh, stop the Scrooge act. They celebrate Christmas here," I said. "They exchange gifts. It's not like we *invented* the custom. How did the tests go?"

"About the way you'd expect. So, how much did you spend?"

"On the tree, you mean?" Of course he didn't mean on the tree. "A quarter—big deal. You have to admit it's the most unusual Christmas tree we'll ever have."

Aaron gave me a grudging smile. "It'll definitely be the cheapest."

The week before Christmas Roberto made his diagnosis: Aaron was anemic and had a severe vitamin B deficiency. The treatment was as simple as knocking back a handful of vitamins before every meal. Although Aaron still had trouble with his right eye not focusing, his limp disappeared practically overnight, and so did his headache—the one that had bothered him since his fall.

But his headache returned when the registrar at San Carlos told him it was too early to register for spring term—he'd have to come back in mid-January. Aaron met with some of the anthropology faculty and got the paperwork straightened out with profuse apologies on their side and promises to send copies to his draft board. But he'd still have to come back in January to register for spring classes.

Three days before Christmas, around midnight, I dreamed I was being chased by skeletons clacking their teeth at me. I woke up to find myself still in our room at the *pensión*, my mouth dry and my heart thudding against my ribs. The noise grew louder. Panicked, I looked around the room to see where it was coming from. Aaron. He was shivering so hard his teeth rattled.

I shook him awake. "Aaron, what's the matter?"

His teeth were chattering so hard he had to say, "I'm cold" three times before I understood him.

I laid my wrist against his forehead. "But you're burning up with fever!"

"I need more blankets."

We didn't have more. I helped him into socks and a sweater, folded my half of the blanket over him, and curled up against his back. It took him an hour to warm up enough to fall asleep.

When I woke up the next morning, he was sitting by the window in the weak winter sun, fully dressed, wrapped in the blanket. "How do you feel?" I asked apprehensively.

"Weak. And helpless."

"Do you want breakfast?"

He shook his head.

"Do you want me to call Roberto?"

"No. I'm already in his debt. And I know what this is—I don't need a diagnosis."

"What is it?"

"A malaria attack. I got sick last summer." I didn't know what to say. Aaron was supposed to be the strong one. I was the sickly, accident-prone one everybody had been worried about. "I took a codeine," he added. "It'll kick in soon—you go to breakfast."

"Can I bring you anything?"

He shook his head again.

When I came back from the dining room, our maid was there, unobtrusively mopping and dusting. I saw her glance at Aaron from time to time. Like everybody else in the servant class, she was Indian, a middle-aged woman dressed in thin, hand-me-down Western clothing. She wore her hair in a single braid down her back the way Petrona Xi wore hers. Explaining that my husband was sick, I asked if we could have more blankets. She nodded silently. When she finished making the bed, she left.

"Are you sure you don't want something hot to drink? I can get coffee from the kitchen," I said. "It'll help you warm up."

Aaron was thinking about it when there was a soft knock on the door. "*Para su marido*," the maid said in a low voice, holding out two blankets. For your husband. As I took them, she slid a tiny white pill into my hand.

"*Gracias*," I said in surprise. She nodded and slipped away. "What is this?" I asked Aaron, showing him the pill. "Does she know you have malaria? I'm not sure you ought to take it."

"She knows." Aaron gestured at the clay water jar that stood on the bedside table, its mouth covered by an inverted clay tumbler. "Pour me some water, please. And give me the pill."

She knew. She came from a culture so poor that a visit to someone like Roberto Rendón was as impractical as visiting Paris, yet so attuned to suffering she would give a stranger—a *gringo*—medicine to ease his pain.

By the following day, Aaron's fever had disappeared. When the maid came, he tried to hand her the equivalent of twenty dollars American. It was a very materialistic, very American thing to do. But it was the only thing we *could* do. To her it represented a small fortune, but her face remained neutral. Almost brusquely she indicated that she wanted Aaron to leave the money on the bedside table. When we came back from breakfast, she and the money were gone.

Although it was easy to fault Lawrence's factual information in *The Plumed Serpent*, he had captured the Indians' so-called stoicism perfectly—the need to observe the proper rituals, to keep the correct distance between themselves and other people, and themselves and their gods. This sense of being one prayer away from disaster permeated their lives. Was it their surroundings—their daily struggle with the rain, the dryness, the heat, the brilliant, cold nights, all the deadly creatures lurking in the rainforest—that made them such fatalists? Or was it something in their most basic beliefs about themselves? Expect the worst—anything else is a gift.

But their beliefs gave them a resolve we didn't have in the States. They were a courageous people. The odds weren't in their favor, but they never stopped trying. In their view, no matter what happened to them, something else—something worse—*could* have happened, but didn't. What Lawrence failed to capture was their compassion and their fondness for joking around. I suspected he didn't pick up on their sense of humor because he didn't have one himself.

The Sunday before Christmas, an elderly European woman with a heavy accent—everybody called her "The Countess"—donated a crate of strawberries to the *pensión*'s kitchen so we could all have fresh strawberries for breakfast. It was a wonderful treat—fresh strawberries in December. When Aaron and I thanked her, she tipped her head and waved her hand dismissively the way the pope did. I wondered how she had ended up here, and if she really was a countess.

We celebrated a cautiously optimistic New Year's Eve at the *pensión*. Aaron said he felt well enough to take a quick vacation in Cobán, high in the mountains of Alta Vera Paz, the Kekchi's homeland.

For me Cobán was love at first sight. In a letter to my parents I wrote, "We're staying in the most beautiful *pensión* imaginable—steak every night, a fire in our room, the best coffee in the world, tame red and blue parrots in the courtyard. As the altitude is around five thousand feet, the temperature sinks to two-blanket level at night. Days are sunny, mountains breathtaking. I'm running out of adjectives."

But after Cobán, it was all downhill.

Aaron and I took a bus to the next big town, heading for Puerto Barrios on the coast so we could catch the *Heron* back to Punta Gorda. It was nearly noon, and while we tried to decide whether to wait three hours for a connecting bus or hitchhike, we ate a cheap lunch at a little roadside café. The soup had an acidic, unappetizing flavor, and we left before finishing it.

The sun was too hot for the clothes we'd put on that morning. After sweating by the side of the road for nearly an hour, waiting for the bus, we watched as two Guatemalans in a pickup slowed down for us. Aaron and I exchanged glances. Yes, we'd accept a ride. Anything to get out of this heat.

The truck was fairly new, but the men both needed a shave. The one riding shotgun got out and climbed in back without saying a word. He also needed a bath, and the skin around his eyes looked tight, as though he didn't smile much. The driver wore a similar expression. "I don't like this," I murmured to Aaron. "I'm staying back here with you." The acidic taste of the soup lingered on my tongue.

In Spanish Aaron told the guy who had gotten in the bed of the pickup with us that I preferred to stay where I was, but the man simply looked at him. As the driver revved the engine and took off, the man squatted against the window behind him, looking steadily at me, then at Aaron, who looked steadily back at him. I sat on top of Aaron's rucksack, futilely smoothing down my skirt. Aaron sat on the tailgate.

For the rest of the afternoon—bouncing over a rough road in the unrelenting sun—I wondered if the driver was deliberately hitting every pothole he could find because he was trying to bounce Aaron off the tailgate. Aaron, who later admitted he'd wondered the same thing, finally left his perch and squatted next to me, where we kept a watchful eye on our traveling companion.

By the time the men dropped us off in Puerto Barrios, both of us felt sick. Aaron shoved a handful of money at the driver. It wasn't gas money, it was an after-the-fact bribe—to thank them for not raping me and shoving us both off the tailgate of the truck where our decomposed bodies wouldn't be found for months. The driver accepted the money, and after his buddy climbed back in the cab, they drove off. I had stomach cramps and was so weak-kneed I could hardly walk.

We checked into the first hotel we came to. It was dirty and roach-infested, and—according to Don, who had a good laugh over it afterward—one of several whorehouses in town. It had only one bathroom, in a shed on the roof. The shed had no sink and no running water. The toilet was an open sewage pipe in the floor. Aaron and I used it only once—it was too far away. For the next two days, we lay side-by-side in bed, rigid as corpses, getting up only to vomit or move our bowels. Sometimes we had to do both at once, and resorted to the pitcher and washbowl in the corner of the room. The entire room smelled like rotting soup.

The following morning, bleary-eyed and miserable, we staggered to the dock to wait for the *Heron*. The customs officer, a Maya boy who looked like a Cub Scout and spoke less Spanish than I did, demanded to see our passports. When we produced them, he took mine, clicked his ballpoint pen, and proceeded to copy it, word for word. By the time the *Heron* arrived he was less than halfway through. With a groan Aaron slipped him some money. The boy indicated that I and my passport could leave. On board the *Heron* I paid for two one-way tickets to PG. When the purser asked who the other ticket was for, I pointed to Aaron and explained that he was still talking to *migración*.

The purser swore and spat over the side. "Guatemala's president, Ydigoras Fuentes, he hire these stupid Indians from the provinces and give them one gun and one uniform and pay them couple *quetzal* a month. This could be his army. See, he don't want no smart people in the army. He *want* it the stupids. This way he know the army not going get together and say, 'Hey, we got to get rid of this guy.' They not going get together. How they could do that? Nobody talk the same language!"

Half an hour passed. Finally Buster Hunter blew the *Heron*'s whistle—a blast that under different circumstances would have lifted me five feet off the deck and blown out my eardrums. I kept my eyes on Aaron. More money changed hands, and finally Aaron dragged his rucksack up the gangplank. We both toppled into the lower bunk of the first empty cabin we saw and stayed there until we reached PG.

When we crept onto dry land, Don took one look at us and doubled up laughing. If I'd been hoping for sympathy—which I was—I'd come to the wrong man.

"You're not sick," he scoffed. "Look at you—all that good living in Guatemala City is what's done you in. You're fat as Christmas geese, the pair of you! Cirila'll fix you right up. I told her to make *escabeche*. Nothing like chicken *caldo* to cure what ails you."

My grandmother couldn't have said it better. I looked Don in the eye without smiling. "Happy New Year to you, too."

He grinned like a cheeky little boy. I was so mad at him that by the time we got to his house I'd forgotten about my gurgling stomach and was actually hungry.

Escabeche comes from the Spanish word *escabechar*, "to pickle," and the soup contained more than enough vinegar and *chile* pepper to burn out whatever bacteria still lurked in our intestines. Cirila told me the dish was reserved for special occasions. Like my grandmother, Don didn't go in for displays of emotion. You had to look for it between the lines—or in the soup he served you.

The next morning he drove us to San Antonio and dropped us off. We paid Father Cull a visit to let him know that Aaron was all right. He seemed glad to see us, and told me in the coming weeks that I could expect visits from everybody from the local school superintendent to George Price, the first minister of British Honduras. He never told Aaron he was glad his illness hadn't been serious. You had to read between the lines with Father Cull, too.

XXXXXXXXXXXXXXXXXXXXXXXXXXXXXXXXXXXXXXXXXXXXXXXXXXXXXXXXXX

ESCABECHE

This is how Cirila cooked *escabeche*, although I have substituted chicken breasts for a freshly killed free-range chicken. I've probably taken other liberties as well.

4 skin-on, bone-in chicken breasts, all visible fat removed
8 cups chicken broth, preferably homemade
2 dried *chiles arbol*, broken into small pieces (including seeds)
2 teaspoons dried thyme
½ teaspoon dried oregano
2 cloves garlic, minced
1 teaspoon salt
2 large white onions (about 1½ pounds)
¼ cup vinegar
ground cayenne to taste (optional)

Heat the stock in a large, heavy pot over high heat. When it comes to a boil, add the chicken, *chiles*, thyme, oregano, garlic, and salt and bring to a second boil. Cook about 1 hour, covered, at a slow simmer, until the chicken is tender but not falling off the bone. Remove chicken from the pot; cover soup and continue to simmer. While chicken cools, bring a kettle of water to a boil and slice the onions into thin rings. Discard the skin and bones from the chicken and shred the meat. Return to pot.

Place sliced onions in a colander. Pour the boiling water from the kettle over them and drain thoroughly before you add them to the soup. In *escabeche*, the onions are a vegetable. You don't want to overwhelm the chicken with the flavor of onions.

Add the vinegar 1 tablespoon at a time until you like the taste.

Simmer an additional 5 minutes to allow the flavors to blend. The onions should be slightly crunchy.

Serves 4–6 people.

FOURTEEN

Food Feud

"Hold on a second," I told Aaron as we walked past Tommy Salam's store on our way to Rio Blanco. "I forgot something."

"Won't it wait?"

"I want to buy cigarettes."

I couldn't believe those words had just come out of my mouth. I hadn't *planned* to do this. When I saw the look on Aaron's face, I immediately tried to justify my behavior to myself, even as I walked into the store. It was my money—no different from using it to buy a piece of material for myself in the market in Guatemala City. Well—maybe a little different. Aaron had never forbidden me to buy material. But his original argument had been that I couldn't smoke because the Maya women didn't smoke. That had turned out to be less than truthful. Aaron didn't mind if I smoked somebody *else's* cigarettes. Somewhere along the line his argument had changed. Smoking cigarettes was okay. *Buying* cigarettes was not.

I came out of Tommy Salam's with two packs of Colonials. Aaron was furious, but he didn't say anything. That didn't mean he accepted my tobacco rebellion. All it meant was that he didn't have the energy to fight right now.

It had been a cool, clear morning; now it grew progressively hotter the farther we walked. By the time we reached the Santa Cruz turnoff, we were both sweating. I didn't realize how much I had missed my bush house in the jungle until I saw the Rio Blanco River, its stippled surface flashing in the sunlight.

"I want to bathe," I said impulsively. Everybody said that, even the kids who just liked to dog-paddle in the pool by the falls.

"Not now. We can do that after we unpack and relax."

"I'm sorry," I said, and meant it. "I'll only be a minute." Stripping off my sweaty clothes, I splashed to the opposite shore and tossed them on the bank. "Why don't you join me? It'll relax you. It's good water," I added, risking a joke.

"Look. I'm tired, okay? It's been a rough trip and I want to get back."

No jokes. I set off downstream, where the water deepened, and slid the elastic off my ponytail. I didn't need a bath—I had showered at Don's. I needed something else. I remembered my first sight of the river when Aaron and I had hiked in from San Antonio with all our belongings: I'd wanted to roll in it. Pushing off with both feet, I dove forward, my arms outstretched, and rolled sideways. As the water closed over my head, all the stress and fears and concerns of the past weeks dissolved. I was suspended in the shimmering water, my body as weightless as an egret feather. It felt like being baptized.

When I surfaced, flinging my hair out of my face, two men headed for Santa Cruz stood talking to Aaron, who had already crossed the river. They were Maya, but I didn't recognize them. Probably from Pueblo Viejo, I thought as I tucked my legs under me and treaded water. We greeted one another politely, the way the Maya always did, eyes averted, me naked and neck-deep in green water. The men continued across the river, paying no more attention to me than I paid to the tiny ever-present, ever-curious fish.

I was home.

Aaron noticed it first—only a few small children ran out to greet us. The rest of the village looked either deserted or at war. For the first time I could remember, the door to Silvaria and Enriques's house was closed. As we got closer to school, we saw that the door to Dolores and Joaquin's house was closed, too. Lucia and Crispino's house was likewise shut. The same with Mateo and Micalia Ical's house. As I bent to scratch a sand fly bite, I remembered that home was also a place where somebody had made *obeah* against somebody else—and that the "somebody else" might be us.

Later. Even if everybody in the village had turned against us, I'd deal with it later.

Our house was just as we'd left it. The pot I had used to heat coffee water still sat half full over a dead fire. A letter to Barbara remained in my typewriter, the paper draped limply over the platen.

"I wonder what's going on?" I asked the Answer Man.

"A plague? Rape and pillage? How the hell should I know?"

"Why don't you take a nap and I'll make something for lunch?" I suggested, trying to sound conciliatory and wifelike. The timing of my impulse buy had been terrible. I *knew* the trip had been hard on him, emotionally as well as physically. "How does that sound?"

Without answering, Aaron fell into his hammock backward, with his right arm flung over his eyes to block the world out. Silently I lit the fire. With no advance warning, Dolores probably hadn't made any extra *tortillas*, so lunch would be out of a can. After we ate I'd pay Lucia a visit and find out what was going on.

While I waited for the water to boil, I unpacked my new "things"—my candles and my embroidered diamond-weave material. I had the same dishware every woman in Rio Blanco did, blue and white speckled tin. But one of my plates had sprung a leak, a serious problem when nearly everything I cooked was soup or stew. From now on the leaky plate was going to hold candles. I shook out the material and placed it, full length, on the table next to where I usually sat, then set down the plate with the candles on it, along with my purple ashtray and my two packs of Colonials. When I stepped back to view the results, I had to laugh. All I needed was a saint's statue and I'd have an authentic Kekchi *santos* table.

Without announcing herself, Paulina walked in the door carrying freshly made *tortillas* and a bowl of steaming chicken *caldo*.

"Oh, wonderful! Food! Thank you, Paulina," I said warmly. "How are you?"

"I am well, Teacher." Eyes downcast, she sidled back out.

Aaron sat up and we exchanged glances. Something was definitely going on. Not until Maxiana and Natalia came over about half an hour later did we find out what. Joaquin Choc and his father and brothers were feuding with everybody else. The village *was* at war.

The basic story was this: soon after Aaron and I had left for Guatemala, Eustaquio Tux came home drunk from San Antonio, leading José's mule. On his way past Florencio Choc's house—Florencio was one of Joaquin's brothers—Eustaquio observed, out loud, that Florencio's yard was messy (true) and made a bad impression on people entering the village (also true.) At that, all three Choc brothers ganged up on him and beat him senseless. After the mule returned without Eustaquio, José Tux and his sons went in search of him. When they found him, still out cold beside Florencio's chicken coop, his brothers carried him home while José Tux took up the matter with José Ical, who walked to Pueblo Viejo and returned with the Kekchi policeman. The Chocs greeted the policeman with machetes. Without saying a word, the policeman turned around and walked back to Pueblo Viejo. The next day a uniformed Garifuna policeman drove in from San Antonio, armed. He informed the Choc brothers they were guilty of assault and fined them ten dollars each, a lot of money for subsistence farmers.

Between the ties of blood, marriage, and other ceremonies, the feud divided the village nearly in half. The Choc faction—which included two of the three Choc families, the Boh family, Juan Oh and his son John, and Martín Ical's family—had cut their bean fields by themselves and had not been invited to participate in planting the communal rice field.

So many new people had moved into Rio Blanco in the past few months that the men had voted to have their own *alcalde* so they wouldn't have to depend on the one in Pueblo Viejo. But now the Choc faction opposed the plan, even though the villagers had elected Enriques Choc as the second *alcalde*, or assistant mayor. José Ical had been elected first *alcalde*, which explained why he was the one who'd gone for the police.

"We can't take sides," Aaron cautioned me.

"But everybody knows that José Tux treats you like family. They know Evaristo wants us to be Fidel's godparents and that Lucia treats *me* like family."

"But we can't play favorites," Aaron insisted.

"Okay. I won't."

I was as good as my word. No matter who brought me food, I thanked everybody equally.

Nearly once a day someone, usually the woman of the household, came to our door carrying something to eat. For me this was a delightful and unexpected windfall, like eating out every night, even though I'd never seen some of the food before, let alone considered it edible. Bernarda Xo, who lived with her young husband near the river crossing, brought me an armadillo that had been boiled in its shell with an overabundance of *chile* pepper. It looked like roadkill and tasted like strips of wet tennis ball. But it was food. Score one for the Chocs.

The next day José Ical's wife—her name was Paula, and she *was* older than he was—gave me some sugarcane and a bowl of homemade cocoa. Score one for the Tux faction. Unlike the ceremonial drink of parched cocoa beans ground with black pepper, this beverage looked and smelled as though it might actually taste like chocolate.

But I was reluctant to drink it. Aaron decided he had definitely seen Laura, the old *curandera* from Pueblo Viejo, burning candles in the schoolhouse that night, not Paula. Therefore the cocoa didn't contain poison or some mind-bending herb. Since he was so sure of himself I made him drink it first.

Lucia brought over three eggs and some *k'ib*, cut from the heart of a cohune palm. She told me to boil the palm hearts while I fried some onions and *chile* peppers, then stir the eggs, add the palm hearts and onions, and scramble the mixture.

The following day Alejandro Mijangre's wife gave me some *pibil*—seasoned pork wrapped in banana leaves and roasted in a pit over hot coals. The English-speakers called it barbecued pork. In the Yucatan, where it is very popular, it's called *cochinita pibil.* Score: Tuxes 3, Chocs 1.

Goyita Boh gave me some "antelope" meat. Chocs 2.

Sebastian Garcia's shy wife appeared at my front door long enough to hand me a bowl of *watusi,* bush rabbit. Tuxes 4.

Miguel Choc brought over some fungus he had found on a dead tree in the bush. He assured me it was edible. When I asked Lucia about it, she said to add it to my beans, that it tasted like meat. She was right. Years later, when I ate my first portobello mushroom, I immediately thought of *ok'ox,* the brown, spongy fungus that tasted like meat. Tuxes in the lead, 5 to 2.

A few days later Valeria Choc ran through the back door, not a scrap of clothing on, calling excitedly, "*Iguan,* Teacher! *Iguan!*" Dolores had spotted one while the family was bathing. Aaron carried his rifle down to the river, Valeria leading the way, and shot it. He gave it to Dolores, saying she should give us some after it was cooked, along with a few eggs, if it was a female. Dolores chopped it up and cooked it with *chile*—skin, toes, eggs, and all. The meat tasted like frog's legs, and the eggs—a whole string of them, each smaller than the previous one—tasted like the yolks of small, hard-boiled chicken eggs. Chocs closing the gap: 5 to 3.

Mateo found a tree in the bush filled with honey and sold the honey for five cents a pint. I tried to buy some, but he insisted on giving it to me. It was runny and slightly sour and full of bee body parts. Aaron said it came from the same stingless bees that produced black wax, and that the Maya had been gathering honey from them for thousands of years. Advantage Tuxes—6 to 3.

One morning a woman who had moved into the village while we were in Guatemala brought over some *tortillas* and a big bowl of barbecued pork. Her name was Juanita Bul. She spoke excellent English—another San Antonio Mopan—and said she was married to Jaime Bul. They had one son, too young to be in school. As soon as she spotted Thompson's book, she asked if she could look at it.

"I have seen this book before," she told me. "I like to sew, but some of the old patterns, women don't make like that anymore." She showed me photos of the embroidery that the Mopan women sewed around the neck and sleeves of their *huipiles* and sat on the bench for the next hour, totally absorbed in the book. When she gave it back, she showed me photos of the San Antonio men who worked for Thompson when he excavated Lubaantun in the 1930s. "My father, he knew these men. They were his neighbors. I could come back and look at this book again?"

"Of course." I didn't have any idea whose side she was on. We just enjoyed the pork.

Aaron happened to be home a few days later when Nicasio arrived, carrying a shoebox-sized package wrapped in *mox* leaves. "You like to eat? My brother Francisco shooted two like this." It was a curassow, a bird the size of a domestic turkey, sliced surgically in half by one adept stroke of a machete—plucked and ready for the pot. It was about seven pounds of meat, and pushed the Tuxes securely in the lead at 7 to 3.

"Yes, we like to eat this!" I said fervently. I had a lot of food obligations to repay. "Please tell Francisco that Teacher says thank you."

Nicasio grinned and galloped out the door.

Aaron, who had been catnapping in his hammock, looked at the package speculatively. "How are you going to cook that?" From his tone of voice I knew he was envisioning a succulent, skin-on roast turkey. But my failed bread experiment had made me leery of makeshift ovens.

"I'm going to make soup. Not *caldo*. Just plain old American-style soup."

He didn't try to talk me out of it.

After starting a fire, I severed the wing, drumstick, and thigh from the carcass—cutting fowl into portions I would have recognized in a supermarket was a newly acquired skill—so the meat would fit in the pot. I planned to add water, salt, black pepper, and onions, and that was it. No outlandish herbs or *chile* pepper. Just a nice, bland soup like the ones I'd grown up with.

Not ten minutes later, Lucia came in with Natalia, asking if she could buy some meat. I forked the drumstick out of the pot—Lucia probably liked the feet and I didn't—and carved out half the breast meat. When she tried to pay me, I refused. Seconds after they returned home, Natalia came back with two grapefruit and two limes.

I couldn't resist dipping a spoon into my "American" soup. Its meek, watery taste appalled me. I flung handfuls of thyme and *chile* peppers into the pot, along with some *samat* from our yard. Just before serving, I squeezed the juice of half a lime into each bowl.

"This is good," Aaron said around a mouthful of *caldo*, curassow, and flour *tortillas* dripping with butter. "But it's not how my mother makes turkey soup."

It wasn't how my mother made it, either.

One afternoon when I went down to bathe, the woman ahead of me suddenly stepped off the trail into the river without breaking stride. Thousands of single-minded army ants had converged on the path as far as the waterline. There were so many I couldn't see the ground underneath them. By the time I had bathed and got water—I could balance a full pail on my head all the way home now, but I still had to steady it with my hands—the ants were gone.

Aaron planned to leave in a couple of weeks for San Carlos to register for spring semester. He had lost nearly twenty pounds, but he felt and acted so much better that he might never have been sick at all. His main concern was building up his stamina, since he planned to walk part of the way in order to visit some Kekchi villages in Guatemala.

One cool, bright morning he decided it was a perfect time to map the village in order to determine who lived where. It would also give him some exercise. I was typing a letter to the University of Michigan requesting readmission for summer semester when Dolores brought over a string of fish. They were trout-sized, and she said Joaquin had caught them that morning using *chalam*. Although everybody who spoke English called *chalam* a "fish poison," the translation wasn't totally accurate. The Maya would dam up a portion of the river and toss in some *chalam* leaves. Whatever was in the leaves disoriented the fish, and they floated to the surface. At that point the fisherman waded in, clubbed them on the head, and tossed them into a henequen net, or *champa*.

In addition to the fresh fish, Dolores also brought a bowl of fish stew that smelled strongly of ground allspice. I thanked her and submerged the fresh fish in water, figuring they'd keep longer that way. When Aaron came back, we would eat the cooked fish for lunch.

In spite of the chilly morning—I had my sweater on—Dolores was naked from the waist up. I started to ask if she wasn't cold, but she interrupted me. "Where you husband could be?"

"He's map—drawing a map of the village so he knows where everybody lives."

She gave me a blank look.

"Gone."

"He come back soon?"

"Probably not."

She licked her dry lips. "You don't have baby?"

"No. Not yet." Aaron and I had agreed to wait until he finished his Ph.D. before starting a family.

"How you could do that?"

"Do what?"

Dolores looked at me as though I were retarded. "Make it so you don't have baby."

I reached for a cigarette. If I didn't know how to explain that Aaron was mapping who lived where in the village, I wasn't going to make much headway trying to explain birth control pills. "Don't the women use something?" I asked. "You know—bush medicine?"

Dolores made a noise of disgust in her throat. "Rum and lard." As I was wondering whether alcohol would pickle the sperm, she added, "It don't do nothing."

Buying condoms in Toledo District—where the only church was Catholic and Father Cull's word was law—would be nearly impossible, and I doubted she could convince Joaquin to use them even if she found some for sale. "In the United States, you'd need to see a doctor," I said slowly, thinking aloud. "He'd prescribe pills—that's what I use. But you can't buy them in Toledo District." I didn't think she could buy them in Belize City, either, even with a doctor's prescription—she didn't have the money. She probably didn't have enough money to see a doctor in the first place. She probably didn't *have* money, period. Her husband Joaquin had it.

"So you don't got nothing?"

"I'm sorry, Dolores. I wish I could help you."

Wordlessly she turned and walked out the door. Only then did I see the fresh welts crisscrossing her back.

Aaron decided to leave for Guatemala the following week. He didn't know how long he'd be gone. My twenty-first birthday was coming up, but his choices were leaving me here alone and registering for classes at San Carlos, or staying for my birthday and getting drafted. When I told him I was worried about him making the trip by himself, he admitted he had arranged for Manuel Xi from Crique Sarco to walk with him partway to Guatemala City. Just in case.

The villagers, it turned out, were worried, too, but not about Aaron. No good to leave your woman home alone, one-one, they all but told him outright. (The Maya said very few things outright.) I couldn't figure out what they thought might happen. Lone travelers sometimes came through the village, but the dogs set up such a ruckus it was highly unlikely that I'd have any unwelcome visitors. Since I had no intention of wandering around in the bush by myself, I wasn't concerned about *sisimitos*, and the *ixtabai* preferred men. I wasn't seriously worried about *obeah*, either. Whatever the black candle business had been about, it didn't involve us.

The day Aaron left, José Tux stopped by late in the afternoon. Since we both spoke beginner Spanish—a lot of hand gestures, everything in the present tense—we communicated fairly well. As José drank his coffee, he told me how glad he was that the children were learning to read and write. He was the only man in the village, quite probably the only man in Toledo District, polite enough to begin a conversation by praising his hostess.

Then he paid me another compliment—that Aaron and I had always been willing to eat the Indios' food. I nodded, pleased, thinking about the times we had visited people's houses and gamely choked down pigs' brains, *caldos* containing various unnamed innards, and flour *tortillas* wrapped around scraps from a cow's skull.

Finally, circuitously, José got around to the point of his visit: the villagers wanted to buy a *santo* of Santa Elena, their patron saint, and have a celebration. Did I think that was a good idea? I told him I thought it was a wonderful idea. A village-wide party would give people a reason to put the feud behind them. José nodded—that had been his intent. And another thing: the men wanted me to write a letter to the first minister of British Honduras, George Price, to let him know that they had elected an *alcalde*. I told him I'd be happy to write the letter.

Since it was now nearly dinnertime, José—who had said what he came to say—thanked me for the coffee, wished me a good evening, and left.

I had just started dinner when Paulina shuffled over, looking put-upon, followed by Valeria and Lute. All three sat on a bench and looked at me expectantly.

"Do you want something?" I asked Paulina.

"No, Teacher."

Valeria stuck her thumb in her mouth. Finally Lute said, "Make we stay with you, Teacher." They had obviously been ordered here by Dolores, who wanted to make sure that *somebody* from the Choc faction was with me, especially since my previous visitor had been a Tux.

I sighed. "Are you hungry?"

"No, Teacher," they said in unison.

Good. At least Dolores didn't expect me to feed them.

The kids alternately watched me eat dinner and flipped through magazines until I decided I was going to bed. "Time to leave," I said briskly, clapping my hands in dismissal. Three pairs of eyes locked onto mine. Nobody moved. "Stay" apparently meant "stay the night." How were a little girl, her eight-year-old brother, and her thirteen-year-old sister going to protect me? And from what? They probably didn't know either. In resignation I gave them Aaron's big sleeping bag and told them they could sleep in his hammock.

Sometime in the middle of the night, I woke up to see a flashlight beam darting along the floor. I caught my breath and sat up. Lute had turned Aaron's flashlight on, and in the ring of light I saw something scuttle sideways, something insectlike and sand-colored. It was a scorpion, the first I had ever seen. Handing the flashlight to Paulina, Lute crept across the floor, picked up the flat "warming rock" I kept next to the fireplace, and dropped it on the scorpion. His sisters sucked in their breath in admiration, and I vowed never again to put my sneakers on without looking inside first. Lute climbed back into Aaron's hammock and we all went back to sleep.

After school the following afternoon, Maxiana came over with fresh *tortillas* and a bowl of chicken in *samat*. She said her father had sent her over to keep me company. After we ate I stretched out in my hammock with a book of Aesop's fables in Spanish that I had bought in Guatemala City.

"Teacher, your hammock," said Maxiana, frowning.

"What about my hammock?"

"Is too short. Here, I show you."

Mystified, I climbed to my feet. Standing on a *banco*, Maxiana patiently untied the knots at the foot end of the hammock and then retied them to the next beam. That didn't make the hammock any longer, but it was farther off the floor and formed a more gentle curve. I wouldn't wake up in the bottom of my hammock curled into a fetal position any more. How simple. How life changing.

"Maxiana, why is everybody so worried about me?"

"We like you, Teacher."

"Well, thank you. I like you, too. But nothing's going to happen to me."

"One lady, alone in her house—no good."

"But *why*?"

Just then Paulina and Valeria showed up, Paulina looking even more sullen; that night the three girls shared Aaron's hammock. John Oh, Juan's handsome young son, seemed to be living with the Chocs, and I wondered whether Paulina would ordinarily be sharing *his* hammock.

It was Maxiana who explained the facts of life to me. No widow ever lived by herself—she moved in with one of her married children. If her children didn't live nearby, or if she had no sisters or brothers willing to take her in, she might consent to be some hard-working man's second wife. Being female and alone was bad luck—lone women *attracted* bad luck. If the villagers let me stay by myself, something bad was sure to happen.

I assured Maxiana that nothing would happen, and that I didn't want to hear any more stories. I could have saved my breath. The third night Maxiana and Natalia arrived as soon as I came back from bathing. They carried dinner—chicken *caldo*, *tortillas*, and candy that Maxiana's mother had made from sugarcane syrup and toasted sesame seeds. It crackled like peanut brittle. The kids called it *wangla*.

Just before I blew out the kerosene lamp, Lute slipped in the front door. "My mother say I spend the night with you," he announced. He didn't seem at all put out by the prospect of sleeping in a sleeping bag with two girls, although Maxiana shot him a dirty look when she thought I wasn't watching.

Evaristo stopped by to say the men wanted to write their letter to George Price. He was all dressed up—hair carefully parted and combed, trousers creased, shoes and socks, a belt. He looked tense and out of sorts.

"Something wrong?" I asked as I gathered up my things.

"I go to San Antonio to borrow money from my uncle, so I can buy Pavian Chen's old house. He builded it maybe three years ago, before he moved, and I want to buy it for the wood—I don't want to live there. But my uncle say he's not a rich man, just a poor Indian living out in the bush, like me. So I got to build a house by myself."

"Won't José help you?"

Evaristo relaxed long enough to grin at me. "When José come back from selling beans, he was drunk-drunk and belittled me. So I take Aleja and Fidel to my father's house. José won't be at the meeting. He got *goma* too bad."

"What's *goma*?"

Evaristo's grin widened. "Hangover."

"Shouldn't somebody else be here?" I blurted out. "Like Lucia?"

At that he laughed outright. "Yes, my sister get vexed with me, I talk with you one-one. When I first came back, everybody wanted me to get married quick-time. A man like me, not married, is a threat to other men's wives."

With Evaristo's looks and confidence, he had clearly been a ladies' man. Lucia had good reason to worry. But then there was Silvaria's brother, Julian Jimenez, also not married. I doubted he was a threat to anybody's wife, but I could be wrong. "So that's why you're in such a hurry to build your house."

"Yes. I have my family, it's time I have my own house. Besides, I bought Aleja some dresses, but Ana, she refuse to let Aleja wear them. She says they're too short."

It was my turn to laugh. I'd had similar conversations with my own mother.

Evaristo walked ahead of me to school, carrying my typewriter. I carried a pen and paper and the kerosene lamp. Men from both factions had already assembled inside. Clearing a spot on the table, I turned up the wick in the lamp. In the flickering light I rolled a sheet of paper into my typewriter. I typed the date, "Rio Blanco, Toledo District, British Honduras," skipped two lines, and typed "Dear Honourable Sir." Then I waited for instructions.

Evaristo, dressed in his *ladino* Sunday best, looked as though he belonged to a difference class of people than these thin, barefoot men in tattered shirts and patched, ill-fitting pants. But they argued back and forth as equals, deciding how best to present their case. When they had agreed on what they wanted to say, they dictated the letter to Evaristo, who translated it into English.

Nearly two dozen men were in the room. I typed everybody's name at the end of the letter, then read the names aloud to make sure I hadn't missed anybody. José Ical, who spoke a little Spanish, reminded me that four men weren't here, including José Tux. I had to type in their names, too.

"Why? They didn't write this letter."

"But they're part of the village," José explained patiently, in Spanish. "Their names must be on the letter. The letter comes from the whole village."

I looked at Crispino. Somebody translated my question. He looked back at me and nodded. I turned to Evaristo. He nodded, too.

"Okay, José Tux. Who else?"

Since John Oh had agreed to take the letter to San Antonio the next morning—he had to get his birth certificate from Father Cull in order to marry Paulina—my last official act was to forge four crosses for the four absent citizens. Of all the men present, only Evaristo and Leonardo Ical could write their names. Silently I made a vow. By the time I left, all the kids in school except the very youngest, who were still struggling with capital letters, would be able to sign their names.

XXXXXXXXXXXXXXXXXXXXXXXXXXXXXXXXXXXXXXXXXXXXXXXXXXXXXXXX

SESAME COCONUT CRUNCH

Maxiana introduced me to *wangla*, and many years later Francisca Bardalez was kind enough to re-create the recipe for me in her kitchen in Big Falls.

The Kekchi call sesame seeds *hoholin*; *wangla* is the candy. But most Belizeans call the seeds themselves *wangla* and use them in confections of all kinds. Since sesame seeds are expensive in the States, I use a mixture of sesame seeds (or pecans) and coconut. The candy is so easy to make and takes so little time that it's worthwhile experimenting with other nuts, including the obvious one—salted peanuts.

2 cups sugar

1 cup sesame seeds

1 cup sweetened dried, flaked coconut

In a small cast-iron skillet, lightly brown the sesame seeds. Remove them to a paper towel.

Butter a cookie sheet and pour the sugar into a medium-size nonstick frying pan. Cook uncovered over low heat, stirring constantly. As soon as all the sugar is dissolved (it should be light brown), remove it from the heat. Working quickly, add the sesame seeds and coconut and stir until each flake of coconut is well coated.

Pour mixture on the cookie sheet, making sure to tip the frying pan away from you. (Remember—the candy is 30-plus degrees hotter than boiling water.) Do not scrape the bottom because the mixture is hottest there and has probably crystallized.

When the candy is cool, break it into pieces.

Feeds 1–2 sugar addicts.

FIFTEEN

*"You Need a
Second Husband"*

I didn't plan to celebrate my twenty-first birthday. Who would I celebrate with? Aaron was still in Guatemala, and the Maya didn't understand the importance of this particular rite of passage, since most girls were married at fourteen and mothers at fifteen.

I got up early, as usual, lit a fire, and cooked breakfast. As usual. Just another ordinary day in the bush. I hadn't even gotten a birthday card from my parents. But it *wasn't* an ordinary day. In my culture turning twenty-one was a big deal—the first day of my life as an adult. I not only wanted to celebrate, I wanted company.

So I washed my face, laced up my sneakers, tied both doors closed, and walked the twenty miles to San Antonio, where I hitched a ride from a shopkeeper on his way to PG. He dropped me off on Don Owen-Lewis's doorstep, where I announced I'd come to spend my birthday with him. Don, who was eagerly anticipating his move to Big Falls, admitted he had already started packing. We would both celebrate!

That night Cirila, the kids, Don, and I ate dinner in much less time than it had taken Cirila to prepare it, the fate of all good cooking: *escabeche*, rice, and flour *tortillas*, with fresh pineapple for dessert. After

Cirila and I finished the dishes, she sent the kids to bed and left me and Don in the living room to talk. Aaron had been right—this appeared to be standard practice among both Mopan and Kekchi Maya. Whenever we visited Lucia and Crispino in the evening, Lucia withdrew to the kitchen, although their house was so small she could hear our conversation effortlessly and often interjected comments—usually quite pointed ones. Sometimes I stayed with Aaron. Sometimes I joined her and Natalia in the kitchen.

"What's that smell?" I asked Don, rubbing my road-weary feet—they weren't accustomed to four-hour jaunts. A sweet, exotic scent drifted in through the screened windows.

"Night-blooming jasmine," Don replied. "Feet hurt?"

I glanced at him suspiciously. If they didn't hurt, why would I be massaging them? "In Rio Blanco the scent wakes me out of a sound sleep sometimes. Some of the women plant flowers around the *milpas.*" Dolores, to my surprise, was one of them. "The only ones I recognize are poinsettias and birds of paradise."

Don and I were chain-smoking Colonials and drinking rum. He had turned the generator off for the night, and the Coleman lantern threw dramatic, exaggerated shadows on the walls. "The Kekchi like pretty things as a rule, although I doubt your husband would agree." Don raised the rum bottle and looked at me.

I extended my glass. "He wouldn't?" Aaron and I had never talked about "pretty things," even though Cirila kept hibiscus blossoms in small vases throughout the house. Whenever Don came back from the bush, he brought her wild orchids.

"He thinks the Kekchi have no artistic sense, no appreciation of beauty," Don said, filling both our glasses. "He's always going on about the baskets they make and pointing out how functional they are. Same with the pottery—no designs, very little use of color. Strictly utilitarian."

"But look at their music," I protested. "We have an entire orchestra in Rio Blanco! Several men play the violin or viola—I can't tell the difference—Alejandro Mijangre plays the flute, José Ical plays the *marimba*, and Sebastian Garcia plays the harp. I've heard somebody playing a guitar, too, but I don't know who it is. The music is different from ours, but it's beautiful. And they're all skillful musicians, especially Sebastian."

Don grinned.

"Are you humbugging me?" I demanded.

"Now why would I do that? Ask him yourself. 'No artistic sense.' That's what he keeps telling me."

"Or the women's clothes," I said indignantly, downing another swallow of rum. "A Kekchi skirt must be insanely hard to weave with all those different colors. Even their food can be artistic. Look at what they start with. Corn. And look at how many dishes they make out of it! I can think of at least half a dozen right off the top of my head, and no two women cook them the same way!"

Don shrugged elaborately and crossed his arms behind his head. "You'll get no argument from me."

I slumped in my chair. I would from Aaron—he'd tell me sewing and cooking were women's work, and that I was stretching the point to call any of it "artistic." "How long did it take them to accept you?" I asked in a small voice.

"Not very long, really. But I was lucky."

"Because you spoke the language?"

"Well, that helped. But mainly it was because of a silly little incident that happened shortly after I moved here from Crique Sarco. I'd just got the Toyota, you see, and I drove into PG one day to pick up supplies. And, as usual, I ended up carrying some Kekchi passengers. Well. I finished my shopping and I'm sitting there in the Toyota, waiting. I'd told them, 'Now don't make me late, goddamn it,' and of course it was 'Oh, no, Mr. Lewis, we'll be *right* back.'

"So here I was, parked in front of one of the shops, no sign of the silly buggers anywhere, so I went inside and bought a small box of raisins. I'm very fond of raisins and don't often have the chance to eat them, but since I was sitting here anyway, waiting, why not?

"So. I'm in the Toyota, tossing down raisins. And here come the Kekchi, who don't eat raisins. They don't even know what a raisin is. But there's a small, very hot red pepper that grows here. The women dry them before using them, and they turn dark red, almost purple.

"Anyway, I'm driving back to Machaca, eating raisins, gesturing, talking about this and that, and all of a sudden I realize it's quiet as a goddamn tomb behind me. Nobody's saying a word. Finally I looked in the rear-view mirror. Have you ever had a dog watch you eat? Watch you poke your fork into the meat, raise it up, put it in your mouth? That's what this lot was doing. They thought I was eating *chile* peppers! Oh, God, but I laughed! And d'you know, from that moment on, nobody questioned a thing. I could have asked them to build a ladder to the moon and they'd have tried to do it, just because they thought by God, this one's *mucho hombre*, and if he says we can build a ladder to the moon, we bloody well *can*.

"You've heard that, haven't you, when somebody gets drunk? *Soy hombre! Soy mucho hombre!* Well, that's what they thought I was. Quite the man." Don laughed, pleased with himself, pleased with life.

I laughed, too, but I kept wondering when the Maya would accept *me*.

The next morning I woke up late. My head throbbed, my tongue felt coated with algae, and my feet were so sore I could hardly get out of bed.

I had just finished my third cup of coffee—breakfast smelled dangerous—when Alfonso Godoy from the Forestry Department stopped by. He was a well-fed, mustachioed *ladino* wearing a gold pinky ring, his dark hair gleaming with hair oil. He was on his way to San Antonio. Did Mr. Lewis need anything? he asked, smiling broadly.

"No, but this footsore young *señora* needs a ride to San Antonio," Don told him, straight-faced. "D'you think you can do that for her, Alfonso?"

Alfonso stroked his mustache between his thumb and index finger and thought he could.

"What a coincidence he stopped by!" Don marveled, giving me a crooked grin. "Now all you have to do is walk back from San Antonio—be home before you know it. Safe trip and all that."

If it was a coincidence, I was Joan of Arc. I felt like throwing my arms around Don's neck and kissing him, but it would have embarrassed him.

Alfonso Godoy was so overwhelmed by the solemnity of his duty that he didn't say a word to me. His hair oil was as strong as the night-blooming jasmine but not nearly as pleasant. I was praying that last night's dinner would stay put when Alfonso took a sudden, unscheduled detour into the bush and pulled up next to a thatched-roof shelter. A small sign identified it as the property of the Forestry Department.

"Where are we? Why did you stop?"

Without answering he opened the door on my side and motioned for me to get out. As I limped after him up to a raised wooden platform, a crowd of men appeared silently out of the jungle in pairs and small groups. They crowded around the foot of the platform, which held several uncomfortable-looking wooden chairs. After seating me in one of them, Alfonso sat down beside me and delivered a brief speech, first in Spanish, then in English. The men were part of a work crew—most carried machetes—and Alfonso explained what he wanted them to do while he drove me to San Antonio.

Why had he detoured to make this speech? I wondered. The men didn't care where he was taking me.

Alfonso made a big show of helping me back to the Land Rover. As soon as he started the engine, I gagged. "Alfonso, may I open the window, please?" Unhappily he touched his hair, then nodded. For the rest of the trip, I knelt on the front seat with my head out the window, nose sniffing the wind like a hound. Now that I wasn't half delirious from hair oil fumes, I understood why Alfonso had called the meeting. He wanted his men to see me sitting next to him, to realize that he had been given the honor of escorting me back to where I lived. He had been showing me off.

In silence Alfonso drove me through San Antonio, past Santa Cruz, and right up to the Rio Blanco River. I thanked him profusely—I felt very flattered—gave him some of the pineapple Cirila had sent back with me, and thanked him again. One short hike and I was home. An adult.

At last.

"The old lady that live by Sebastian, she say Natalia going die," Lucia told me, her voice a strained monotone.

Natalia slumped listlessly on the bench in front of me as I examined her. I'd been home less than a week, and it was late afternoon, almost dinnertime. "That old lady talks nonsense," I told Lucia sharply. "Don't listen to her."

Lucia didn't answer.

Natalia's face was dirty, her dress torn, her elbows scraped and bloody. Most of the bruises looked superficial, but her hair was matted with blood and I couldn't tell where it was coming from.

"What happened, exactly?" I asked Lucia.

She said that Natalia had been on her way back from Garcia's house when a dog chased one of their pigs. The pig, trying to escape, had knocked Natalia down and trampled her.

Finally I discovered the source of the bleeding—a deep, inch-long gash behind Natalia's left ear. Hoping that I was doing what a doctor would, I snipped off her hair around the cut, told her she was a good girl, swabbed the wound with peroxide, applied a bandage, prescribed half a codeine, and told her she was a good girl again.

The cut was clean. The problem was Natalia—she appeared to be in shock. I'd never had a head wound as a kid, unless I counted the time I fell off a galloping horse (the saddle had slipped) and knocked myself out. What were the warning signs of concussion? Did Natalia have any?

"She'll be fine," I assured Lucia cheerily. "She probably won't feel like doing much the rest of the day, though."

Lucia nodded, her face carefully composed. All that gave her away was the sweat on her upper lip. Crispino had a son by an earlier marriage, but Natalia was their only living child—according to Father Cull, they had buried four others. As Lucia and Natalia walked out the door, the little girl wobbled like a drunk. I hoped fervently that what I'd told Lucia about the old lady was true.

That night only Maxiana stayed with me.

The following morning Lucia and Natalia came back, Natalia clinging to her mother's hand. She had been delirious during the night, Lucia told me—not the best news I'd ever heard. Carefully I removed the bandage, holding my breath as I tried not to pull her hair out with the adhesive. The wound was deeper than I remembered, but to my relief it looked absolutely clean. I gave Natalia another half a codeine, dabbed more peroxide on her scalp, and rebandaged the cut.

"I'm pretty sure she's all right," I told Lucia. "The wound isn't infected. It will take a while to heal, though." What bothered me was Natalia's passivity. Normally she was very independent, especially for a girl—smart and a little sassy, just like the daughter I hoped to have one day. Maybe half a codeine was too much. Maybe she *did* have a concussion. "Have you thought about taking her to the nurse?"

Lucia didn't bother answering. And in all honesty—having just made the trek to San Antonio myself—I knew it was physically demanding, especially for a nine-year-old with a head injury.

The next morning Natalia came over alone, carrying half a dozen chicken *tamales* and some dried chickpeas. The cut was healing fine, but she still acted as though she were sleepwalking.

"Does your head hurt?" I asked.

Natalia stared at the ground.

"Do you hurt anywhere else?"

A small, negative headshake.

I knelt in front of her and smoothed back the fine hair around her face. "Good morning, Natalia," I said in my "Teacher" voice. "How are you today?" Then I switched to a little girl's falsetto. "I am well, Teacher, thank you. And how are *you*?" We had gone over the words in class—how to greet people in English, how to say good-bye—but I couldn't coax her into saying them.

The following day Lucia came to do laundry alone.

"Lucia—oh, my God! Where's Natalia? Is she all right?"

"When she fall, she lose she soul," Lucia said, her voice matter-of-fact, as if this happened all the time. "Is call it *espanto*. Crispino and me, we take she to Laura in Pueblo Viejo. Laura going keep Natalia one week."

Laura was the *curandera*. The Maya believed that if somebody was injured or badly frightened—women were particularly vulnerable—her soul left her body but continued to hover around. It was the *curandera*'s job to coax Natalia's frightened soul back into her body.

As soon as Lucia left, I looked up *espanto* in my Spanish/English dictionary. Its first meaning was "fright." Its second and less reassuring meaning was "ghost."

"Teacher!" Lute raced through my back door, panting and out of breath.

I looked up from my hammock. It was my lunch hour, and I was reading one of Don's books called *Amazon Town: Man in the Tropics* by Charles Wagley, who maintained that people needed more vitamin B in the tropics than they did elsewhere, and that foods containing it, such as pork, had less of it than they did in temperate climates. Too bad we hadn't known that when Aaron's leg first started bothering him. "What is it, Lute?"

He grabbed a *Dick and Jane* book and flipped through the pages. When he found what he was looking for, he shoved the book under my nose. It was the chapter where Dick and Jane's parents take them to the zoo.

"You eat like this?" He pointed to the picture of a rhinoceros.

"We don't have those here, Lute. They live in Africa."

"No, Teacher! My father kill one in his *milpa*! You want some meat? I get you some!"

Rhinos *did* live in Africa, didn't they? Suddenly I had my doubts. I'd been wrong about the vampire bats. "Yes, I would like some meat."

Lute tugged on my arm. "Then come with me to my house, talk to my mother. Please, Teacher?"

I let Lute lead me by the hand to petition Dolores, who said I could have meat if I excused Lute from school to help his father. She said the English name of the animal was mountain cow, but the Maya called it *tsimin che*, bush horse. I much preferred the "cow" designation.

Shortly after I let school out, Lute stumbled through my door again, his clothes smeared with blood, carrying a lump of meat wrapped in *mox* leaves. He was followed by Gonzolo Ical, who was carrying—a foot? It had four hard toenails that looked very much like ponies' hooves, but all on the same foot. I'd never seen anything like it.

After Lute handed me the meat, he took possession of the foot. He was going to keep it, he said proudly. Then Micalia materialized in my kitchen along with Lucia, Goyita, Paulina, and Juanita Bul, the San Antonio woman interested in embroidered *huipil* designs.

"Juanita, how do you cook this?" I asked.

She looked at me, her expression serious. "We don't eat it."

I turned to Lucia, who shrugged. "*Pues*, I don't know. I never eat like so."

"Paulina?"

Paulina shrugged, too. "I don't know, Teacher."

All these women in my kitchen, all claiming they didn't eat mountain cow.

I took another look at the foot. By now it had attracted Hermalinda and Ambrosia Ical, Epijenia Garcia, and half a dozen men.

"Ambrosia. Are you taking some home to your mother?"

"No, Teacher. We never eat mountain cow."

Even if it was a rhino—which I doubted—carnivores like lions and humans ate them. I'd seen enough Disney documentaries to know that. So why didn't the Maya, who lived here?

I unwrapped the *mox* leaves and looked dubiously at the meat. It was bright red with no fat, connective tissue, or bones. All meat—and, apparently, all mine. I reviewed my arguments again. I—am a carnivore. (Okay, omnivore.) This "mountain cow"—is an herbivore. (Anything that ate corn and wasn't a bird or a bug qualified as an herbivore in my book.) Omnivores eat herbivores. What was I not getting here?

After Lute carried the foot home in triumph and the last visitor had drifted away, I pondered my options. It seemed a shame to throw out a piece of meat just because half a dozen women were reluctant to eat it. I had lived here long enough that the Maya philosophy of waste not, want not had become part of my own thinking—especially when it came to meat.

I cut off a steak-sized slice and seared it in lard over a hot fire. I wasn't willing to risk rare, but I'd risk pink. The meat tasted like filet mignon. I cut off a second, bigger slice. It was even tastier than the first one.

The next morning Lucia came over carrying a bowl of black bean *caldo*, but it was an excuse. "You eat the mountain cow?"

"Yes, and it was very good. You sure you don't want some?"

She looked me up and down. I didn't have a fever, I wasn't writhing in pain, and I hadn't broken out in spots. "Maybe little bit."

I gave her about a third of the meat I had left and wondered what to do with the rest. I knew I should ask Ana Tux how to smoke it, since I'd seen meat drying over her fire. But my feet were still tender, and I didn't feel like walking a mile to her house and back in order to find out. After a breakfast of scrambled eggs and mountain cow steak, I diced the remaining meat into stew-sized pieces and lined them up on top of my machete blade, directly over the banked coals, the only way I could think of to smoke the meat. I left them that way when I went to class.

At lunchtime I stoked the fire again. I smoked the meat the rest of the afternoon, and that night I heated a few pieces in the frying pan with a little lard. Salted and rolled into a hot *tortilla*, the smoke-flavored meat was delicious. But I was unwilling to trust my drying methods past the fourth day—the temperature was already in the eighties.

The mountain cow turned out to be a tapir. A single animal could destroy a *milpa* in one night, and corn was their favorite food. But because tapirs are nocturnal, the Maya seldom caught them in the act of eating it. That was the only reason the women had been reluctant to accept the meat. They had told me the truth—they'd never eaten tapir before.

Luckily I never thought of consulting J. Eric Thompson, who contends that "[t]he outstanding non-edible animals are the jaguar (*balam*) [and] the tapir, also known locally as the mountain cow." In reality, if the Maya were really desperate for meat, they'd eat even jaguar. So would the Creoles, as I discovered years later when Gail Miller of the Belize Forums gave me a cookbook called *Silly Bug and Bittle Recipes*, 4th ed. (Crooked Tree Village Creative Woman's Group Cookbook, 2004.) One recipe calls for a skinned "tiger" paw (all Belizeans call the jaguar "tiger") and "1 set of tiger equipment scraped clean and diced." The recipe is for Tiger Prick Soup.

The third week after Aaron left I ran out of firewood. Except for a few big pieces I would have to split, I didn't even have kindling. Aaron also hadn't gotten around to cutting the weeds around the house, so I did, using his machete. I was getting fairly proficient with one. After I finished I borrowed an ax from Lucia. But I wasn't nearly as good at chopping wood, and managed to get two trophy-sized blisters, one on each hand, without splitting a single log.

That afternoon Crispino backed in a load of wood for me and split the big pieces. Luis, Maxiana's younger brother, stacked an armload of balsa wood inside my back door for kindling. The wood was so soft I could split it with a table knife. I made another batch of *comal* cookies and delivered them to Lucia and Candelaria, to say thank you.

The following morning after breakfast, I grabbed the toilet paper and slid my feet into an unlaced pair of sneakers I kept in the corner to go bush. I should have learned my lesson when I saw the scorpion Lute killed. I couldn't get my right foot all the way into my sneaker. There was an obstruction in the toe, something soft and yielding. I slid my foot out, and a plate-sized tarantula scrambled over my foot.

I screamed. The spider rocked back on six of its eight hairy legs and waved the front two as if daring me to come closer. This one wasn't getting away, I vowed, picking up Aaron's machete. I held it over my head in both hands like a broadsword, brought it down directly in front of me, and sliced the tarantula in half. Using the machete blade to scrape up its remains, I walked out the door yelling "Breakfast!" and tossed them to Micalia's chickens.

When Father Cull stopped by on his monthly visit, he commented in my ledger book about the "remarkable progress" the kids were making and told me I'd be responsible for getting them through their first communion. I was too surprised to ask how.

After thinking it over, I walked to the schoolhouse that night while the Maya made their confessions and waited for them to finish. I had a bandana that I sometimes wore as a sweatband, and when Father Cull and I were the only people in the room, I tied it over my head kerchief-style and asked if he would hear my confession.

He pulled back as though I had walked through the door naked. "I can't do that—you're not Catholic!" His face was ruddy in the lantern light; I think he was embarrassed for me. "When can you have the children ready for their first communion?"

"Well, that's what I'm trying to do. I understand they have to confess before they take their first communion, and I thought I'd have a better idea what's involved if—"

"I'll send you some pamphlets."

So much for rehearsal.

Two days later Lucia and Crispino came to visit after dinner. Behind them was Natalia. She flashed me a shy grin. I wanted to grab her and tell her how beautiful she was and that I'd missed her. Instead I treated her the way her mother probably had—I teased her. "How's the girl with the *cau li holom*?" How's the girl with the hard head?

"Good evening, Teacher. My head is good. And your head?"

"My head is good, too. When did you come home?"

"Yesterday, with my father."

Lucia explained that Crispino and Joaquin had carried Father Cull's church paraphernalia to Pueblo Viejo, his next stop. As soon as Natalia saw her father, she begged to go back with him—her soul had been restored and she was ready to go home. The gash behind her ear was completely healed.

I had just put a pot of water over the ritual fire to make the ritual cups of coffee when big Julian, Sylvaria's brother—the one who had worked in Scotland during World War II—shuffled in. "Good evening, Missus." He looked nervous.

"Julian, why so dressed up? You have shoes on—and a tie!" And wool trousers with a crease in them! "Would you like some coffee?"

"Yes, Missus. Thank you."

Only then did he seem to notice I had other visitors. After greeting Lucia and Crispino, he checked to see that his fly was buttoned before he sat down. Aaron had asked him once why he didn't get married—did he plan to live with Silvaria the rest of his life? He answered by saying that if he married, his wife would want new clothes, and once he bought her new clothes, she would leave. This sounded so far-fetched we wondered if it had actually happened to him.

He climbed to his feet again. "I'm going, Missus. I come back some other time."

As he disappeared out the back door, Mateo Ical sauntered in through the front door.

I sighed. Would *Mateo* like coffee?

Yes, he would. While I waited for the water to boil, he made himself comfortable in my hammock and started talking to Crispino. While Father Cull and the bishop of British Honduras were here, Saturnino, his oldest child, would be confirmed. Did Crispino know what confirmation involved and how much it cost?

Confirmation? I thought. The bishop of British Honduras? What else had Father Cull neglected to tell me?

Crispino relayed what he knew about confirmation. To my surprise I could follow the conversation fairly well, although I still couldn't speak more than nine words of Kekchi. When Crispino said that Saturnino would receive an additional name afterward, Mateo asked what name they had given Natalia. Crispino thought for a minute but was unable to recall it. Still speaking Kekchi, he asked Natalia what her name was.

Without hesitation she answered, in English, "My name is Natalia

Bah." Everybody laughed, especially Teacher, who had taught her to say those words.

Then the conversation drifted to Evaristo's new house. Mateo asked if Evaristo intended to have it blessed. Crispino said yes, he did. Mateo agreed that was smart. He'd heard of a man in San Antonio who had gone crazy because he hadn't gotten his new house blessed, and it was haunted by animals. When Father Cull blessed it, babies and monkeys ran out.

Silently I spooned *café listo* into my speckled blue and white mugs. So Natalia's soul had returned from the land of the spirits, and Father Cull blessed houses as a sideline. What next?

I passed coffee around, and the men continued to talk about San Antonio. Since Mateo was in my hammock, I sat on a bench near the door. Natalia immediately climbed in my lap, something she did all the time when her parents visited. My coffee was halfway to my lips when Lucia hissed at her daughter. Obediently Natalia slid down and went back to her mother.

What had I done wrong this time? Now that Natalia had her soul restored, she couldn't sit in my lap anymore?

True to his word, Julian came back the following evening. He was wearing the same clothes he'd worn previously, a long-sleeved shirt, wool trousers, and a tie. Like Evaristo he was tall for a Maya, long-legged and lean, but unlike Evaristo he had no clothes sense, very few teeth, and no curiosity about his place in the world—either the natural one or the spiritual one.

After pouring coffee for the two of us, I offered him a cigarette. He accepted, and we reclined in our respective hammocks, both doors open to catch any stray breeze, smoking and chatting about how his sister couldn't seem to have girl babies and how Cresencio and little Julian had to scrub the dirty dishes in the river using sand and ashes. That wasn't a suitable job for *boys*, he insisted.

Good for you, Silvaria, I thought.

After finishing his coffee Julian asked offhandedly, "Your husband not back yet?"

"No, not yet. Soon, though."

Julian looked past me, seemingly debating something. He must have been seventeen or eighteen when he went to Scotland, and World War II ended in 1945, so he'd been back here eighteen years. Julian was probably in his late thirties—Don's age. He looked fifty.

"Maybe your husband gone and left you," Julian observed, still not looking at me.

"No, he just went to Guatemala City."

"What is your first name, Missus?"

The only other person who had asked me my name was Lucia. When I told Julian, he wanted to know how old I was. I told him that, too.

"You think about taking one next husband?" he asked.

"Why would I want to do that? One is plenty." I didn't add that I was finding life much more interesting *without* a husband.

"No, Missus Joan. You need a number-two husband. The one you got, he isn't here now."

Julian's decades-old trousers, how nervous he'd been yesterday—I should have seen this coming. "He'll be back," I said, trying to keep a straight face.

"You shouldn't be alone so much," Julian continued earnestly. "You need one husband *here*—then you could stay in Rio Blanco. Nobody wants you to leave."

"I have to cook dinner now, Julian. I think you'd better go." If this conversation went on any longer I was going to start laughing.

Julian left. But I had to tell somebody—it wasn't every day that a man volunteered to be your second husband—so I sat down to write Barbara.

But I couldn't get started. In perplexity I lit a cigarette and stared into the gathering darkness. Julian hadn't pulled me behind somebody's hog pen and tried to wrestle my underpants off. Instead, he had dressed in his best clothes and come courting. Twice. Even if his intentions weren't honorable, strictly speaking, his actions had been. No matter how laughable I thought the situation was, I couldn't laugh at *him*. I'd write to Barbara about something else.

xxxxxxxxxxxxxxxxxxxxxxxxxxxxxxxxxxxxxxxxxxxxxxxxxxxxxxxxxxx

CHICKPEA SOUP WITH *CILANTRO* AND PASTA

The Maya cooked all beans more or less the same way, but I like the taste of *garbanzos* more than I do other dried beans. I still occasionally prepare them, particularly if they taste like something else. Garlic, for example. Add a cup of cooked, diced chicken and you have a meal.

> ¼ cup olive oil
> 2 cloves garlic, crushed
> 6 cups chicken stock
> ½ cup dry pasta, preferably small shells or elbows
> 2 cups cooked chickpeas (*garbanzo* beans)
> 2 tablespoons fresh *cilantro*
> salt and black pepper to taste

Heat the olive oil slowly in a large, heavy pot. Add the garlic and sauté until translucent. (Do not let the garlic brown.) Add the stock and turn heat to high. As soon as the stock comes to a boil, add the pasta and cook according to package directions. When the pasta is al dente, add the chickpeas, *cilantro*, salt, and black pepper, and cook until heated through.

Serves 4 people.

SIXTEEN

The Earth Is a Cornfield

One sultry March afternoon, Mateo, Joaquin, and Jesús raced each other through the back door of my house like teenagers. But instead of greeting me, they crowded around the front door and stared intently at the trail. Since this usually meant a stranger was on his way through, I put my book down—I was halfway through Simone de Beauvoir's *The Second Sex*, a provocative discussion of the "otherness" of women—and joined them. Sure enough. The stranger was taller than the Maya men accompanying him, wore laced paratrooper boots, and toted a heavy rucksack.

When Aaron saw me, he broke into a shambling run, and I shoved past the onlookers in my doorway. But at the last second, surrounded by the men, he pulled back, then relented just as I pulled back. I walked next to him to the house, thinking that he'd been gone almost a month. We had wanted to kiss—we should have kissed. *One* of us should have insisted.

"What a trip!" Aaron slung his rucksack on the table, sat down, and unlaced his boots. All the men following him and the men who had watched his arrival from our house gathered around him in an expectant semicircle.

"Are you legal?" I asked, crouching at the fireplace, match in hand.

"As far as San Carlos is concerned, yes. We'll know about my draft board by next month, if I'm lucky."

"I missed you," I said softly.

"I missed you, too." With a grunt Aaron pulled his socks off and examined his toes. "I picked up some kind of jungle rot—my skin is sloughing off. Throw these into the fire, will you? Lucia won't want to get close enough to them to wash them."

"Oh, I almost forgot! We both got readmitted to Michigan for summer term."

"Great!" Aaron straightened in his chair. "That means we can start wrapping things up here."

"Start wrap—but *why*? Summer school doesn't start until June!"

"We should be ready to leave in May, just in case San Carlos screws up again and we have to go back to Guatemala City."

"But I'm not ready to leave yet! I haven't taught the kids everything they need to know. I'm not *finished* here!"

The men crowded closer.

"Well, I am. I've visited every Kekchi-speaking village in British Honduras and conducted dozens of interviews in Guatemala. All I have to do to keep San Carlos happy is write an eighty-page report for *Guatemala indígena* before the end of the semester. Then we can pack up and get the hell out of here."

He was right about his socks. When they caught fire, the smell was so rank I had to move away. Why were Aaron and I willing to fight in front of onlookers but hadn't been willing to kiss?

Aaron had barely been home a week when Evaristo invited us to the blessing of his new house.

"Is Father Cull here?" I asked in astonishment. It was much too early for his monthly visit.

"No. I asked José to bless my house. You could bring your clock, Missus? José say he needs to know when midnight comes."

After dinner Aaron and I walked to the Tuxes' house, carrying the alarm clock, which Ana set on the *santos* table along with five candles. The candles had been made from the wax of the stingless bees, which was black. As Aaron kept reminding me, the Maya—who made their own candles—were pragmatists. The couple in the schoolhouse that night had probably burned black candles for the same reason Ana Tux was burning them tonight. Black was the only color they had.

In quick succession Ana beheaded, plucked, and dismembered three chickens and threw them into a huge pot boiling over the fire. Aleja, big-eyed and bashful, served us coffee. For the next few hours, Aaron and the menfolk conversed in Kekchi while I talked to the children. Periodically I glanced at the clock.

"It's midnight," I told Evaristo. All conversation ceased. Ana picked up a raw chicken heart, wrapped it in a *mox* leaf, and set it on the *santos* table. She did the same with the other two hearts. Then she placed live coals in the *censario*, a handmade clay incense holder suspended inside a web of henequen, and dropped *pom*, incense, on the coals. The sweet, smoky smell filled the room.

With Ana leading the way, swinging the *censario*, we walked single file to Evaristo and Aleja's new house. Ana and I were the only women—not even Aleja accompanied us. José and Eustaquio each carried a bucket, one filled with chicken blood, the other with cacao.

After Ana had set the food offerings on a table in the center of the house, José swung the *censario* over them and lit the five black candles. The smoke from the incense drifted slowly upward—a living link to heaven, to catch the gods' attention. Evaristo placed a candle on each of the four corner posts. A chill ran through me as I watched the wavering candles. Like the Christian Trinity, the Chac had more than one manifestation—four, in this case, one for each direction. According to the ancient Maya, there were three worlds. One was the temporal world. The second was just like the first—a cornfield—but in the sky, where the gods lived. The third was below them—the underworld, the home of the dead. (I'd been reading Thompson's book myself.) On the slabs of carved rock that archaeologists call stelae, the god of the north was always white. The eastern god was red, the god of the south was yellow, and the god of the west was black, the color of death.

Praying in a low monotone, José took a rum bottle from under the table, uncorked it, and sprinkled the table with rum. I couldn't understand anything he said—he was using words I didn't ordinarily hear. Suddenly he stopped speaking. After a short silence Ana prompted him. José finished the prayer, then splashed rum on all the corner posts and both doors. Returning to the table, he unwrapped the *mox* leaves. After placing the chicken hearts on a *tortilla*, he held them up to the center of the house. As Ana swung the *censario*, José prayed some more and laid an offering on each corner post. Dipping his hand in one of the buckets, he smeared blood over all four posts—the four corners of the world. Ana added more incense to the coals and swung the *censario*. José forgot the words again, and again Ana prompted him. When that didn't help, she finished the prayer herself. José rubbed cacao over the posts and prayed again, his voice a murmur.

After repeating the ritual at each door, José, Ana, and Evaristo carried the buckets outside and sprinkled the ground around the house with chicken blood and cacao. I shivered. I couldn't help wondering if their ancestors—the same ones flitting around jungle paths on All Souls' Day—would have used human blood and a human heart.

When we returned to the Tuxes' house, José lit another candle on the *santos* table, burned more incense, and prayed again. With that the ritual ended, and even the sleepy children ate a late dinner of chicken stew and fresh *tortillas*. This time, all of us ate together.

The *caldo* was excellent—Ana was a very good cook—and it contained a chewy, strong-tasting green that resembled spinach. It was one of the few green vegetables I'd eaten here. "Ana, what is this?"

She didn't answer; she probably didn't speak English.

"We call it *callaloo*, a bush green. It grows everywhere," Evaristo said dismissively—meaning that it grew wild. His tone of voice suggested that Ana should have served us something more formal, more befitting the occasion.

By the time Aaron and I got home, it was two in the morning. "Did you like that bush green?" I asked. "I'll ask Lucia to show me where it grows. What did Evaristo call it again?"

"We still haven't seen anybody die here," Aaron said, as though replying to my question.

Since there was nothing else to say, I stretched out in my hammock and tried not to cry. Although I had asked Aaron about his trip several times, I had no idea what he'd done in Guatemala—whether he'd seen Roberto and Joanne Rendón again, if his paper would be published once he finished it. He spent more time writing up his field notes than he did talking to me.

I lay awake in the darkness a long time, returning to the same three topics again and again: that Aaron and I seemed to have nothing to say to one another, and that somebody in the village *was* dying, although not physically.

According to Lucia, when Aleja told Evaristo she was pregnant, he decided his smartest move would be to leave Rio Blanco and go be a *chiclero* again. He had never wanted to be a farmer—that's why he'd run away from home in the first place. But Aleja told her father, and José took Evaristo aside and laid out the alternatives. Either Evaristo married Aleja, or José would nail his skin to a wall, or turn him into John Crow, a buzzard, or just lay him out in the *camposanto*. Those were his choices. And Evaristo, the man who could visualize the solar system and had once sneaked a drink of sacrificial wine while waiting to see Father Cull—to see if he would live to tell about it—knuckled under to a little old man half his height and three times his age because he was a Maya, and in his bones he believed the old *ak'tul* could really do it.

So Evaristo was a farmer now, waiting for his corn to ripen and his second child to be born, just one more poor Indian living out in the bush.

As if I didn't have enough to think about, another topic stuck in my head, tenacious as prickle grass. Did civilizing the Maya mean losing rituals like the one I had just witnessed—rituals their ancestors had performed before the birth of Christ? It would be like asking modern Greeks to disavow *Antigone*, or the present-day inhabitants of Rome to raze the Coliseum in order to build condos. It seemed to me that anyone determined to "civilize" the Maya should give them something of value equal to what they would lose. It also seemed to me that teaching the Maya to speak English was not of equal value.

What the kids really needed was someone to teach them about their own history—the ancient Maya civilization in all its grandeur—so they realized they were more than a bunch of "poor Indians living out here in the bush." But I wasn't that person. I didn't know enough.

Slowly, as the days grew increasingly hotter, the tempo of life picked up. Everybody seemed *busy*—women scurried to each other's houses, men sharpened their machetes and talked. For the first time I heard the name Tzultak'a spoken aloud—not publicly, but in low voices, whenever the men got together. Yes, their prayers had been answered. The rains had finally stopped, and the bush was drying out. Soon they could cut the bush. When it had dried, they would burn it and plant their *milpas* in the thin, fertile soil—where, José Tux told Aaron, they would pray to Tzultak'a again.

In extremis—especially when it came to the corn crop that the Maya equated with life itself—they didn't depend on the god of the Roman Catholic Church. Whenever the Maya planted their corn, blessed a house, or carried a baby astride their hip for the first time, they invoked the same gods their ancestors had—Tzultak'a, the "mountain and valley" god, or the Chac. It was the old gods—buried in the airless rubble of as yet undiscovered tombs—who still dominated the most important rituals of their lives, alive and potent in spite of four hundred years of Christianity.

A letter from the Honourable George Price arrived. He was very pleased with the villagers' willingness to participate in local government, but their request for a mayor, an *alcalde*, had to go through proper channels.

In the meantime, he had authorized money for a bulldozer to widen and level the road from Santa Cruz to Pueblo Viejo, as per the villagers' earlier request. Father Cull had been right—the first minister was planning to visit us. I wondered if he was up for reelection.

That night José Ical blew the conch shell to announce a meeting at school. Every man in the village showed up to hear Aaron read Price's letter and try to explain what "proper channels" were. They were happy to hear about the road and discussed buying a patron saint for the village again. Crispino had done some comparison shopping. A statue of Santa Elena cost forty-five dollars, while the combined cost of *santos* of San José, San Antonio, and Santa Maria was only sixteen dollars. The villagers decided to buy those three statues as soon as they finished planting. They could buy one of Santa Elena later.

The minute the road was passable, the bulldozer arrived in Santa Cruz. It was so loud we could hear it long before we saw it—a dull, discordant roar that crept slowly closer and closer. The day it crossed the Rio Blanco River, everybody in the village crowded into our house and watched silently as it rumbled into view, spewing dirt and rocks. Everybody knew Alex Williams, the Creole operator, who had lived in Toledo District his entire life. When Alex finished work for the day, José Ical invited him for dinner, and Alex left the bulldozer parked by the school. The men crowded around the huge machine, running their hands over it and examining its parts. Mateo stood next to it, staring at it intently. It was late afternoon, and the sun caught the high, sharp planes of his cheekbones. He and the bulldozer did not look as though they should be occupying the same space.

During the day smoke lingered in the humid air and refused to dissipate. The men were burning the dry bush in preparation for planting. Joaquin invited Aaron to watch him burn his *milpa*. I tagged along, too.

"Will you look at the size of that stump?" Aaron pointed—the root buttresses were so big the men had been forced to build a platform to reach the main trunk. "And they have metal axes. The ancient Maya used stones."

The fire's violence was frightening. Joaquin had left some cohune palms standing, and when the fire reached them they exploded. Burning pieces of bark and liana flew through the air with a humming noise.

"Enriques told me it's the sound of burning snakes," Aaron commented.

Petrified lightning, screaming snakes, the Maya had a vivid imagination.

As soon as the soil was cool enough, Joaquin and his father would plant corn in the thin, ash-covered soil. Until that happened, everything we ate, even the water we drank, tasted like smoke. But the sunsets were spectacular.

The villagers seemed to have arrived at an uneasy truce. By the end of the week, all of our neighbors were hosting rowdy parties that didn't break up until the early hours of morning.

Just after daybreak I awoke to a shrill scream. Leaping out of my hammock, I yanked the front door open to see who was being murdered. But the shrieks had stopped. In her yard Silvaria cradled a pig's head in her lap, a calabash positioned carefully under the gash in its throat to catch the blood. Children, her own and other people's, big-eyed and silent, examined the pig. *Ki kam*. Dead. Shortly before I left for school, Silvaria stopped by and invited us to dinner.

That night Aaron and I found out what all the noise and hilarity were about. Enriques was ready to make plantation, and—according to Evaristo—had to abstain from sex before planting or the corn seeds wouldn't germinate. He had to abstain after planting, too, so birds wouldn't eat the young sprouts. Probably to keep his mind off what he was missing, he invited the men and their families who would help him plant to his house for a party—pork *caldo* and a game called *buluk* that the Maya played only when they planted corn. It involved a row of about two dozen dried corn kernels, individualized tokens such as the ones used in Monopoly, and more dried corn kernels, black on one side and white on the other, which the men tossed like dice to see how far they could move their tokens. Two men could play, or twenty—the more the better. Sometimes the games lasted all night. Once the Choc brothers arrived with Juan Oh and his son John, the first game started.

Aaron used shotgun shells for his tokens; Enriques used dried beans. Alex, who had walked in from Pueblo Viejo, where his bulldozer was parked, used wooden matches. Julian, who resolutely avoided eye contact with me the entire night, used coins. I had broken my promise to myself and told Aaron about Julian's proposal, thinking it might get him talking. It didn't. His only comment had been "To know them is not to love them." But for tonight, at least, he seemed more open, more relaxed. He even seemed to be enjoying himself.

The girls helped their mothers while the boys watched the game intently, hollering encouragement to their fathers or brothers. A few of the older boys, like Cresencio, were allowed to play, but Lute and little Julian, who were too young to count reliably, were not. As the men played *buluk*, Silvaria and her daughters-in-law kept us supplied with the chewy drink made from cacao beans and black pepper that didn't taste anything like chocolate.

After the men finished their game, we ate dinner. Aaron asked why it was necessary to invoke Tzultak'a at every stage of planting. His question was greeted with silence. Then Juan Oh, whose mother had been Kekchi and who admitted he might not remember *exactly*, said they prayed to Tzultak'a before they cut bush to ask for protection against snakebite and falling trees, and to be forgiven for scarring the deity's face—almost exactly the explanation José Tux had given Evaristo. Before they dropped seven dried corn kernels into holes they had poked into the ash-covered ground with a stick, they prayed for a good crop. As Juan talked, some of the other men broke in to clarify or correct what he said.

Silvaria had made an excellent pork *caldo*. I had rolled up my *tortilla* and was using it to shovel chunks of pork into my mouth the way the Maya did when I encountered a piece of meat that bounced away from my teeth like rubber. I shifted it to the other side of my mouth. It was tube-shaped, like a Life Saver candy, and bristled with small, stiff hairs. Then I realized what it was.

Hastily setting my bowl down, I sprinted outside and threw up. I had discovered something else I would not—*could* not—eat. A pig's anus.

As soon as dinner was over, the men started another game. Because ten men were playing, it didn't break up until well after midnight. Most of the women had left hours earlier—their part of the ritual was finished. The next morning, at midday, they would walk to Enriques's *milpa* with Silvaria, carrying pork *caldo* and *tortillas* for the men.

"Have you seen Thompson's book lately?" Aaron asked, rummaging through the clutter on the benches. "I can't find it."

"I loaned it to Juanita Bul—she wanted to copy some embroidery patterns."

"Shit! And you fell for that?"

His anger was so unexpected it felt as though he'd thrown a rock at me. "What do you mean? Fell for what?"

"She borrowed it because Jaime, her slimeball husband, wants the planting prayers!"

Jaime, a slick talker with a thin, haughty face, had rapidly made himself either the village's most popular resident—if you happened to be a borderline alcoholic—or its least popular. He claimed he had moved out of San Antonio because all the good *milpa* land was played out. He started to build a house, but the location he chose was in the middle of Sebastian Garcia's rice field, and Sebastian made him stop. So Jaime and Juanita and their son moved in with Martín and Fernanda Ical—the two women were sisters. Jaime paid for his keep by buying rum in San Antonio, bringing it back to Rio Blanco, and selling it by the glass. The practice was illegal, and it meant that a lot of men were drunk most of the time. But now, apparently, Jaime intended to clean up his act and plant corn.

"If he wants the prayers," I said, "why not let him have them?"

Aaron gave me a long, hostile look. "José told me if anybody wants to learn the prayers, he should pay for them. I told Jaime that and he laughed in my face."

"Who's he supposed to pay? Thompson?"

"Jesus, Joan. Pay *me*!"

"Why? Do we need the money?"

"That's not the point."

"Then what *is* the point? You're an anthropologist—people give you information. You don't pay them for it. If you give *them* information, why should they have to pay *you*?"

"Why are you passing judgment on something that doesn't concern you? I don't come to school and tell you how to teach!"

"You just called me stupid for giving Juanita the book. That 'concerns' me."

"Then forget I said it."

I stared at him. I'd fought with my mother like this—words with barbs on them, meant to tear flesh—but never Aaron. I had never been this angry at him before. Or this disappointed in him. "Look. We agree— Jaime's scum. But he doesn't know the prayers and you won't teach him. Thanks to some teacher in San Antonio, he can read English. He wants to copy down the prayers in Thompson's book so he can plant his corn the old way, using the old prayers. I think that's very resourceful."

"The *point* is, I told him I would teach him the prayers if he paid to learn them. But he's too cheap. So he sent his wife, on some ridiculous pretext that suckered you in, to 'borrow' Thompson's book."

"So he lied and I'm stupid. Personally, I think a modern-day Maya getting ancient Maya planting prayers out of a book is pretty funny!"

"You have a weird sense of humor."

"You have a weird sense of priorities."

We left it at that.

Aaron and I spoke to each other very politely but only when necessary. When he said he was going to Big Falls to talk to Don about the paper he was writing, I was relieved. If I was by myself, I wouldn't have to be polite. Then I felt guilty for feeling relieved.

That night I had a houseful of visitors—Lucia, Crispino, Natalia, Evaristo, Maxiana, and old Marto, Lucia and Maxiana's father. Lucia kept a strict eye on her daughter, to make sure the little girl didn't try to sit in my lap again, but I'd figured out what was going on. She didn't want Natalia to get too fond of me. "The Kekchi shy away from close relationships," Don had told me once, in a rare serious moment. "Life is so tenuous here—people are always moving away, dying, some goddamn thing."

It was Marto, Maxiana translating, who asked me the question I had been dreading ever since Aaron came back. "Teacher—my father wants to know when you are going to leave."

"School is over in May," I said carefully, with the sick, stone-in-the-stomach feeling I got whenever I told a lie. "But we'll be back next year." It was what Aaron had instructed me to say. In reality, we couldn't afford to come back unless he got some serious grant money.

"Not June?" Evaristo looked surprised. "Father Cull said you would be here until June."

"When did you talk to Father Cull?"

Evaristo grinned. "When you and Mr. World were in Guatemala, we had a meeting with Father Cull. José Tux came too, and Aleja's brothers, Sebastian Garcia, José Ical—a lot of people."

I waited.

"We wanted to know how to make you stay here."

The stone in my stomach got bigger. "What did Father Cull say?"

Evaristo's grin faded. "That we could do nothing. You would have to decide yourself."

"If you go, I'm going with you, Teacher," Natalia exclaimed into the silence. Lucia had warned her daughter away from me a little too late.

"I also," Maxiana added in her quiet voice.

"Why you have to leave?" asked Lucia. "We don't want it you go."

"I wish we could stay longer," I said, on the verge of tears. "But we'll be back next year."

Evaristo shook his head. "You won't come back. You soon forget about Rio Blanco."

How casually people can break each other's hearts.

The villagers received another letter from the Honourable George Price, who announced he planned to visit Rio Blanco and would be happy to listen to the villagers' concerns while he was here. There was only one problem. He was coming the same day that Father Cull and the bishop would be here for the children's first communion.

Thanks to Jaime, who had reverted to his old ways once he'd finished planting his *milpa*, the village was awash in rum for a week before their arrival. Lucia said Jaime was a "bad man" and that somebody should tell the *mayordomo* about what he was doing. So Aaron told José Ical, who was too drunk to understand the problem.

Then Major Glynn Lewis, a friend of Don's and head security officer of the British Army in Belize City, stopped in to visit, and I asked him to stay for dinner. Glynn was a big, boisterous, red-haired man with a booming voice and an iron-fisted handshake. Everybody in the village was intensely curious about him—all that red hair and those freckled arms. When dinner was over, Aaron walked with him to the river, where Glynn had parked his Land Rover.

Thirty seconds later Jaime was at my door, his thin face contorted in rage. "Why did you ask the British Army to come here?"

Keeping my own face absolutely expressionless, I said, "I didn't ask him to do anything." That much was true—Glynn had just stopped by to say hello. "He heard that somebody in the village was selling rum illegally and he wanted to know who."

"What did you tell him?"

"That I'd heard the same thing. I wonder who complained?"

"I think *you* complained, Missus."

"What my husband and I talked to Major Lewis about is none of your business, Jaime. *Pues*, it's getting late. I think you'd better leave."

Jaime turned away, cursing in English, so I understood how angry I had made him and how frightened I should be.

"First communion this morning," I wrote to Aaron's sister Ginger. "Confirmation next week when the bishop comes. Total chaos because Father Cull doesn't speak Kekchi and his translator was absent when we rehearsed yesterday. As a result, one little boy had already taken communion before he was supposed to. Confirmation should be interesting—I wonder if the bishop speaks Kekchi."

Bishop Hodap did not speak Kekchi, but he did speak fluent Mopan. Another American Jesuit, he was everything Father Cull was not—open, friendly, talkative, with the ability to put people instantly at ease.

The children were all dressed up, cleaner than I had ever seen them except for their first day of school. All the little boys—including Mateo's son Saturnino, who looked miserable—had on long-sleeved white shirts with starched collars. After the bishop anointed them, they tied white handkerchiefs over their heads.

People were already walking home when the Honourable George Price roared through with his private motorcade, which included a separate vehicle for his photographer. He probably expected a more enthusiastic welcome, but half the village was drunk and the rest of us were exhausted.

Price walked around the schoolhouse while his aides pleaded with people to come out of their houses and talk to him, or shove their babies in his face while the photographer's shutter clicked. Price saw Dolores watching the proceedings from her doorway and posed next to her. *Click.* Mateo, slack-jawed and drunk, staggered up. Price grasped his hand. *Click.* Then the aide spotted me.

"The people want a bridge," I said as Price shook my hand. *Click.* "When the river floods they can't get their produce to market." But the first minister had already moved on. After posing for a few more photographs, he climbed back in his Land Rover and left for Pueblo Viejo, waving. He had been in and out of Rio Blanco in ten minutes flat—José Tux and his family, who didn't know that Price had arrived, were still on their way home. The men hadn't had a chance to talk to him about anything.

Early one Saturday morning, Aaron and I set out for San Antonio to buy supplies—onions, kerosene, sugar, flour, peanut butter, and instant coffee. We both had a lemonade and I bought four packs of Colonials.

We were just leaving Tommy Salam's store when a drunk hailed us. Aaron hadn't been exaggerating when he said he'd visited every Kekchi village in Toledo District, no matter how tiny. He was the first anthropologist to study the Kekchi of Toledo District, and everybody knew him, or at least knew of him. Breaking into a big smile, the drunk lurched toward us, stopping just in time to avoid toppling into Aaron's arms. Both Aaron and I expected him to greet Aaron—*hombre al hombre*, man to man. Instead he peered into my face. "You could be Teacher, yes? From Rio Blanco?"

Dumbstruck, I nodded. Yes, I was Teacher.

He held out his hand. Like the Garifuna man on the *Heron*, the Maya didn't really understand the concept of a hand*shake*. Most simply held hands with me for a few seconds and then dropped theirs. That's what this man did, except he didn't want to let go. He clutched my hand, nodding and smiling and swaying. "When you going come to my village?"

"What village is that?" I asked. He dropped my hand to turn around and point. Somewhere in that direction—whatever that direction was.

"*Aha*," I said. Yes, of course.

"Is good you come here," he said solemnly.

"Thank you."

"How long you going stay?"

"Until May."

"Then you go back to the States?"

"I'm afraid so."

"You going come teach in my village?"

"No, I'm sorry. I promised Father Cull I would teach in Rio Blanco."

"I see." He frowned. "*Pues*—is good I see you."

He hadn't wanted to talk to Aaron. *I* was the one he wanted to talk to. Whatever my personal misgivings, he valued me for who I was and what I had accomplished, not for who my husband was and what *he* had accomplished.

I took his hand in both of mine and smiled at him. "Thank you."
So what if the guy was drunk?

XXXXXXXXXXXXXXXXXXXXXXXXXXXXXXXXXXXXXXXXXXXXXXXXXXXXXXXXX

CALLALOO

The Maya often use bush greens in their cooking, and this "chewy spin-ach" is one of the most common. It's a variety of amaranth that grows wild throughout most of Belize. The Maya commonly add it to *caldo*, as Ana did, or boil it in water 10 or 15 minutes and eat it separately.

> 1 pound *callaloo* leaves, sorted and washed (you can also use
>   spinach)
> 2 large cloves garlic, pressed or minced
> 1 tablespoon butter
> 2 tablespoons olive oil
> a pinch of cayenne (or to taste)
> salt

Melt the butter in a cast-iron skillet over low heat. Add the olive oil, garlic, cayenne, and salt. Do not let the garlic brown. Tip skillet to distribute the butter and oil evenly over the bottom of the skillet.

Turn heat to high, add *callaloo* leaves, cover the pan, and cook 3 or 4 minutes. The mixture will cook down rapidly. Remove cover and stir. (If you used spinach, it's ready to eat.) Lower the heat, cover pan again, and let the mixture cook at least 5 more minutes. Continue to cook and stir until the *callaloo* is thoroughly cooked and limp.

Serves 2 people.

XXXXXXXXXXXXXXXXXXXXXXXXXXXXXXXXXXXXXXXXXXXXXXXXXXXXXXXXX

BUSH GREENS AND *GARBANZOS*

> 2 cups cooked *garbanzo* beans (chickpeas)
> 1 tablespoon olive oil

    2 cloves garlic

    ½ onion, diced

    ¼ can of tomato paste (or a handful of sliced cherry tomatoes)

    1 cup chicken broth

    2 packed cups of shredded greens (*callaloo*, spinach, collards, chard, etc.)

    ½ teaspoon salt

    ¼ teaspoon black pepper

    a pinch of cayenne (optional)

Sauté the onions and garlic in olive oil until limp. Add tomato paste and cayenne; cook 1 minute. Add stock gradually, stirring. When well mixed, add *garbanzo* beans. Bring to a boil. Add greens and cook 2 minutes (for spinach) to 10 minutes (for everything else).

Serves 4 people.

a Feast among the Fallen Gods

The men held another meeting and decided to buy the three *santos* and bring them to the village as soon as possible. That meant the *fiesta* would be in two weeks. First they would welcome the saints' statues to Rio Blanco, and after the prayers and singing—Teacher and her students would be responsible for the singing—the villagers would hold a feast, followed by a dance. One of those secular dances Aaron didn't like. With rum. They had to pay the musicians, didn't they?

Each man in the village agreed to contribute seventy-five cents. Even the two young bachelors, Leonardo Ical and John Oh, had to pay up. That's when I discovered that John was working off the price of "buying" Paulina as a bride by helping Joaquin in his *milpa*—otherwise Joaquin wouldn't consent to a wedding.

Crispino collected the money and told Aaron what names to put on the list. Only seven of the men paid. The others said they had to sell something first. *To get seventy-five cents?* I thought. But sure enough— first thing the next morning, Francisco Tux took José's mule to San Antonio with a load of dried corn.

I spent part of each class period, morning and afternoon, going over the songs we would sing. I even gave "The Star-Spangled Banner" another try, starting in a lower key. This time I managed to sing it through to the very end. Paulina looked disappointed. "Okay, now *everybody's* going to sing it. 'Oh, say can you see, by the dawn's early light'—come on. Sing!" After we got through that twice, we sang "God Save the Queen."

The following Thursday every able-bodied woman in Rio Blanco convened in Lucia's kitchen. Each family had donated a chicken, and three widows from other villages—including Laura, the *curandera* from Pueblo Viejo—were working in exchange for meals. Inside Lucia's house a dozen babies hung from the rafters in their tiny hammocks. I didn't see how the women had enough elbow room to cook.

A case of rum arrived Friday morning, before the *santos* did. The official ceremonies began late that afternoon, after the men had cleared Mateo and Micalia's house of furniture and removed her clay fireplace. They also cleaned the interior of the schoolhouse, pushing desks and chairs along the walls and dragging the table closer to the door. Some men cut fresh cohune fronds and covered the door frame with a palm-leaf archway. When the *santos* arrived, the men placed them on the table beneath a smaller arch of palm fronds. After the *fiesta* the saints' permanent dwelling would be a niche in the far corner.

While it was still daylight, a procession began at the Tux household and wound its way toward the village. At the head of the procession was José's grandson, four-year-old Felipe Tux, so clean he still looked wet, carrying a flickering white candle. He was followed by Jesús Boh beating a drum, Marto Choc swinging incense, José Tux with a heavy wooden cross on his shoulder, and Alejandro Mijangre carrying a small bundle wrapped in a silk scarf.

"What's in the scarf?" I whispered to Aaron. "Some kind of religious relic?"

"I don't know. So many Maya ceremonies were absorbed into seventeenth-century Catholic ritual that it's hard to tell what's what." He and I had reconciled our differences the way his sister said married people usually did—in bed. But I had never heard him admit to an inadequacy before. Was he having a malaria relapse? I eyed him obliquely. No. He was simply exhausted—I could see it in his face. He really didn't care anymore. The only thing he cared about was going home.

When the procession arrived at Mateo's, José Tux instructed his son Francisco, the last member of the procession, to fire two shots. At that, Mateo joined them and the group continued on to the school—which by now had clearly metamorphosed into the church—where Francisco fired two more shots. The men entered the building. José set the cross on the table next to the saints, and several men stepped forward to toss brilliant red blossoms around the *santos'* feet.

As the sun went down, people gathered inside Mateo and Micalia's house to wait for the musicians. To my surprise they had imported a harpist from Santa Cruz instead of asking Sebastian. To make sure nobody started playing it before he arrived, he had removed the first six strings.

Since nothing much was happening except drinking, Aaron and I went home to get some sleep. We woke up about ten when the harp player arrived and the music started. As soon as we sat down—benches had been set against all four walls—Crispino handed us the first two bowls of chicken *caldo* and told us to eat. Right behind him, a succession of children trooped in carrying more *caldo* and heaping plates of *tamales* and *tortillas*.

All the women were dressed in their newest, most fashionable clothes—Juanita Bul, Jaime's wife, had incorporated one of the designs in Thompson's book into her blouse. The floor of the house was fragrant with allspice leaves. As we ate, the musicians tuned up—a violinist and a guitarist, with a young man beating out the rhythm on the harp box. The onlookers, women as well as men, offered rum to one another straight out of the bottle. The recipient took a few swigs and passed the bottle back.

When Mateo fired his shotgun—he was already drunk, and I had no idea why anybody would trust him with a gun—the music began in earnest. At first only the children danced. Then Mateo, who could barely navigate, staggered around the room, dangling a clean white handkerchief and shouting "*Ma xahoc!*" Dance with me—I'm available. One of the widow ladies got up and danced a small circle in front of him to signify her acceptance, her arms spread to hold her long skirt off the floor. Then Evaristo, Jesús Boh, Sebastian Garcia, and Alejandro Mijangre circled the room. As the women rose from their seats and bobbed in front of them, more men flooded the dance floor.

Aaron and I had a few drinks, watched the dancing for a few hours, and went home.

I woke up very early the next morning to the sound of another hog being slaughtered. I rolled over with my hands over my ears. Somebody shoved the front door open and staggered inside.

"What the hell are you doing?" Aaron yelled, sitting up in his hammock. "*Elen!*"

My hammock was closer to the doorway than Aaron's, and the man swayed toward me, a big, sloppy grin on his face. I hit the floor running, forgetting that I'd set a mousetrap by the table. In my haste to get away from him I stepped on it. It snapped shut on my toes. I howled and hopped on my other foot, struggling to pull my toes free. When the man laughed, I lost my temper. "Get *out* of here, damn you!"

He gave me another wet grin and stumbled forward. I was so mad I did something I'd never done before. I put both hands on his shoulders—I was taller than he was—and swung him around until he faced the door. Then I gave him a good hard shove. As he staggered outside, I yanked the door closed behind him and tied it. He loitered for a few minutes, peering at us through the wallboards and giggling. Aaron told me to ignore him. I would have preferred to shoot him.

When the drunk finally staggered off, Aaron and I escaped out the back door to Lucia's. The women were already hard at work chopping up pork for *caldo* and scraping the hair off the pig's skin to make *chicharrones*. Crispino welcomed us with bowls of *chicha*. Corn beer wasn't exactly what I had in mind for breakfast, but I sat in a vacant hammock with my calabash, taking small sips. Aaron went back outside, where most of the men had congregated. Nicasio and Luis stuck their heads in the door, saw me, and ran over. Both looked very grown up in new long pants and belts and long-sleeved white dress shirts. Nicasio told me proudly in English that he had "danced all night."

That afternoon the saints officially arrived as if they had just crossed the river, and everybody in Rio Blanco turned out to welcome them. A group of women including Lucia, Dolores, Ana, and Laura led the procession, all swinging *censarios*. Next came three men, each carrying one of the *santos*, then José Tux with the cross followed by Alejandro—still cradling the mysterious bundle in his arms—and finally me and the schoolchildren. Since none of us knew what we were supposed to be doing, we all kept a close eye on José Tux. He was the only one not improvising.

This time I had dressed up. My hair was knotted in a French twist, and I wore my Madras wraparound skirt and a short-sleeved black blouse—not the smartest decision I'd ever made. It had rained during the night, and the day was so hot and humid my clothes stuck to me. Under the cloying incense I could still smell the jungle.

The kids and I sang almost every song I had ever taught them—the national anthems of two countries, nursery rhymes, lullabies in English, liturgical music in Latin, "The Children's Mass," and "Row, Row, Row Your Boat." I drew the line at "The Alphabet Song." Gradually I stopped singing so I could listen to the children—their high, clear voices ringing in the fluid air.

At the halfway mark, the shelter at the crest of the hill where the rest of the villagers were gathered, the procession halted and we stopped singing. Sebastian, seated at his harp, began to play a slow, simple melody in a minor key that I had never heard before. The saints were placed carefully on a table sheltered by palm fronds. After José said a few prayers, women handed out calabashes of coffee, cacao, or *lab*, the sweetened corn gruel I'd first tasted in Crique Sarco. I took coffee—fresh coffee that had been ground this morning. Another group passed out sweet *tortillas*. Each bore the imprint of a leaf that a woman had painstakingly stamped on the wet dough to form a design. I teased my salivary glands by allowing each bite to melt on my tongue.

After refreshments the procession resumed, but the kids and I had reached the end of our musical repertoire. I looked questioningly at José. What did he want us to do next? He gestured at the *santos*, which I interpreted as "Then sing all the songs you know all over again."

José and the other men carried the cross and the *santos* around the church three times, with pauses for incense and prayers at all four corners, before carrying them through the palm fronds arching over the doorway. As soon as the *santos* had been placed inside their shelter on the table, Marto laid a china plate in front of them, and all the children in the village old enough to walk stepped up to cross themselves and pray before putting five cents in the plate. After the adults took their turn, the saints were carried to Mateo's house, where Mateo welcomed them by firing his shotgun. The men placed the *santos* in an alcove near the musicians. The bundle in the silk scarf disappeared as mysteriously as it had appeared. I never did find out what was in it.

Everyone in the village, plus guests, crowded inside the house. As soon as we were seated, the women served us pork in *caldo*, *tamales*, and fresh *tortillas*. The saints were also given food, and someone hung a cloth in front of them "so they could eat in peace," an English-speaker from Santa Cruz told me.

On the second night of the *fiesta*, Sebastian was the harpist, and when he tuned his instrument, the other musicians, including Joaquin, began tuning up as well. Last night had just been a warm-up—an excuse to drink rum. *This* was the real *fiesta*. Even the drunk who had walked in on us this morning had sobered up and wanted to dance, and I noted with pleasure that women from the Tux family were dancing with Choc men, and vice versa. José Tux's idea had worked. The feud was over.

At the end of each dance, the men were required to drop five cents into a plate. Their offerings were carefully eyed by a committee of elders—José, Enriques, Marto, and Mateo's father, who were all doing a commendable job of staying sober. Avelino Garcia and Asunción Choc weren't as successful, and Jaime, Francisco Tux, and Martín Ical were all drinking heavily. After dancing with Fernanda, Jaime neglected to drop a coin into the plate. Marto, Evaristo's father, accused him of cheating. Jaime called Marto a liar. Evaristo got vexed and accused Jamie, in English, of being a troublemaker and a sonofabitch. While Evaristo's sisters and mother-in-law subdued him, Mateo took a swing at Jaime. Crispino and Joaquin rushed Mateo out the door.

This was why the police were supposed to be here—to make sure everybody behaved. But Crispino and Joaquin, who agreed on little else, had apparently agreed that there would be no Garifuna police at this feast. Then they had gone one step further and appointed themselves as peacekeepers.

After a few minutes Mateo staggered back inside to dance. This time José Ical's daughter Ambrosia accepted his invitation. But Mateo immediately picked a fight with Jaime again, and Crispino and Joaquin hauled him outside again. This time he didn't reappear.

Even though the dancers paired off male-female, they never touched one another, and the woman chose the man she wanted to dance with. After watching a few dances, Aaron commented that the system gave everybody an opportunity to participate—wallflowers were strictly self-imposed.

People kept buying rum for the musicians, and as a result the dancing lasted only until nine thirty, when the musicians passed out. Most of the villagers, women as well as men, were drunk. I sat on the bench inhaling the scent of allspice, sharing a bottle of rum with Laura, the *curandera*, and Eusebio Tux. The three of us pretty well killed it. Aaron was drinking with the former *alcalde* of Pueblo Viejo and Ana Tux. As soon as José was relieved of guarding the money plate, he joined his wife, and our two groups merged. After the bottle had gone full circle a few times, the *alcalde* bought a new one. Sometime later José said to Aaron in Kekchi, "I never expected white people to come live with us poor Indians in the bush." He sounded puzzled and genuinely touched.

When the second bottle was empty, Aaron and I helped each other home and fell, fully clothed, into our hammocks. At midnight gunfire woke us up. Mateo was yelling at Jaime, but I didn't feel like getting up and finding out why. Aaron mumbled something, ran out the door, and was sick.

The next morning the village was strangely quiet. I couldn't tell if Aaron was snoring or groaning. Outside it spat rain, but I saw signs of life at Lucia's, so during a lull in the drizzle I ran over. I had *goma*, but I'd had worse hangovers in college. Lucia and Crispino were handing out pig's liver *caldo* to everybody sober enough to eat it. (And *chicha*, for anybody hankering for the hair of the dog.) Other than that, nobody paid any attention to me—I was just another casualty of the feast. Every adult there had *goma*.

Avelino Garcia was perched on a three-legged stool, his new white shirt smeared with mud from spending the night on the ground outside the church, and John Oh sat on the floor holding his head. Marto limped around his daughter's house like an old dog afraid to lie down because he wasn't sure he could get up again.

I sat down in the only vacant space—next to Avelino on the stool. Maxiana handed me a bowl of *caldo*. As I sipped it, waiting for it to cool, about a dozen people, all bedraggled-looking, stumbled inside Lucia's house for nourishment and then, fortified, stumbled back out into the intermittent rain.

Aaron never did get up. A few men asked where he was, and when I told them he had *goma*, they looked amused and—something else, something too subtle for my soggy brain to comprehend.

The *caldo* had the rich, smoky flavor of liver and blood and *chile* pepper. As my headache ebbed, my body relaxed. I was aware of the hubbub around me but didn't feel obligated to take part in it. Nobody seemed to care. Nobody even seemed to be watching me. I stopped chewing and looked craftily around the room. Not a single soul so much as glanced in my direction.

A revelation propelled me into sobriety. Nobody had stared at me for months. I had been so preoccupied with my failures as a cook and my faltering marriage that I hadn't noticed. That's why everybody had seemed pleased when I told them that Aaron had *goma*. He'd gotten drunk, just the way they had. To us, it would have been like inviting people from another country to join us for a New Year's Eve party, and looking on with pleasure as they eagerly took part in the festivities. The Maya had accepted us. Yes, we had our own language and quirky gringo habits, but scrub off our culture and we were ordinary people who liked to drink and dance—just the way they did.

Sometime before lunch I went home. Aaron was awake but told me that pig's liver *caldo* didn't interest him in the slightest. I fixed him coffee and oatmeal and hovered over him until he ate some. But when I heard music coming from the Icals' house again, I went out to take a look.

Marto, seated like a sleepy Buddha behind the collection plate, explained that because all the rum hadn't been sold—even though Mateo was doing his best to finish it off single-handedly—there would be more dancing.

I ran home and told Aaron I intended to go back. I wanted to dance. He gave me the kind of look people give lunatics. "Have a good time."

"Oh, spoilsport—come with me. How can you go hunting with these people, accept invitations to a *hetz mek* and a house blessing, get drunk with them, and then not dance with them? It doesn't look hard—kind of like a foxtrot. Just shuffle your feet."

While Aaron feigned sleep, I washed my face and changed into my Guatemalan skirt and the Mopan blouse that Lucia had embroidered for me, and promised myself that I *would* dance today. Of course I had told myself that yesterday, but it hadn't happened. My pep talk to Aaron had been directed at both of us.

I stood indecisively in the doorway. "Well—if you change your mind, you know where to find me."

Aaron didn't answer.

"I'm sorry about the business with Jaime and the planting prayers."

Still no answer.

"You did figure out that Dolores is Mopan, didn't you? And that

Lucia speaks Kekchi *and* Mopan? The younger girls all speak Kekchi because Candelaria is Kekchi. The boys speak Mopan."

Nothing.

Slowly I walked up the hill to the Icals' house.

The musicians looked like zombies, but they played gamely, if not always on key.

To my surprise a lot of people were here, even more than last night. Enriques, José Tux, and Mateo's father had joined Marto behind the money plate, pale but sober.

I sat out the first dance because I'd arrived in the middle of it. But when the next dance started, I waited until Eustaquio Tux stood in front of me, dangling his handkerchief and calling "*Ma xahoc*" before I rose from the bench.

As I swung past the door, holding my skirt out, bobbing and weaving the way the other women did, I saw Aaron. The musicians—who suddenly sat up very straight with big smiles on their faces—played louder and faster. All around me people hissed excitedly, "*Mira—li maestre!*" Look at Teacher!

Across the room a man yelled encouragement, and the English-speaker from Santa Cruz started bawling directions at me like a caller at a square dance. As I'd told Aaron, the dance resembled a foxtrot—a series of tiny, mincing steps—and I concentrated on matching my steps to Eustaquio's, who looked as though a jaguar had fallen out of a tree on top of him and then run away. The musicians played at least four times longer than they usually did. When the dance was over, I sank into the nearest empty spot—which happened to be behind the collection plate. Mateo's father leaned over and said to me solemnly in Kekchi, "You are just like an Indian." Speechless, I nodded. It was one of the most gracious compliments I had ever received.

The *alcalde* from Pueblo Viejo passed a rum bottle in my direction, but before it reached me, Marto, then the English-speaker from Santa Cruz, and then Crispino asked me to dance. None of them bothered with the formality of circling the room. They simply walked up and asked me to dance.

This time when I sat down—my legs were so weak I was shaking—Aaron had saved a place for me, a rum bottle in his hand. Smiling, he held it out. From the other end of the bench, José Ical grinned and gestured. I took a slug and handed the bottle back to Aaron, who downed a swallow, tried not to make a face, and passed the bottle down the bench back to José. Everybody who handled it took a swig.

When the musicians began to play again, I whispered to Aaron, "Ana Tux is sitting right over there. Why don't you ask her to dance? She'd love it."

Gamely Aaron cut across the dance floor and danced a circle in front of Ana, an endearingly goofy grin on his face, his hand outstretched but empty. He'd forgotten his handkerchief. Ana giggled like a little girl and heaved herself to her feet. People started to yell and clap. When the dance ended, Aaron sank down next to me. Two bottles made their way toward us, one from either end of the bench.

But for some reason it never occurred to either of us to dance *together.*

The *fiesta* ended that afternoon, and the saints were carried back to their shelter in the church. Then the original procession—headed by Felipe Tux with his candle and José carrying the cross, but minus the bundle—returned to the Tuxes'. The villagers made a profit of twenty-one dollars. Another *fiesta* and twenty-four dollars more and they could afford a statue of Santa Elena.

Although Aaron and I didn't leave until May, the saints' feast marked the end of our stay for me because it was the last happy occasion I remember.

By the time we left, all my older students could write their names.

✕✕✕

FEAST-DAY *CHILE VERDE*

The Maya made pork *caldo* the same way they made any *caldo*, by simmering the meat with onions, *chile* peppers, thyme, and other seasonings. Properly cooked with a lean piece of meat, pork *caldo* can be delicious. My version is closer to a stew than a soup, and with its abundance of green *chile* peppers—please read the caution that follows—and *tomatillos*, it closely resembles the classic green *chile* of Mexican cooking.

If you can't find fresh green *chiles* and fresh *tomatillos* in the supermarket, substitute canned.

Caution: This dish isn't scald-your-taste-buds hot because you remove the *chile* seeds—which *are* hot. I suggest that you wear rubber gloves. Contrary to popular opinion, if the *chiles* are fresh enough, you do not need to char or remove the skins.

> 5 pounds pork shoulder (sold as "pork butt"), trimmed of fat and cut into stew-sized pieces
>
> 3 tablespoons canola oil
>
> ½ large white onion, diced
>
> 6 cloves garlic, minced
>
> 2 teaspoons ground cumin
>
> 2 teaspoons oregano
>
> 1 teaspoon thyme
>
> 1½ teaspoons salt
>
> 1 teaspoon ground black pepper
>
> 4 dried *chiles arbol*, torn into small pieces, seeds included
>
> 5 mild green Anaheim *chile* peppers (about 3 cups) or 4 seven-ounce cans diced green *chiles*
>
> 3 mild green *pasilla* or *poblano chile* peppers (about 2 cups)
>
> 10–12 fresh *tomatillos*, husked (about 2 cups) or 2 twelve-ounce cans diced *tomatillos*, drained (if necessary, substitute green tomatoes)

Remove stem ends of *chile* peppers and slit in half lengthwise. Remove seeds and dice. Remove stem ends of *tomatillos* and dice.

In a large, heavy pot, sauté onion and garlic in 1 tablespoon oil. Remove to a large bowl and set aside. Brown pork in small batches in remaining oil. As they're done, add them to the bowl.

When all the pork is browned, return it to the pot with the remaining ingredients and simmer, covered, about 2 hours. Adjust seasonings.

Serve over rice with small dishes of chopped fresh cilantro, shredded Monterrey Jack cheese, and lime wedges for garnish.

Serves 7–10 people.

AFTERWORD

Halfway to the Belize City airport our taxi blew a tire. I waited by the side of the road under the shade of a tree. My mind felt like an uneasy mixture of vinegar and cream—it kept separating. For the past year I'd been desperate to leave British Honduras, yet now that deliverance was only hours away, I didn't want to go. How had that happened? More to the point, could I stay here and continue to teach?

Doubtful. Aaron, I knew, would leave with me or without me. In Father Cull's quest for a teacher, he had been willing to overlook the fact that I wasn't Catholic. So had Bishop Hodap. But I doubted either one would be eager to take on the double whammy of a non-Catholic separated from her husband. And without a husband, who would make plantation for me? Who, for that matter, would make *tortillas* for me?

As I watched the cabdriver—a sweating, cheerful Creole—half of me hoped he wouldn't get the spare on in time and that Aaron and I would have to postpone, or rethink, going back. The other half of me wanted him to get the tire on as fast as possible so we could get on with our lives.

When we landed in New Orleans, my first impression was of an overwhelming number of people. In the women's restroom, the overhead lights were so harsh they hurt my eyes. The room looked bitterly antiseptic, everything made out of steel and white porcelain. No trees. No corncobs. No pigs twitching their corkscrew tails in anticipation.

I needed a quarter to use the toilet—that was a first. I could wash my hands for free, but I had to pay to use the toilet? Was Aaron facing the same predicament? Did he need a quarter to use the urinal?

As I stood fuming and indecisive—I didn't *have* a quarter; I didn't have any American money—a stewardess entered. She was a pretty blonde wearing bright red lipstick, her eyebrows penciled in, her hair carefully coiffed and sprayed. She obviously hadn't expected pay toilets either. Lips pursed, she stared at the coin mechanism. "Well, shit," she drawled, teasing out the final word until it had two syllables.

No, I wanted to tell her. It's pronounced "shet."

Fishing a nail file out of her purse, she winked at me and jimmied the lock. I had a nail file, too, and after wrestling briefly with my conscience, I used it. The door opened like a cheap magic trick. The first American woman I'd met on American soil had assessed the system and shown me how to beat it by breaking the law.

Welcome home, I told myself.

Ann Arbor was more reverse culture shock. I tried to hold on to my hard-won independence, but Aaron was trying just as hard to return to our pre–British Honduras status quo. The Answer Man was back—the anthropologist two years older than his impractical writer wife. So was Mr. We'll-Do-It-My-Way.

I went shopping one afternoon to fill up the gaps in my closet. When I came back, Aaron asked to see what I'd bought. He wouldn't admit it, but he wanted to see how I'd spent "his" money—even though I was ironing shirts for our Armenian landlady and had another part-time job as a salesclerk at the natural history museum on campus.

"Okay." I was willing to play along. Aaron's request seemed harmless enough. He sat at his desk in our three-room apartment and I stood next to him, digging various articles of clothing out of my shopping bags and dropping them in front of him on the desk. "A litter of underpants. A flock of blouses. A gathering of—oops, only one dress. Short-sleeved. And a gaggle of slacks." One pair I was especially fond of was a vivid paisley print with splashes of lime green and lavender.

Using his pencil, Mr. We'll-Do-It-My-Way pushed the slacks off his desk. "Take them back. They'll make you look like you live in Miami Beach."

I chose to follow his suggestion.

At a faculty party shortly after that, in a wealthy part of Ann Arbor, I drank too much because I couldn't find anybody to talk to. I wanted to sit down, but all the chairs were occupied. Aaron was deep in conversation with one of his professors—a big, blustery man, renowned for his many books and his three ex-wives, who broke off to look at me when I joined them. After a brief nod, he turned his attention back to Aaron. I backed into the wall and slid down it until I was on the floor with my legs crossed in front of me. When I lit a cigarette, Aaron's professor glanced at me again. His gaze lingered on my legs. "She's pretty," he told Aaron, as if I were deaf or in another room. "She'll be an asset to your career."

I reacted to these expectations by digging my heels in, exactly the way Petrona Xi would have if she'd been heading down a steep hill. That's how I felt—as if I were skidding downhill into a future I didn't want. I couldn't seem to make Aaron understand that living in Rio Blanco had changed me. The best I could do was point out that, to me, the dance that had concluded the *fiesta* was an accurate indication of women's status in Maya culture: if they chose to, they could remain on the sidelines. Or they could choose to dance. Lucia spoke her mind in mixed company. Ana Tux prayed to the old gods when her husband forgot the words, and no lightning bolt struck her dead.

I knew that if I wanted to live with the degree of independence I had enjoyed in Rio Blanco, I would have to claim it. My culture didn't offer me the choice. Neither did my husband. Several months later, it came as no great surprise to either of us when the word "divorce" came up in conversation.

In the years that followed, I tried every once in a while to put my British Honduras stories down on paper, but I never got very far. I had never evaluated why a single year out of my life continued to loom so large.

"How did I *feel* about living in a bush house in the jungle, learning to cook over an open fire?" I asked myself sternly in a journal entry.

"It was an adventure, and I was an adventurous kid. I was twenty years old and trying to create a life of my own, as distinct from my parents' lives. I had intellectual pretensions and looked down on a lot of people, but I was also a romantic and I wanted some kind of rapport with the Maya. But the Maya didn't know they were supposed to be noble savages and kept behaving like people—and I ended up having to make the same decisions I would have made in Verona. Do I like you? Why? *Because you're curious. You're smart. You have a sense of humor. I like your take on the world and I want to find out more about you.* Why do I dislike *you*? *Because you're none of the above, have no conscience, and remind me of Jaime Bul.*

"Did the people matter to me? *Of course they did. Maybe it's possible to fall in love with a country—I did—but I fell in love with the people first.*

"*Did* living there change me? How?"

Yes it changed me, but I wrestled with the question for almost fifty years before I could answer it. I brought my idealism to the Maya—my *willingness* to fall in love, and my desire to help—and they repaid me with their friendship.

A fair trade, all things considered.

But then I think about Cirila and Lucia and Maxiana and all the other women who accepted a white stranger into their lives and taught her how to cook, and I have to confess I got the best of the bargain.

To order or obtain more information on these or other University of Nebraska Press titles, visit www.nebraskapress.unl.edu.

ALSO BY JOAN FRY

The Beginning Dressage Book
(coauthor) Arco Publishing, 1981.
Reprinted Lyons Press, 2003.

Backyard Horsekeeping:
The Only Guide You'll Ever Need
Lyons Press, 2004. Revised
edition, 2007.